America and the World, 1898–2025

Other Books by the Author

America and the World, 1898–2025

Achievements, Failures, Alternative Futures

Walter C. Clemens, Jr.

St. Martin's Press
New York

AMERICA AND THE WORLD, 1898–2025
Copyright © Walter C. Clemens, Jr., 2000. All rights reserved. Printed in
the United States of America. No part of this book may be used or
reproduced in any manner whatsoever without written permission except
in the case of brief quotations embodied in critical articles or reviews. For
information, address St. Martin's Press, 175 Fifth Avenue, New York,
N.Y. 10010.

ISBN 0–312–22878–3 (cloth)
ISBN 0–312–23638–7 (paper)

Library of Congress Cataloging-in-Publication Data
to be found at the Library of Congress

Design by Letra Libre, Inc.

First edition: September 2000
10 9 8 7 6 5 4 3 2 1

for
Julian Benjamin,
Olivia Ellen, and
Rose Elizabeth Clemens

CONTENTS

ACKNOWLEDGMENTS

The author wishes to thank all those who contributed to the surveys underlying chapters 1–3. Taken together, the contributors had expertise on every part of the world and on problems ranging from arms control to foreign aid to international law. Their answers could not establish the truth in any absolute sense, but their replies pointed to an expert consensus on some points. Both their agreements and disagreements enlarged my perspectives and stimulated my own reading and thinking. None of the contributors would agree with everything in this book; some disagreements among contributors are noted in the text.

The 1976–1977 surveys were facilitated by Samuel F. Wells, Jr. at the Wilson Center; the 1987 survey by Joseph S. Nye, Jr. at the Harvard University Belfer Center for Science and international Affairs; and the 1999 survey by Andrew Bacevich, Director of the Boston University Center for International Relations.

Professors Hermann Fr. Eilts and David Mayers contributed to the surveys in 1987, as did Bacevich in 1999. Eilts reviewed nearly the entire manuscript and made many useful comments, as did Professor Lincoln P. Bloomfield at MIT. Mayers and Bacevich kindly reviewed parts of the manuscript in 2000.

The book's interpretation of complexity theory owes much to the writings of Stuart Kauffman and to discussions with him in Santa Fe. The book's analysis of power and interdependence owes a great deal to the writings of Robert O. Keohane and Joseph S. Nye and to seminars with them at Harvard University. Lincoln P. Bloomfield at MIT introduced me to scenario-writing and simulations as ways to outline alternative futures.

The analysis also benefits from seminars at the Belfer Center and the Davis Center for Russian Studies at Harvard University, the Center for International Studies at MIT, the Center for International Relations and the Institute for the Study of Conflict, Ideology, Policy at Boston University, and from comments by Stephen Miller, Steven Walt, Stephen Van Evera, and Hans Ulrich-Seidt at a conference "NATO: The First Fifty Years and Beyond" held on June 21, 2000 at the American Academy of Arts and Sciences.

Dr. Randall Forsberg, president of the Institute for Defense and Disarmament Studies, kindly provided her graphs showing trends in U.S. defense spending and procurement, shown in chapter 4.

All cartoons are Copyright Jeff Danziger, 1997–2000. Would that the words of political scientists cut so deeply as his images!

Ali Ho Clemens of Internet Presence, Inc., provided many graphics as well as crucial moral support and reflection.

Karen Wolny, Gabriella Pearce, Ruth Mannes, and Meg Weaver at St. Martin's Press were unstinting in their encouragement and assistance. The index was prepared by Asbed Kotchikian.

Some reports on the surveys first appeared as op-ed essays in the *Christian Science Monitor.* Parts of chapter 5 appeared in *International Journal* and *Communist and Post-Soviet Studies.* The book develops many themes set out in the author's *Dynamics of International Relations: Conflict and Mutual Gain in An Era of Global Interdependence* (Lanham, Md.: Rowman & Littlefield, 1998). A parallel survey on Soviet achievements and failures appeared in the journal *Survey* and in my book, *Can Russia Change? The USSR Confronts Global Interdependence* (Boston: Unwin Hyman, 1990).

The book is dedicated to my grandchildren with the wish that they and theirs can live in peace, prosperity, and freedom.

CONTRIBUTORS

Many historians and political analysts graciously contributed to this book by responding, in writing or in interviews, to surveys conducted in 1976–1977, 1987, and 1999. The 1976–1977 survey elicited responses from persons associated with the Woodrow Wilson International Center for Scholars: Henry Steele Commager, J. William Fulbright, George F. Kennan, Jon B. McLin, John G. Palfrey, George Packard, George Rentz, Irving Richter, and Samuel F. Wells. Commager, Fulbright, and Kennan did not reply in writing but in long interviews. Diane S. Clemens at the University of California in Berkeley also contributed a written response to the survey.

Respondents to the 1987 survey were former Wilson Fellows Frans A. M. Alting von Geusau (The Netherlands), Yves Boyer (France), Peter Clausen, C. J. Hill (UK), Alan K. Henrikson, Takeshi Igarashi (Japan), Josef Joffe (Germany), Lawrence S. Kaplan, Sanford Lakoff, John Norton Moore, Charles C. Moskos, David McLellan, Henry R. Nau, Harry Howe Ransom, Herbert Spiro, Ronald L. Steel, John A. Thompson (UK), Leopold Unger (Belgium), Kenneth N. Waltz, Robert Wesson, M. C. Young, and Boston University professors Hermann Fr. Eilts, José E. Garriga-Pico, Roy A. Glasgow, William R. Keylor, William V. Shannon, Frank Zagare, Howard Zinn. Their responses (28) amounted to about one-third those solicited in two mailings in 1987. All respondents were U.S. citizens or residents except as indicated. Former U.S. ambassadors Eilts and Spiro were born in Germany; professor Garriga-Pico in Puerto Rico; professor Glasgow in Trinidad and Tobago.

Boston University faculty responding in 1999 were Andrew Bacevich, William Keylor, Max Otte (Germany), and Maria Rodriques (Brazil). From further afield, Bruce Cumings responded from the University of Chicago; J. David Singer from the University of Michigan; and John Nolte, New School of Social Research.

America and the World, 1898–2025

FRAMEWORK:
AIMS, METHODS, THEORIES

Aims and Methods

This book seeks guidelines for United States foreign policy in the first decades of the twenty-first century. To do so, it begins by searching the record of America's achievements and failures in the twentieth-century world. When and why did U.S. policies succeed? When and why did they fail? Did successful policies bear any distinguishing traits? How important were individuals—from Teddy Roosevelt to Bill Clinton—in shaping success and failure? How important were domestic and global forces?

From analyzing the past, the book turns to America's global prospects in the first quarter of the twenty-first century. What are the country's tangible and intangible assets relative to other actors? What alternative futures may emerge? What lessons—what guidelines for policy—spring from looking back and looking ahead? How can we act so as to avoid chaos and improve prospects for a world in which Americans and the rest of humanity live in peace and interact for mutual gain?

Distilling Wisdom from Experience

The book's interpretations are the author's. They flow from the author's research into arms control issues between Washington, Moscow, and Beijing and a synthesis of theoretical perspectives described later in this "framework" chapter. The analysis benefits from the evidence presented in major texts by diplomatic historians so different in outlook as Walter LaFeber and Walter McDougall.[1] Last but not least, the book's interpretations tap the opinions and distill the wisdom of more than fifty leading experts on foreign policy who generously responded to surveys asking them to list the major achievements and failures of U.S. foreign policy since 1900 and the factors that gave rise to them. Respondents ranged from George F. Kennan and four other retired ambassadors to historian Henry Steele Commager to journalist Josef Joffe to neorealist political scientist Kenneth N. Waltz and radical critic Howard Zinn.[2] The experts agreed on many points and disagreed on others; there were majority and minority viewpoints. Some respondents empathized with U.S. foreign policymakers; others expressed anger and impatience at their shortcomings.

Can We Define the Bottom Line?

What is "success" in foreign policy? Respondents to my surveys were asked to judge success by the extent to which a given policy met the goals that its creators in Washington set for it. But motives are hard to assess. And so respondents tended to evaluate U.S. policies by their contribution to the country's interests, regardless of the ostensible or hidden motives behind the policy. The respondents tended to look beyond near-term success (even though it might help a president win reelection) to the policy's longer-term consequences for the national interest—as they understood it.

Appraisals reflect values. Thus, the U.S. invasion of Grenada in 1983 could be seen as standing up for a position or as "bullying and shooting from the hip." But Republicans as well as Democrats gave high marks to the 1978 Egyptian-Israeli accords mediated by President Jimmy Carter at Camp David. One expert explained that "Camp David can't be seen as anything other than Americans using our power and leadership to bring peace to the world."[3]

History provides a trove of experience that can be mined to learn what happened and why. The quest can be both interesting and useful. But we need a method—a framework for analysis.

This book's standard for evaluating a policy's success is whether, after three years, it enhanced United States fitness—the country's ability to cope with complex challenges and opportunities—at home and abroad. This concept of fitness derives from complexity theory, as outlined later in this chapter. This standard might seem noncontroversial, but assessing alternative policies gives rise to hard choices, as illustrated in box 1.[4]

Let us clarify the standard by which we evaluate policy outcomes. First, it focuses on results—not inputs. A policy may be well formu-

---

Box 0.1. The Many Meanings of Success

Consider the many factors a member of the U.S. House of Representatives might weigh when deciding whether to approve continuing U.S. economic assistance to a developing country. Does the aid program satisfy a moral imperative to help the less fortunate? Has this aid raised the recipient country's living standards? If so, has it reduced emigration to the United States?

Does aid create business opportunities for U.S. firms? Should Washington demand a sharp rise in economic growth or be content with marginal gains? Might other kinds of aid have been more cost-effective—basic education rather than hydroelectric projects?

Has this aid won influence for United States? Has it led the recipient to align with us on key issues at the United Nations? Has our aid influenced the recipient country to abjure nuclear weapons?

Does the program take funds from more important undertakings at home or abroad? If this aid program is worthwhile, should it be enlarged? Could it be down-sized without damaging its thrust?

The Congresswoman also deliberates how her vote will shape her career and personal interests: "Will my vote make the White House more supportive of programs for my district? Will my stance win or lose votes for me at home? Will it generate campaign contributions for me from firms doing business in the target country?"

---

lated but fail when poorly implemented.[5] Successes may be easy wins or long-shot victories. Even if achievements depended heavily on favorable circumstances, we place them in the plus column; if a policy failed against the tide, we count it a failure. Still, the standard takes into account assets and context. It asks: How well did Americans use the resources available to deal with the problems at hand? Did they succeed against the great odds or fail despite propitious conditions? Note that inaction as well as action can be "policy." Inaction can result from ignorance, an inward-looking worldview, or a specific decision, for example, not to arm or to intervene.

The standard requires us to prioritize in light of potential gains and risks. We must answer tough questions: What if a policy improves the trade balance but degrades the environment? What if an antimissile defense shields Americans from a North Korean attack, but provokes Russia into building more missiles?

Fifth, the standard focuses on the greatest fitness for the greatest number. A policy outcome favorable to a certain geographical region, an ethnic group, or business interest *could* enhance the country's overall fitness. But this is not guaranteed. A private gain could be a public loss.

Sixth, the standard requires us to define expectations in a meaningful way. If we set the bar high, U.S.-led interventions in Bosnia and Kosovo probably failed. If we place the bar lower, perhaps these interventions will appear more successful.

Few policy outcomes can be deemed a complete success or failure. Even the greatest achievement is only a partial success. Each has a downside. Today's success may be tomorrow's loss. Often, the seed of failure resides in the fruit of victory—and vice versa. Most failures are partial—especially if we can learn from them.

The illustrations that limn this book suggest the paradoxes inherent in evaluating policies. What one person sees as success may appear a failure to others. The book's graphs on military spending and acquisitions make a similar point. For some, U.S. defense outlays are excessive; for others, insufficient. No matter how big or small, the outlays may go for unwise missions or purchases.

No book can provide the last word on foreign policy. But this book's juxtaposition of achievements and failures, its portraits of alternative futures, and its outline of policy implications should stimulate further efforts to learn from the past how to forge a better future.[6]

Let us analyze the assumptions that undergird this book's interpretations.

Theoretical Assumptions

Politicians may think that their decisions are responses to "facts," "national interests," and "pressures"—not to theories. But each of us filters reality and acts on the basis of certain expectations and beliefs—implicit if not explicit theories. Each politician's view of "national interests" reflects a theory.

This book argues that success in foreign affairs is more likely when a policy accords with a synthesis of several interrelated theoretical perspectives:

The explanatory power of these perspectives can be checked against the track record of U.S. policy. But first let us examine each concept in more detail. We begin with assertions about shared vulnerabilities.

1. The Nature of Global Interdependence

Human communities have long been interdependent, but their interdependence escalates with technological change. This trend, discerned by Karl Marx and Friedrich Engels in 1848, grows ever stronger.[7] Global interdependence becomes a fact of life.

Interdependence is more than interconnectedness. It is a relationship in which the well-being of two or more actors is vulnerable, or at least sensitive, to changes in the condition or policies of the other.[8] It means mutual dependence—a domain between the extremes of absolute dependency and complete independence. Interdependent actors are linked so closely that a change in the conditions or policies of one actor will impact the other in ways that it cannot easily change. Thus, they may help or harm one another.

Global interdependence affects states, while globalization ignores them. Globalization is the process by which global forces—from ideas to electronic mail to epidemics—transcend state borders.

Given the facts of global interdependence and the forces of globalization, global actors—states and nonstate actors—may try to claim values at others' expense or create values for mutual gain.

2. The Model of Complex Interdependence

The relations between states and societies can evolve from interdependence to approximate a model of complex interdependence with

---

Box 0.2. Varieties of Interdependence

Sensitivity means liability to costly effects imposed from outside before any policies are devised to cope with the new situation. Vulnerability means continued liability to costly effects imposed from the outside despite efforts to alter or escape the situation. Interdependence may be symmetrical or asymmetrical, but if a relationship is extremely one-sided, one party will be dependent—not interdependent.

Symmetrical vulnerability. The United States and Russia remain vulnerable to missile attack by each other. *Asymmetrical vulnerability.* Russia is much more dependent economically on the West—especially for credit—than vice versa. *Sensitivity.* If Russia does not import U.S. grains and chicken, or if Washington blocks their delivery, each side will be inconvenienced. But neither side is without recourse. American farmers can shift to other crops or markets, and Russians can buy grain from Australia, Argentina, or elsewhere.

---

a strong capacity to diminish discord and sustain peaceful cooperation. This model is marked by three features:[9]

1. A complex agenda with no hierarchy. There are many issues on the agenda. No single one stands out so that, unless it is resolved, the entire relationship is in jeopardy.
2. Interaction at many levels of government and society. Multiple channels connect the societies—not just meetings of ministers and presidents.
3. Bargaining without coercion. Negotiations continue on many issues but military threats are virtually unthinkable.

Complex interdependence makes the participants stronger than the sum of their parts. Peaceful cooperation is both a cause and a result of complex interdependence. Starting in the late nineteenth century, Canada and the United States moved toward complex interdependence, even though their governments and many basic values remained distinct. Starting in the 1950s, all West European countries moved in an ebb and flow toward complex interdependence. Russia and the United States tried to move closer in the early 1990s but withdrew from each other later in the decade. Thus, complex interdependence is a model toward which states may move or from which they may withdraw.

3. The Nature of Power

Humans—especially when the stakes are high—are tempted to grab what they can. Cooperation and reciprocity must often be induced by skillful use of soft or hard power. Soft power persuades or coopts; hard power commands or coerces. Soft power inspires consensus (agreement); it coopts others to embrace the same goals. It uses the power of example or the lure of a reward to motivate. Hard power uses mainly tangible assets—economic and military—to compel or coerce others to change their course, but it may also use intangible assets, such as scarce information. Besides soft and hard power assets, an actor on the world stage needs "conversion" power to transform these assets into fitness and influence—the ability to alter others' behavior. Conversion power requires wisdom, foresight, leadership, skill, and other qualities, both tangible and intangible.[10] The qualities a diplomat needs to translate hard and soft power into constructive outcomes are analyzed in chapter 3.

Cooperation achieved by consensus and cooption is likely to be far more stable than that produced by coercion or command. West Germany in the 1950s became a willing partner in a security community that evolved from the European Recovery Program (Marshall Plan)—quite unlike the grudging German participation in world affairs under the Versailles Peace Treaty.

4. Mutual Gain Theory

Mutual dependencies bring both danger and opportunity. A wise foreign policy will not assume that politics is a zero-sum struggle or that win-win solutions are always possible. Neither cynics nor martyrs do well in the give-and-take of world affairs.

Mutual gain theory is normative, but is also helps to analyze the past, describe the present, and anticipate future contingencies. American and other global actors are more likely to enhance their objectives if they can frame and implement value-creating strategies aimed at mutual gain than if they pursue value-claiming policies for one-sided gain. Exploitation may yield short-run benefits for one side (at least for parts of that society) but tends to boomerang in the longer run so that total costs outweigh unilateral benefits. The "longer run" may have once been measured in decades or centuries, but in a world of escalating interdependence, it becomes ever shorter, so that profitable exploitation is difficult to sustain longer than, say, a decade.[11]

Mutual gain theory argues that policies oriented to conditional cooperation for mutual gain are more likely to enhance an actor's interests than zero-sum competition. The qualifier "conditional" is necessary because humans are not angels. The success of cooperation depends upon reciprocity—promoted by self-interest, sanctions, and safeguards.

The stronger side—for most of the twentieth century, the United States—can afford to initiate cooperative policies with rivals as well as with established partners. Even so, the initiator must also make clear that continued cooperation depends upon reciprocity.

5. The Value of Open Communication

Mutual gain policies require open communication at home and abroad. The more that all parties communicate, the greater the prospect of finding solutions useful to all sides—"good" outcomes if not "great"; and certainly not "poor" or "catastrophic." The more voices and interests have access to relevant information and can make themselves heard, the less chance of miscalculation. The more that intelligence estimates are shared within society, the more likely that policy initiatives will succeed—at least in peacetime. If the parties are at war, they have reason to mask their actions, but even belligerents can gain from discussing how to limit their conflict.[12]

The foreign policy of the world's first and greatest mass democracy has been "subject to broader public scrutiny and influence than that of any great power in history."[13] Has this been an asset or a liability?

Some negotiations are better conducted without publicity. Also, so long as deep rivalries persist, human societies will need to gather intelligence on each other's capabilities and intentions. How to balance the conflicting pressures on the behalf of "open" and "closed" diplomacy is not easy. Much depends on time and place, and the nature of the competition. Our survey of twentieth century diplomacy in chapters 1 and 2, however, shows that openness has facilitated major foreign policy successes while secrecy has often been counter-productive.

The utility of openness probably increases in a time of information revolution and escalating global interdependence. States rich in natural resources will continue to dominate world politics in the information age, but they will rely less on traditional resources and more on their ability to remain credible to a public with increasingly diverse sources of information.[14]

6. Complexity Theory

Complexity theory as developed at the Santa Fe Institute is interdisciplinary, but rooted in the life sciences. It modifies Charles Darwin's emphasis on natural selection as the key to evolution. It treats "fitness" as the capacity to cope with complex challenges.[15] In the 1990s many businesses sought advice from complexity theorists on how they should organize to cope better with complexity.[16]

Complexity theory suggests that all life forms exist on a spectrum ranging from ultrastability (ordered hierarchy) to instability (chaos). Fitness is found in the middle range of the spectrum between rigid order and chaos.[17]

Complexity theory stresses the importance of agent-based systems. These are networks in which independent agents, each following a few rules, self-organize to form an emergent phenomenon without central direction from above. Thus, many species interlock in a coral reef and shield one another from predators, temperature extremes, and strong currents. Without planning, they cooperate for mutual gain.

When organisms associate in the symbiosis of a coral reef or other ecosystem, the resultant structure is called an "emergent property." It is "order for free." The system offers protection against the ravages of storms and alien species, but it is fragile. A coral reef, for example, can be broken by strong currents or killed by temperature change. But many ecosystems endure for long periods. Their fragile equilibrium is called self-organized criticality. Like the coral reef, every durable ecosystem is an emergent phenomenon.

Insects that live in colonies seem to have their individual agendas. Yet the group as a whole appears to be highly organized. The seamless integration of all individual activities appears to take place without supervision. Instead, cooperation seems to be self-organized. The interactions of individuals appears simple but they manage to solve difficult problems, such as finding the shortest path to a food source.

The collective behavior that emerges from a group of social insects is called "swarm intelligence." It offers an alternative way of designing systems that traditionally required centralized control and extensive preprogramming. It counts on autonomy and self-sufficiency in an effort to generate systems that adapt quickly to fluctuating conditions.[18]

Social science as well as biology suggest that a society's well-being—its overall fitness—may depend upon a capacity to cooperate both within and outside the group. To sustain our common life support system, humans need to cooperate—not try to ride free on others' labors. Mutual gain can be an emergent property of humans' coevolution with one another and with other life forms.

Fitness Landscapes.   Complexity theory suggests that coevolution can be mapped as a rugged landscape in which the relative fitness of each organism is shown as a peak rising or falling as a consequence of coevolution. As in an arms race, the peaks of a predator and its prey may gain or decline according to changes in their offensive and defensive capabilities. If attackers acquire more lethal weapons, the fitness peak of the prey will drop. If individuals among the prey population acquire characteristics that reduce their vulnerability, their peaks will rise.

Indicators of Societal Fitness.   For a human society, fitness is the ability to cope with complex challenges and opportunities at home and abroad; to defend society and its values against internal and external threats; and to provide conditions in which its members can choose how to fulfill their human potential.

How does fitness differ from power? Like power, fitness has many dimensions. It is a deeper condition from which material, intangible, and other kinds of power and influence can emerge.

Societal fitness must be evaluated relative to conditions at home and across borders. There is no one measure of fitness, such as population growth or nuclear arsenals or energy consumption per capita.[19] Still, a society's infant mortality rate provides a first approximation, for it reflects many dimensions of fitness. The United Nations Development Programme's Human Development Index

(HDI) provides additional standards. The HDI assesses each country's attainments in physical health, education, purchasing power, gender equality, and other indicators of justice. A society with a low infant mortality rate and a high HDI is fitter than a society with high infant mortality and a low HDI.

A fit society is one that helps its members to fulfill their human potential. The United Nations Development Programme evaluates societies by their capacity to give their members *choice*. The Human Development Index provides a set of yardsticks to evaluate this capacity. But the conditions it measures merely set the stage for human fulfillment. A developed society can facilitate and even encourage, but not ensure, a good life for its members.

A society may be internally fit but weak in the international arena. Overall fitness requires a capacity to defend against external threats and, in a world where peace is indivisible, to contribute to collective action against aggressors and violators of human rights.

Each human society—each state—interdepends with others regionally if not globally. The fitness of regional and global systems can be measured by their ability to foster peace, economic well-being, justice, liberty, and environmental quality as well as cultural, scientific, and spiritual development.[20]

A world system in which many people die needlessly lacks fitness. The twentieth century witnessed more than 100 million excess deaths from war—about half of them in the 1940s. But the death toll from wars pales next to the damage to public health from underdevelopment, racial and ethnic discrimination, and gender bias.[21]

Human fitness is jeopardized by authoritarian rule. Communist systems led the twentieth century in demicide (killing one's own or another people) and politicide (killing political foes). Among the peoples who suffered from Soviet demicide and politicide were Balts, Ukrainians, Kazaks, and Chechens.[22] Demicide and politicide are abhorrent but also dangerous to others. A society willing to kill its own people is a menace to humanity.

A system in which millions—indeed, billions—of people are at risk from violent death also lacks fitness. If even a fraction of the U.S. or Russian nuclear arsenals were fired, millions would die. Even more millions would become ill from the effects of radiation and pollution. Nuclear winter might set in.[23]

Fitness requires both order and freedom, but a fit society will avoid the Scylla of rigid hierarchy and Charybdis of social chaos.

Survival—in politics as in evolution—is determined not just by natural selection but by self-organization. Fitness in the information age requires a capacity to process information about many variables and deal with them efficiently.

This book assumes that Americans should strive to make their country more fit—not to build up wealth, power, or influence for their own sake. Power in all its forms can be useful and sometimes necessary, but should not be seen as an end in itself. As we shall see below, the United States was the world's sole superpower as one century ended and another began, rich and accomplished in many fields, but with deep social cleavages and domestic problems that undermined its quality of life and weakened its influence in world affairs.[24]

7. Liberal Peace Theory

Fitness through self-organization rather than top-down organization by autocratic fiat lies at the heart of liberal peace theory. Writing just a few years after the American and the French Revolutions, Immanuel Kant explained the inner logic between self-rule and peace. The first and basic key to peace, Kant argued, is "republican" or representative government—not monarchy or direct democracy (then shaking France). Republicanism is synergistic. Kant assumed that it would contribute to and gain from international organization and law, the spirit of trade, and an enlightened culture of mutual respect.[26] Similar assumptions underlay the views of both Republican and Democratic Party internationalists in Washington throughout the twentieth century—from Theodore Roosevelt, William Howard Taft, and Woodrow Wilson to George Bush and William Clinton. These assumptions were also shared by public figures who believed the United States should be an exemplar to the world and those who believed that the United States should actively intervene to shape the world in its image.[27]

Kant's second postulate was that self-governing peoples will tend to form federations to preserve peace and their rights. If an enlightened people forms a representative government, "it will provide a focal point for a federal association among other nations that will join it in order to guarantee a state of peace among nations . . . and through several associations of this sort such a federation can extend further and further."

> ## Box 0.3. How Independent Agents Shaped American Political Culture
>
> "Agency" is an idea that developed in sixteenth century England. It took shape in the Puritan challenge to the monarchical order. For Puritans, the individual became a self-reliant agent able to act freely. Agency, for Puritans, was not servitude but a path freely chosen. However, Puritans did not see agency as individualistic freedom. They hoped that individuals would defer to collective authority and choose to serve a larger vision.
>
> "Agency"—not liberty—was the dominant idea shaping American political culture. An agent might be a congregant who joins an independent church and becomes devoted to its mission. Or a politician in a constitutional government whose demands are tempered by the social contract.
>
> "Liberty" was an idea that inspired American farmers to join political elites in the struggle for independence, but the American Revolution enshrined agency—not liberty. The result was an ongoing struggle between demands for individual freedom and collective order. From the start, untethered liberty was seen as a danger—indulgent and disruptive. But servitude to unquestioned authority was just as troubling. The tension between iconoclasm and conformity in American life often produced a compromise in which freedom served the common cause.[25]

Third, since these representative governments will not accept any other government over them, they accept an enlarged body of international law that will "finally include all the people of the earth." As community prevails among the earth's peoples, "a transgression in *one* place in the world is felt *everywhere*."[28]

Fourth, representative government and law are linked with commerce. The "*spirit of trade* cannot coexist with war, and sooner or later this spirit dominates every people." Those with the most to lose economically will exert every effort to head off war by mediation.[29]

Fifth, common institutions should lead to mutual respect. Language and religion divide men, but "the growth of culture and men's gradual progress toward greater agreement regarding their [common] principles lead to mutual understanding and peace." Kant was also a Green before it became popular. He stipulated that the "right to visit, to associate [with other peoples], belongs to all men by virtue of their *common ownership of the earth's surface* [emphasis added, W.C.]."

Kant urged governments to remember that if their policies attempt to do what is *morally* right, peace and other good results will follow. If each state behaves morally, the space between them can become an extension of the rational political community or "civil society" achieved within each state. The international arena then could be dominated—not by amoral anarchy—but by "pure practical reason and its righteousness."[30]

Kant also realized, however, that the system he outlined would be vulnerable to the wild streak in human nature that could tear down the rule of reason. He cautioned that "from the crooked timber of humanity no straight thing can ever be made." But he hoped that each individual, reaching upward like a tree for air and sun, would grow straight under the canopy of civil society.[31]

The synergy among the conditions forecast and prescribed by Kant interact to form a "social field"—an exchange society with a habit of problem-solving by negotiation and accommodation. Liberal peace theory helps explain why few if any established democracies have ever attacked each other. Peoples that *perceive* one another as democratic have not fought each other. Indeed, they have tended to band together against authoritarians.

8. Convergence of Mutual Gain, Complexity, and Liberal Peace Theory

The postulates of liberal peace theory read like a description of the European Union at the onset of the third millennium and, by extension, the "security community" linking Europe, Canada, the United States, and Japan in networks of complex interdependence.

Liberal peace theory converges with mutual gain and complexity theory. Each urges self-organization to create shared values. Societies based on self-rule are geared to mutual gain and value creation rather than toward exploitation, at least within their borders.

Taken together, the theoretical assumptions of this book predict that a good society is likely to be one self-organized for the mutual gain of its members and, as international conditions permit, for co-operative value-creation with other societies. In principle a society or an international system could also be organized for the common good from the top down by enlightened despots, but this is unlikely. Their vision will probably be myopic due to vested interests and ignorance of local strengths and problems.

The bottom line for U.S. foreign policymakers is that the world contains danger and opportunity. The United States and its people are linked with other actors—countries, peoples, movements, firms, nongovernmental agencies, families, individuals—in networks of global interdependence and globalization. We can seek to exploit one another or create mutual gain.

Let us now look at the U.S. record in the twentieth century. The overview will help us decide whether the foregoing theoretical assumptions should be accepted, refined, or rejected.

Notes

1. Walter LaFeber, *The American Age: U.S. Foreign Policy at Home and Abroad, 1750 to the Present* (2d ed.; New York: W. W. Norton, 1994); David Mayers, *Wars and Peace: The Future Americans Envisioned, 1861–1991* (New York: St. Martin's, 1998); Walter McDougall, *Promised Land, Crusader State: The American Encounter with the World Since 1776* (Boston: Houghton Mifflin, 1997). Most of the topics discussed in this book are analyzed by contributors to Michael J. Hogan, ed., *America in the World: The Historiography of American Foreign Relations since 1941* (Cambridge, UK: Cambridge University Press, 1995).

2. This analysis builds on expert views gathered as written responses by foreign policy specialists to open-ended surveys conducted in 1976–77, 1987, and 1999. The first and second surveys polled scholars and diplomats associated with the Woodrow Wilson International Center for Scholars; the second and third surveys included input from political scientists and historians at Boston University and several other universities. The contributors are listed after the Acknowledgments. Most respondents were academics but many served as government consultants; most were Americans but some were Asian, European, or Latin American. Five had been U.S. ambassadors—George F. Kennan, Hermann Fr. Eilts, John Norton Moore, Herbert Spiro, and William V. Shannon. Ambassador Kennan, Senator J. William Fulbright, and historian Henry S. Commager gave their responses orally. Some of the survey results appeared in op-ed essays published in the *Christian Science Monitor*. A parallel survey on the successes and failures of

Soviet foreign policy was summarized in Walter C. Clemens, Jr., *Can Russia Change? The USSR Confronts Global Interdependence* (Boston: Unwin Hyman, 1990), chapter 1.

3. Political scientist Robert D. Putnam quoted in Alan Clymer, "Camp David at Top in U.S. Policy Poll," *The New York Times,* April 1, 1985, p. A6.

4. To take another example: Consider the program by which the United States buys enriched uranium from Russia. Does the program serve to keep fissionable material from aspiring nuclear powers? Does it improve working relations between U.S. and Russian military and scientific personnel? Does it acquire nuclear fuel for the United States at bargain prices? Does it make U.S. investors richer and take a financial burden from government? Does the program contribute on balance to U.S. fitness?

5. For studies of national and local welfare and environmental programs, see Helen M. Ingram and Dean E. Mann, eds., *Why Policies Succeed or Fail* (Beverly Hills, Ca.: SAGE, 1980) and Aron Wildavsky, *Speaking Truth to Power: The Art and Craft of Policy Analysis* (Boston: Little, Brown, 1979). For other policy evaluations, see Mark G. Field, ed., *Success and Crisis in National Health Systems: A Comparative Approach* (New York: Routledge, 1989).

6. On the Clinton years, see Alvin Z. Rubinstein et al., eds., *The Clinton Foreign Policy Reader: Presidential Speeches with Commentary* (Armonk: N.Y.: M. E. Sharpe, 2000). Articles in such journals as *Foreign Affairs, Foreign Policy, Orbis,* and *The National Interest* have graded the foreign policies of various administrations. See, for example, Stephen M. Walt, "Two Cheers for Clinton's Foreign Policy," *Foreign Affairs,* 79, 2 (March/April 2000), pp. 63–79.

For current materials, use the websites offered by the White House: *http://www.pub.whitehouse.gov*

For Congressional documents: *http://clerkweb.house.gov/doc/docs.htm*

For Department of State briefings: *http://dosfan.lib.uic.edu/ERC/briefing.html*

For Department of Defense materials: *http://www.defenselink.mil/pub/almanac/osd.html;* also *http://www.dtic.mil/execsec/adr_intro.html*

For publications of the Central Intelligence Agency: *http://www.odci.gov/ica/public_affairs/html*

Intelligence: A Consumer's Guide to Intelligence (Washington, D.C.: Central Intelligence Agency, 2000).

To order CIA and other publications, National Technical Information Service: *http://www.ntis.gov*

For publications of the U.S. Government Printing Office: http://www.access.gpo.gov/su_docs/

7. "In place of the old local and national seclusion and self-sufficiency, we have intercourse in every direction, universal interdependence of nations. And as in material, so also in intellectual production." Karl Marx and Friedrich Engels, *Communist Manifesto* [1848] (New York: Oxford University Press, 1992).

8. The argument here follows Robert O. Keohane and Joseph S. Nye, *Power and Interdependence* (2d ed.; New York: HarperCollins, 1989), chap. 1.

9. Keohane and Nye, *Power and Interdependence,* chapter 2, with case studies of complex interdependence in oceans and money in chapter 5, and in U.S. relations with Canada and Australia in chapter 7.

10. Soft, hard, and conversion power are discussed in Joseph S. Nye, Jr., *Bound to Lead: The Changing Nature of American Power* (New York: Basic Books, 1990).

11. Mutual gain theory is developed in Walter C. Clemens, Jr., *Dynamics of International Relations: Conflict and Mutual Gain in an Era of Global Interdependence* (Lanham, Md.: Rowman & Littlefield, 1998). An earlier version was the author's "The Non-Zero Sum Hypothesis and National Self-Interest," paper presented to the Peace Research Society (International), in Vienna, August 29, 1971. The theory builds on Petr Kropotkin, *Mutual Aid* (London, 1902) and David A. Lax and James K. Sebenius, *The Manager as Negotiator: Bargaining for Cooperation and Competition* (New York: The Free Press, 1986). The term "escalating interdependence" was suggested by Karl W. Deutsch in a conversation long ago. See also Robert Wright, *Nonzero: The Logic of Human Destiny* (New York: Pantheon, 2000).

12. This thesis—also advanced in Clemens, *Dynamics of International Relations*—will be examined below in the cases reviewed in chapters 1 and 2.

13. Its policymaking elite was not an insulated imperial class as in nineteenth-century Britain or other great powers. Adam Garfinkle, "The U.S. Imperial Postulate in the Mideast," *Orbis,* 41, 1 (Winter 1997), pp. 15–29 at 16.

14. Robert O. Keohane and Joseph S. Nye, Jr., "Power and Interdependence in the Information Age," *Foreign Affairs,* 77, 5 (September/October 1998), pp. 81–94.

15. Founded in 1984, the Santa Fe Institute attracted scholars so diverse as physicist Murray Gell-Man, economist Kenneth Arrow, and biochemist Stuart Kauffman. For early work at the Santa Fe Institute, Roger Lewin, *Complexity: Life at the Edge of Chaos* (New York:

Macmillan, 1992). Major books by Stuart Kauffman: *The Origins of Order: Self-Organization and Selection in Evolution* (New York: Oxford University Press, 1993); *At Home in the Universe: The Search for the Laws of Self-Organization and Complexity* (New York: Oxford University Press, 1995); and *Investigations* (New York: Oxford University Press, forthcoming).

The Santa Fe Institute publishes the journal *Complexity*. Institute working papers include Martin Shubik, "Game Theory, Complexity, and Simplicity Part I: A Tutorial" (98–04–027); Melisa Savage and Manor Askenazi, "Arborscapes: A Swarm-based Multi-agent Ecological Disturbance Model (98–06–056).

For agent-based systems in social science and an extensive bibliography, Joshua M. Epstein and Robert Axtell, *Growing Artificial Societies: Social Science from the Bottom Up* (Cambridge, Ma.: The MIT Press, 1996); also "Special Issue: Evolutionary Paradigms in the Social Sciences," *International Studies Quarterly*, 40, 3 (September 1996).

Complexity theory has stimulated much work by Robert M. Axelrod, though he has focused on solving complex problems by a variety of methods rather than on applying complexity theory as developed by Kauffman et al. See Robert M. Axelrod, *The Complexity of Cooperation: Agent-Based Models of Competition and Cooperation* (Princeton, N.J.: Princeton University Press, 1997); also Axelrod, "Advancing the Art of Simulation in the Social Sciences," International Conference on Computer Simulation and the Social Sciences, Cortona, Italy, September 22–25, 1997. For an application of complexity theory by a former student of Axelrod, see Lars-Erik Cederman, *Emergent Actors in World Politics: How States and Nations Develop and Dissolve* (Princeton, N.J.: Princeton University Press, 1997).

The utility of complexity theory is assessed by Hayward R. Alker and Simon Fraser, "On Historical Complexity: 'Naturalistic' Modeling Approaches from the Santa Fe Institute," paper delivered at the American Political Science Association Annual Meeting, San Francisco, August 31, 1996; see also Hayward R. Alker, *Rediscoveries and Reformulations: Humanistic methodologies for International Studies* (Cambridge, UK: Cambridge University Press, 1996). For a skeptical view, see John Horgan, *The End of Science: Facing the Limits of Knowledge in the Twilight of the Scientific Age* (Reading, Ma.: Addison-Wesley, 1996), chaps. 5–9. For a more balanced appraisal, see the "Edge of Chaos" and many relevant entries in Ian Marshall and Danah Zohar, *Who's Afraid of Schrödinger's Cat: All the Science Ideas You Need to Keep Up with the New Thinking* (New York: Morrow, 1997).

Complexity theory builds on the work of systems theorists such as Ludwig von Bertalanffy, Ervin Laszlo, and Jay W. Forrester. See Forrester, *World Dynamics* (Cambridge, Ma.: Wright-Allen Press, 1971), adapted in several Club of Rome studies of the global problematique, and evaluated in Walter C. Clemens, Jr., "Ecology and International Relations," *International Journal* (Special issue: "Earth Politics"), 28, 1 (Winter 1972–3), pp. 1–27.

16. For applications to management, Roger Lewin and Birute Regine, *The Soul at Work: Listen, Respond, Let Go: Embracing Complexity Science for Business Success* (New York: Simon & Schuster, 2000).

17. The manner in which some actors pursued fitness from the top down (Tsarist and Soviet Russia) and others by self-organization (from the Hanseatic city-states to post-Soviet Estonia), see Walter C. Clemens, Jr., *The Baltic Transformed: Complexity Theory and European Security* (forthcoming). For historical and systems analysis, see Hendrik Spruyt, *The Sovereign State and Its Competitors: An Analysis of Systems Change* (Princeton, N.J.: Princeton University Press, 1994). Robert Jervis, *System Effects: Complexity in Political and Social Life* (Princeton, N.J.: Princeton University Press, 1997), examines the complex interactions of social units, but says little about self-organization. Compare with earlier work by Nazli Choucri and Robert C. North, *Nations in Conflict* (San Francisco: Freeman, 1975) and James N. Rosenau, *Turbulence in World Politics: A Theory of Change and Continuity* (Princeton, N.J.: Princeton University Press, 1990).

For more recent studies, see Michael Lipson, "Nonlinearity, Constructivism, and International Relations: Or, Changing the Rules by Playing the Game," presented at Annual Meeting, American Political Science Association, Chicago, August 31-September 3, 1996; Matthew J. Hoffmann, "Constructivism and Complexity Science: Theoretical Links and Empirical Justification," presented at Annual Meeting, International Studies Association, Washington, D.C., February 16–21, 1999.

18. Eric Bonabeau and Guy Théraulaz, "Swarm Smarts," *Scientific American,* 282, 3 (March 2000), pp. 72–79.

19. The United States consumes more energy per capita than most countries, and also leads in post-secondary school enrollment and has a low infant mortality. Might we infer that the more energy consumed per capita, the fitter the society? No. Increased energy availability improves the overall quality of life, but only up to a certain level (1.5–2 kilowatts/person)—beyond which the quality of life hardly changes with additional power consumed. Thus, many industrialized countries have infant mortality as low or lower than the United

States but consume far less energy per capita. Japan and the UK, for example, consumed less than half as much energy per capita as the United States in 1990. Philip Morrison and Kosta Tsipis, *Reason Enough to Hope: America and the World in the Twenty-first Century* (Cambridge, Ma.: The MIT Press, 1998), pp. 164–165.

20. Starting in the 1960s, the World Order Models Project laid out a strategy to attain globally a sequence of goals: first, peace; second, economic well-being; third, justice; fourth, environmental protection. See Richard A. Falk, *A Study of Future Worlds* (New York: Free Press, 1975); and Falk, *Explorations at the Edge of Time: The Prospects for World Order* (Philadelphia: Temple University Press, 1992).

21. The death toll from the twentieth century's wars amounted to 1.2 million lives per year, a little more than 2 percent of the total averaged death rate of 55 million per year. This cut less than 1.5 years from the present world life expectancy of 65 years.

    U.S. life expectancy grew by more than 20 years in the twentieth century. But poor people in the United States lived ten years less than middle and upper income groups, and blacks lived a few years less than whites. Morrison and Tsipis, *Reason Enough,* p. 26.

22. Rudolph J. Rummel, *Lethal Politics: Soviet Genocide and Mass Murder since 1917* (New Brunswick, N.J.: Transaction, 1996), p. 6; Clemens, *Dynamics of International Relations,* pp. 288–290.

23. The United States deployed 9,750 strategic nuclear weapons in 1991, many with a yield a hundred times larger than the Hiroshima and Nagasaki bombs. The USSR had an even larger stockpile. Consider what the USSR could have accomplished with an attack using only one or two percent of its arsenal. Using 239 nuclear warheads in a "counter energy attack," the Soviet Union could have crippled U.S. oil supplies and networks and the manufacturing and transportation systems that depend on them. Though the attack focused on energy, 20 or more million Americans would have died. Morrison and Tsipis, *Reason Enough,* p. 35. If START II were enacted, Washington and Moscow would still be allowed arsenals of 3,000 to 3,500 strategic nuclear weapons.

24. The country ranked near the top of the UN Human Development Index, but was also a world leader in the percentage of its population incarcerated.

25. Research by James E. Block summarized in Edward Rothstein, "Dethroning Freedom as Nation Builder," *The New York Times,* January 1, 2000, pp. D1, D2.

26. Text in Immanuel Kant, *Perpetual Peace and Other Essays* (Indianapolis: Hackett, 1983), pp. 107–143.

27. For a survey of both trends, see H. W. Brands, *What America Owes the World: The Struggle for the Soul of Foreign Policy* (Cambridge, UK: Cambridge University Press, 1998).

28. On the Kantian tradition in international law, see David R. Mapel and Terry Nardin, "Convergence and Divergence in International Ethics," in Nardin and Mapel, eds., *Traditions of International Ethics* (Cambridge, UK: Cambridge University Press, 1992), pp. 297–322. For a skeptical view, see Jens Bartelson, "The Trial of Judgment: A Note on Kant and the Paradoxes of Internationalism," *International Studies Quarterly*, 39, 2 (June 1995), pp. 255–79.

29. Kant lived in Königsberg, once a thriving participant in the Hanseatic League of city-states on the Baltic Sea and the Atlantic shores of northern Europe. Subject in 1795 to the King of Prussia, Kant wrote when there were very few representative democracies in the world, but he may have been inspired by the spirit of the "Hansas." He was certainly familiar with British and French writings on democracy and many of the peace plans proposed by other authors.

30. See also Cecelia Lynch, "Kant, the Republican Peace, and Moral Guidance in International Law," *Ethics & International Affairs*, 8 (1994), pp. 39–58 at 57.

31. See the fifth of Kant's nine theses in "Idea for a Universal History with a Cosmopolitan Intent," (1784) in *Perpetual Peace and Other Essays*, pp. 15–39 at 33.

PART ONE

The Twentieth Century

1.

Achievements of United States Foreign Policy, 1898–2000

The twentieth century saw the United States rise to become one of many great powers; then one of two superpowers; and finally, the sole superpower—the global hegemon. Americans—leaders and followers, in and out of government, in groups and as individuals—achieved a dozen fundamental successes in the twentieth century world:

1. Force: The United States and its partners prevailed in both world wars and drove aggressors from South Korea and Kuwait.
2. Governance: Americans helped forge institutions and habits of collective security and strengthened world order.
3. Interdependence: They helped rebuild Europe and Japan and formed a trilateral community for trade and security.
4. Containment: They won the Cold War without a U.S.-Soviet hot war and handled crises such as the Cuban confrontation without suffering a defeat or a major loss of life.

5. Conflict control: They learned, with the USSR and Communist China, how adversaries can mitigate conflict and collaborate for parallel objectives.

6. Arms and arms control: They developed the world's most powerful armed forces but also made arms control an integral part of security planning.

7. Peacemaking: They mediated the peaceful settlement of others' disputes and contributed to peacekeeping and peace enforcement.

8. Free trade and economic development: They promoted free trade and institutions fostering economic development and financial stability.

9. Modeling a Third Way: Their market-based liberal democracy served as a model not just for many former Communists but also for statists in Japan and Europe.

10. Human rights: Americans kept alive and spread the ideals of freedom and fostered human rights—political, economic, cultural, religious.

11. International understanding: They promoted international exchanges—in science, in culture, and other realms—and open communication.

12. Dependability: They forged a strong reputation for reliability as allies.

By the end of the century these twelve achievements combined to shape a unipolar world in which no other power center had the will and ability to challenge U.S. hegemony.

Americans learned how to cope with complex challenges at home and abroad, with globalization and the information age, meeting these challenges mainly by self-organization. U.S. successes in world affairs demonstrated that value-creating strategies for mutual gain enhance the deep, long-term interests of all parties more than value-claiming exploitation for one-sided rewards.

To be sure, Americans failed in many arenas or performed less than they could have, given their resources. Failures will be detailed below in chapter 2. Here we review Americans' achievements in the twentieth-century world; in most cases, we shall see, they were greater than failures in the same domains.

1. Force: Prevailing in War

Restrained by habit and outlook from preparing for war, the United States did not enter either world war until directly challenged or attacked. In each case the United States rapidly mobilized its human and material resources to become a decisive factor in defeating the aggressors. Unlike any other participant in World War II, the United States carried on major campaigns in the Pacific theater as well as in North Africa and Europe. Americans converted civilian assembly lines to military production; applied cutting-edge science and technology to development of new weapons; integrated as never before air, land, and sea forces; devised and implemented strategies to win first in Europe and then in Asia; and successfully collaborated with difficult partners.

Americans used their assets wisely and suffered comparatively few losses. They fought worldwide for four years in World War II but, as we see from table 1.1, lost fewer lives than in their own Civil War—when the country's population was much smaller. While other sources say that almost half a million Americans died fighting in World War II (nearly double the Pentagon's official statistics), even this number pales next to the 25 to 40 million Soviet soldiers and civilians thought to have perished in that conflict. Whatever the broad comparisons, of course, each death meant severe trauma for the victim's family and friends, and a net loss for the country's productive and reproductive powers.

Besides the two world wars, Americans also prevailed in most other twentieth-century military conflicts or reached a draw. Three years of fighting in Korea left both sides close to the 38th parallel— the dividing line when the war began. But Washington succeeded in driving the North from South Korea. In Indochina, however, Americans met a severe defeat, discussed in chapter 2.

Before and after 1945 the United States used force short of war on hundreds of occasions to shape the behavior of other states.[1] The U.S. Navy showed the flag in ports around the world. American planes and missiles went from a low to a high alert status. U.S. forces carried out joint maneuvers with partners such as South Korea. Even the size and composition of the Pentagon's budget carried messages to foes and friends. American strategists studied the diplomacy of power and reflected on how to use force to deter, induce, compel, or coerce.[2]

Table 1.1 U.S. Military Casualties, 1775–1992

	American Revolutionary War, 1775–1783	War of 1812–1815	Mexican War, 1846–1848	Civil War 1861–1865 (Union only)**	Spanish-U.S. War, 1898	WW I, 1917–1918	WW II, 1941–1945	Korean, 1950–1953	Vietnam, 1965–1973	Gulf War, 1991–1992
Total military personnel during the war	ca. 217,000	286,730	78,718	2,213,363	306,760	4,734,991	16,112,566	5,720,000	8,744,00 worldwide; 3,385,000 in Southeast Asia	2,029,600; 467,539 in the Gulf region
Battle deaths	6,800*	2,280	1,733	140,414	385	53,402	291,557	33,629	45,941	148
Other deaths	18,500*	n.a.	11,550	224,097	2,061	63,114	113,842	20,617	10,306	145
Wounded but survived	6,188	4,505	4,152	281,881	1,662	204,002	670,846	103,284	303,648	467
Annual death rate per 1,000	n.a.	n.a.	n.a.	104.4	36.6	35.5	11.6	5.5	n.a.	n.a.

Sources: *Historical Statistics of the United States: Colonial Times to 1970* (2 parts; Washington: U.S. Dept. of Commerce, 1975), Part 2, p. 1140; Congressional Reference Service; *U.S. Military Personnel and Casualties in Principal U.S. Wars* (Washington, Library of Congress, 1973). Updated by the author using Department of Defense sources.

*Battle and other deaths in the first column are from *The American Revolution, 1775–1783: An Encyclopedia* (2 vols.; New York: Garland, 1993), 1, 272. U.S. official sources give battle deaths as 4,435 in the Revolutionary War and give no estimate of other deaths.

**Confederate troops suffered at least 133,821 deaths, of which 74,524 were in battle.

Note: n.a. = not available.

From 1988 to 1999 the total number of U.S. military personnel in foreign areas dropped by more than one half, as seen in Appendix 1. Still, as the century ended, U.S. air, land, and sea forces were deployed far and wide, as suggested in Map 1.1. United States Air Force operations in just one year (Fiscal Year 1998) are shown in Map 1.2.

Map 1.1 Nominal U.S. Overseas Presence

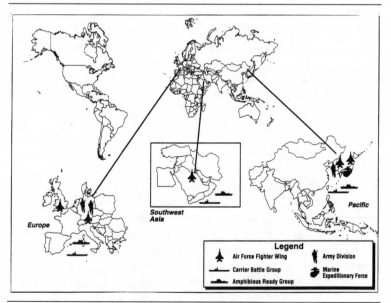

Source: U.S. Department of Defense

Map 1.2 The United States Air Force—Global Involvement

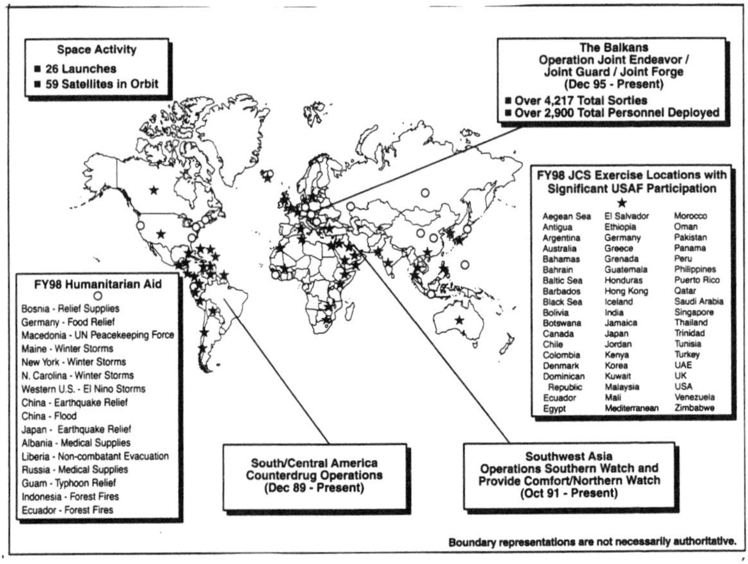

Source: U.S. Department of Defense

In the late twentieth century rogue states and nonstate terrorists had increasingly easy access to explosives and weapons of mass destruction. They could also communicate readily across borders by phone, modem, and other means. Still, the United States in the twentieth century managed to limit damage to its homeland or operations abroad by home-grown or foreign terrorists. Leaving aside the Korean and Vietnamese wars, foreign terrorists attacking U.S. embassies, troop barracks, and airliners killed a few thousand Americans and non-Americans—not tens or hundreds of thousands.

Governance: Collective Security and World Order

In the late nineteenth and early twentieth centuries the United States advocated treaties pledging the parties to settle their border and other disputes by international arbitration. President Theodore Roosevelt, William Howard Taft, and Woodrow Wilson endorsed

Terrorist attacks on the U.S. embassies in Kenya and Tanzania on August 7, 1998 killed 257, including 12 Americans, and injured thousands. In response, the United States fired cruise missiles at targets in Afghanistan and the Sudan. But a far greater worry was the possibility of terrorist attacks using weapons of mass destruction.

this approach to world order. Twenty-two such pacts went into effect under President Theodore Roosevelt and another twenty-one under Woodrow Wilson.

In 1907 the United States sponsored a Central American Court to resolve regional problems peacefully. It functioned well until 1914–1916 when Costa Rica won a decision against the United States, which the Wilson administration disregarded—effectively killing the court.[3]

For much of the twentieth century the United States was the strongest proponent of international organization to uphold collective security—the principle of "one for all, all for one" if any member is attacked.[4]

In 1915 three hundred U.S. dignitaries, many of them Republicans, endorsed a League to Enforce the Peace, and elected former U.S. president William Howard Taft, a Republican, the league's president. The following year the group was addressed by President Woodrow Wilson, a Democrat. He declared that Americans should no longer follow George Washington's admonition to avoid entangling alliances but would join "any feasible association of nations" formed to promote a permanent peace. In 1918–1919 Wilson demanded and got a Covenant of the League of Nations as part of the Versailles Treaty ending World War I. While many U.S. leaders and the public favored some kind of international security organization, many senators demanded clarifications, amendments, or reservations to clarify that the United States was under no obligation to join other states in any form of military or police action, and that U.S. sovereignty remained unbounded. But Wilson spurned any changes to the covenant and the Senate did not consent to the treaty. In consequence, the United States never joined the league.

Despite inward-looking tendencies in Congress and United States public opinion, President Franklin Roosevelt did what he could in 1940–1941 to throw America's weight behind England and against the aggressors. Roosevelt persuaded Congress in March 1941 to approve the Lend-Lease Act authorizing the president to lend and lease military equipment and other goods to countries such as Great Britain whose defense was deemed vital to U.S. security. In August 1941 FDR and British Prime Minister Winston Churchill signed their Atlantic Charter. After a Japanese attack and a German declaration of war brought the United States into the war in December 1941, the United States on January 1, 1942 signed an alliance with Britain, the USSR, and dozens of other countries against "those members of the tripartite pact [Germany, Italy, and Japan], and its adherents with which such government is at war"—a phrase that lightened Moscow's commitments, because it was not then at war with Japan. Despite fears that Moscow or Washington would conclude a separate peace with Germany, the allies maintained a common front until Hitler was defeated. Keeping to Stalin's earlier agreements with U.S. and British leaders, the Soviet Union attacked Japan on August 8, 1945—three months after Germany's surrender, but also two days after the first U.S. atomic bomb struck Hiroshima.

Looking to the postwar world, U.S. planners in 1944–1945 laid the foundations of a United Nations Organization to uphold collective security. Following a suggestion by Republican Senator Arthur H. Vandenberg, the United States offered the USSR a long-term alliance to prevent a resurgence of German or Japanese aggression—a proposal that Moscow did not accept.[5] Instead, Soviet behavior in Iran, Eastern Europe, and elsewhere suggested that Stalin was ready to scuttle the wartime alliance. Soviet representatives at the United

Nations used their veto power to block Security Council action on many threats to the peace.

While the Soviet Union boycotted the Security Council in 1950, the U.S. delegation persuaded the UN body to endorse a collective effort to repulse North Korea's invasion of South Korea. The three-year war was waged mainly by South Korean and U.S. troops, but many other UN members sent contingents. Most important for the United States, UN resolutions added legitimacy to its "police action." The commander of U.S. forces in Korea was designated the commander of UN forces.

To get around a possible future veto in the Security Council, American diplomats in November 1950 persuaded the UN General Assembly to adopt the "Uniting for Peace Resolution" empowering that body to recommend action on threats to the peace when the Security Council did not. An implicit admission that earlier hopes for great power unanimity were unrealistic, the Uniting for Peace Resolution kept the United Nations from becoming an impotent dead letter. In 1956 it permitted the General Assembly to take stands against the French-Israeli-UK invasion of Egypt and the Soviet intervention in Hungary. Even the USSR utilized the resolution during the 1967 Arab-Israeli war. The General Assembly used the resolution in the 1980s to make recommendations on Afghanistan, Namibia, and the Occupied Arab Territories.

The Uniting for Peace Resolution was part of a larger trend in U.S. policy. Faced with an expansionist USSR armed with a veto at the UN Security Council, Washington also organized a network of treaties to provide not universal collective security, but mutual assistance for pact members. Soviet and some other observers condemned these pacts as antithetical to the United Nations, but Washington argued that its alliances were consonant with the UN Charter. Article 51 affirmed the right of UN members to individual or collective self-defense before the Security Council acted to maintain the peace, while Article 53 permitted regional organizations. All the U.S. alliances were strictly defensive in nature. None contemplated partition of others' territories (as did the secret protocols to the German-Soviet "nonaggression" pact of August 1939). If no aggression took place or if the UN Security Council acted against aggression, the U.S.-sponsored treaties would trigger no action.

In September 1947 the United States in Rio de Janeiro signed the Inter-American Treaty of Reciprocal Assistance. The 1947 "Rio Pact" provided for joint action in the event of an armed attack on any member states, with collective measures to be decided by a two-thirds vote. The Senate approved Washington's first regional alliance by 71 to 1, just two months after its signing.

The foundation stone of Washington's defenses against the USSR was the North Atlantic Treaty Organization—NATO—established in 1949. It bound the United States, Canada, Iceland, and nine leading West European countries to collective defense against external attack in Europe or North America (or at sea north of the Tropic of Cancer) until such time as the UN Security Council took appropriate action. Greece and Turkey joined NATO in 1952; West Germany in 1955; Spain in 1982; Poland, Hungary, and the Czech Republic in 1999.

The United States also entered a tripartite alliance with Australia and New Zealand (ANZUS) in 1951 and bilateral alliances with the Philippines in 1951, with Japan in 1951 (revised 1960), with the Republic of Korea (ROK) in 1953, and the Republic of China (ROC) in 1954 (terminated in 1979 and supplanted by the Taiwan Relations Act). Washington formed a de facto alliance with Israel. These pacts and partnerships worked reasonably well, but two other U.S.-sponsored alliances did not—the Southeast Asian Treaty Organization and the Baghdad Pact/Central Treaty Organization, both of which fell apart in the 1970s. Washington's "pactomania" in the 1950s is discussed below in chapter 2.

As relations between the White House and Gorbachev's Kremlin improved, the most successful application of collective security through the United Nations took place in 1990–1991. The Bush Administration pushed through a series of UN Security Council decisions endorsing a collective effort to pressure and, if necessary, oust Iraq from Kuwait. The USSR approved all relevant resolutions while China approved or abstained. Not just European but also many Arab countries took part in the ensuing war against Iraq while Japan helped pay for it.[6]

The UN Security Council obliged Baghdad to accept the dismantling of its weapons of mass destruction under international observation. Until compliance was assured, the UN pledged to maintain economic sanctions. As the 1990s wore on, however, Washington and London were the only permanent members of the Security Council determined to maintain the regime of inspections and sanctions.[7] They bombed Iraq for blocking inspections, but then found the inspection regime difficult to restart. Also, Washington and London liberally interpreted UN resolutions to justify their reconnaissance and their flights over northern and southern Iraq, bombing Iraqi radars and other installations if they threatened the overflights.

The many ways in which the United States bypassed the United Nations, acting alone or with its alliance partners, can be seen as creative responses to UN weaknesses or as sabotage of universal collective security and international law.

NATO is widely regarded as one of the most successful alliances of all time and a major achievement for U.S. foreign policy. NATO passed three tests articulated by a UK official: It "kept the Russians out of Europe, kept the Americans in, and kept the Germans down." NATO proved to be a very unusual alliance. It acquired more members than most alliances; lasted longer; developed more complex institutions; and was more democratic. The United States led but did not dictate alliance policy. Most members (and aspirant members) perceived NATO as an agency for mutual gain—not a tool for superpower dictation, as in the Soviet alliance.[8]

Though we treat NATO as an "achievement," the alliance evolved into a very different product from what U.S. policymakers had intended. The Truman administration in 1948–1949 hoped that Europeans would stand on their own to resist the USSR, bolstered by gestures of reassurance from Washington. The White House did not want an entangling alliance, requiring a major and prolonged U.S. military presence in Europe. But Europeans successfully passed the buck and relied on U.S. leadership and resources for more than half a century. A structural realist might have expected Europeans to align with the USSR against the global hegemon; instead, they allied with the United States against a perceived threat from the USSR or a potential threat from Germany.

Over time, the United States came to enjoy its leading role in NATO. Americans invested far more of their GDP in defense than most of their allies, but U.S. military strength won much influence. This led to contradictory impulses. Self-righteous Americans urged Europeans to invest more for the common cause. When Europeans tried to organize militarily apart from NATO, however, Washington frowned.

Though we rank NATO as a long-term success, it can also be seen as part of an excessive dependence on military instruments to contain Soviet expansion. To be sure, the West's military buildup was stimulated by the Soviet atomic bomb test in 1949 and by North Korea's invasion of the South in 1950—incorrectly assumed then to have been orchestrated by Stalin. But George F. Kennan, while U.S. ambassador to Moscow, reflected in 1952 that a cosmic misunderstanding had taken place: NATO was a military response to a political threat; the West intended its alliance for defense, but the Kremlin—knowing Soviet weaknessess—presumed that NATO was meant to attack the USSR.

When the USSR collapsed in December 1991 and gave way to a still powerful but shrunken Russia, the raison d'être for NATO weakened. Germans, having paid the RAND Corporation for advice, concluded that NATO should become a tool for stability in Europe. German officials argued that NATO had to go "out of area" or "out of business." In part to generate new missions and meet new challenges, the Clinton administration pushed NATO to become a peacemaker beyond its official geographical limits, and a defender of human rights in the former Yugoslavia.[9]

NATO did not fight until the mid-1990s, when it conducted operations "out of area"—not against the USSR but against Serbian warlords. NATO air attacks in 1995, plus Croatian and Bosnian offensives abetted by the United States, helped persuade all parties to accept the Dayton Accords, providing for a Bosnian state policed by NATO and other troops.[10]

Most NATO actions on the behalf of a Bosnian state in the mid-1990s were eventually endorsed by the United Nations. But when NATO in 1999 resolved to protect Albanian-speakers in Kosovo from Serbian repression, it bypassed the UN Security Council, fearing a Russian or Chinese veto. Claiming to uphold both human rights *and* the principle of territorial integrity, NATO attacked Serbian forces in Kosovo and many targets in Serbia proper. When Belgrade agreed to withdraw its forces from Kosovo (at least temporarily), NATO troops entered the territory as peacekeepers while European civil servants endeavored to reestablish economic and social life in a province that, NATO averred, still belonged to Serbia/Yugoslavia.

Did these expansions of NATO's mandate strengthen or weaken the alliance? Did they help or harm the cause of collective security? Would they strengthen or weaken the United Nations?

One could argue that NATO performed a service for its members and for the entire United Nations by stepping into the Balkan caldron where the United Nations and the European Union had proved impotent. Assertions that war crimes and crimes against humanity took place in both Bosnia and Kosovo were upheld by the International War Crimes Tribunal in The Hague. The tribunal investigated but rejected charges that the NATO air campaign in

1999 violated international law.[11] A balanced appraisal of NATO's military actions against Serbia awaits the passage of years to weigh the results and gain perspective. Meanwhile, the dangers posed by NATO's assumption of new tasks out of area, along with its acceptance of new members that were formerly Soviet allies, will be discussed in chapter 2.

3. Interdependence: Building Cooperation for Mutual Gain

Probably the greatest achievement of U.S. foreign policy in the twentieth century was the post - World War II reconstruction of Europe and Japan into a prosperous and peaceful security community. The leading instrument in Europe was the Marshall Plan, under which the United States from 1947 to 1951 extended to Western Europe some $14 billion in loans and credits (more than $100 billion in A.D. 2000 terms). Also known as the European Recovery Plan (ERP), the Marshall Plan exemplified both mutuality and openness in its planning, implementation, and shared benefits.

U.S. support for European integration after World War II, in the words of Josef Joffe, provided an example of long-range vision, one that transmuted explicit restraints on German power in favor of "communitarian constraint," thus evading the mistakes of the Versailles Treaty system imposed on Germany in 1919.[12]

The downside was that the ERP reinforced, though it did not cause, the division of Europe. The Communist states were invited to take part but Stalin ordered them not to do so. Ultimately the Marshall Plan was sold to the U.S. Congress as part of a package of measures to contain Soviet expansion.

Moscow's policies in Eastern Europe underscored the wisdom of the mutual gain strategy underlying the ERP. From 1945 to 1956 the Kremlin took from East Germany and the rest of occupied or "liberated" Eastern Europe plants, products, and raw materials valued at $20 billion. The fruits of this exploitation were bitter. The East European states became impoverished and resentful. Starting in 1953, they rebelled—openly or sullenly—against Soviet rule. In the late 1980s Poland, Hungary, and the other East European states broke from the Soviet-sponsored Warsaw Pact alliance and the "Council of Mutual Economic Assistance" meant to coordinate their economic activities.

As in Europe, so too in Japan: U.S. policies contributed to democratization and peaceful reconstruction. America's partnership with Japan initiated under the post–World War II occupation regime of Supreme Allied Commander General Douglas A. MacArthur was an even more surprising achievement than U.S. cooperation with Europe, because it required each side to transcend racism and a clash of cultures as well as recent sufferings and hatreds.[13]

These peaceful triumphs were far more surprising than U.S. ability to prevail in two world wars and to maintain the world's leading economy—attainments that could be explained by America's material advantages. They contradicted the expectation of Alexis de Tocqueville in the 1830s and many other observers who believed that democracies are incapable of farsighted and sustained efforts in foreign affairs.[14]

Mutual gain policies were more problematic in the Caribbean and Latin America, but Franklin Roosevelt's Good Neighbor Policy, begun in 1933, led to withdrawal of U.S. troops from Haiti and Nicaragua and the establishment of a new relationship with Mexico and other Latin countries, which facilitated effective collaboration during World War II.

The United States gradually modified the imperialist postures it acquired in the late nineteenth and early twentieth centuries. Washington promised and delivered full independence to the Philippines after World War II. Washington also granted either independence or commonwealth status to many of the Pacific Islands under U.S. rule since the nineteenth century or World War II, but it rejected demands by native Hawaiians for independence or even autonomy.

After a difficult half-century, Washington's policies toward Puerto Rico changed after the Second World War, and suggested that mutual gain strategies are feasible even when one side is large and rich, the other small and poor. "Operation Bootstrap" and tax incentives for industry made Puerto Rico a partner in development with the continental United States. Puerto Rico's status as an autonomous U.S. "commonwealth" (1952) did not satisfy the local proponents of statehood or their political opposites, the *independentistas,* but a slight majority of Puerto Ricans consistently voted for continuation of commonwealth status.

John F. Kennedy's Alliance for Progress launched in 1961 tried, with limited success, to promote political stability, democracy, and economic growth. Its vision of a $20 billion, ten-year program for development foundered for many reasons. The major legacy of the Alliance for Progress was U.S. assistance to Latin American armies in counterinsurgency tactics. In the late 1970s President Jimmy Carter strove to weaken dictatorships in Latin America and foster human rights. Both the Kennedy and Carter reforms were scuppered by Latin elites determined to protect their own narrow economic and political privileges. Meanwhile, Washington's fear of leftist regimes anywhere led the United States to continue its familiar pattern of forceful interventions in the Caribbean and Latin America—most of them counterproductive, as detailed below in chapter 2.

Nowhere did the United States intervene more forcefully than in Panama, where—early in the century—it fostered a new state; purchased the right to build a canal; did so; and then claimed "titular sovereignty" in the Canal Zone. The resultant structure—one of the world's great engineering feats—facilitated world commerce and America's two-ocean navy. Faced with mounting Panamanian demands in the 1960s and 1970s, however, the Carter administration agreed in 1977–1978 to return the canal to Panama by 2000; the Clinton administration did so in 1999. The 1977–1978 commitments avoided more bloody riots in Panama and the possible closing of the canal. President Carter and Senate leaders who secured the treaties' approval with but one vote to spare in 1978 "scored the most significant victory in U.S.–Latin American relations since Franklin D. Roosevelt's good neighbor policy four decades earlier."[15] How the new arrangements worked in practice would take years to assess.

Struggling against what it called "isolationist" forces in Congress, the Clinton administration asserted that interdependence is a fact of life—one that Americans should utilize for their good and for that of others. President Clinton urged Americans to reach beyond their borders to shape the revolution tearing down barriers and building new networks among nations and individuals, economies and cultures—globalization. "Our open, creative society stands to benefit more than any other, if we understand, and act on, the new realities of interdependence. We must be at the center of every vital global network, as a good neighbor and partner. We cannot build our future without helping others to build theirs."[16]

This rationale underlay one strand of U.S. policy from the 1940s into the new century.

4. *Containment: Winning the*
Cold War without a Major Hot War

The United States and its partners persisted in a long Cold War that destroyed Soviet imperialism without war.[17] Containment—America's strategy toward the USSR since 1946—helped to "contain" Soviet expansion and set the stage for the collapse of the Soviet empire in 1989–1991. Containment provided time and fertile conditions for the empire to disintegrate from within. Contrary to the forecasts of some theorists, the USSR made no last-ditch stand. There was no transitional war to uphold or seize a superpower's hegemony.

To be sure, the Cold War competition saw each side march more than once toward the brink of war. There were many close calls—the most dangerous in 1962 when the USSR attempted secretly to deploy missiles in Cuba. How the Kennedy White House coped with the ensuing crisis, however, was a major accomplishment. U.S. firmness and some concessions induced a Soviet retreat.[18] Many experts regard U.S. handling of the Cuban confrontation as the second- greatest U.S. achievement in foreign policy in the twentieth century—second only to the Marshall Plan. Whereas the European Recovery Program depended basically on various forms of soft power, U.S. policy in the Cuban crisis relied heavily on military threat as well as persuasion and quid pro quo diplomacy.

When crises developed with Moscow or Beijing over a third region, Washington usually managed a judicious use of firmness and flexibility. Such crises arose over divided Berlin (1948–1949 and 1958–1961), in Israeli-Arab relations (1956, 1967, 1970, 1973), over Iraq (1990 and later), and over Taiwan (in 1954, 1958, 1996, and 2000).

No major fighting took place between U.S. and Soviet or U.S. and Chinese forces except during the Korean War, when waves of Chinese "volunteers" crossed the Yalu River and Soviet pilots masqueraded as North Koreans.

The Cold War competition risked stretching U.S. resources to the breaking point, but the USSR broke first. The burdens of the competition weighed much less heavily on the United States than the USSR. Military and intelligence activities, plus interest on the costs of past wars, consumed about 6 to 8 percent of America's GDP in the 1980s, compared with 15 to 25 percent in the Soviet Union.

U.S. intelligence activities cost nearly $30 billion a year in the 1990s—the lion's share for aerial and satellite reconnaissance, communications interception, and encryption-decryption. Both human- and machine-gathered information helped inform Washington about the strategic assets and plans of its adversaries. Reconnaissance revealed the Soviet missile deployment in Cuba; guided inspectors to weapons sites in Iraq; and alerted the world to North Korea's nuclear and missile activities.

5. Conflict Control: Learning How to Collaborate While Competing

Americans and their major rivals learned how to collaborate for shared objectives even while they competed in other domains. Game theorists pointed out that international politics is seldom a zero-sum game. Rather, a variety of outcomes are possible—victory for one or all parties, losses for one or all sides, victory for one side and defeat for the others.[19]

The shadow of nuclear weapons helped rival countries to grasp that their overarching interest was to avoid Armageddon. Rivals could push and shove in Berlin or the Taiwan Straits, but no party dared drive the other against the wall or threaten its vital interests (as the United States did to China in 1950, precipitating the entry of Chinese "volunteers" into the Korean War). Instead, each side could take initiatives to promote détente—relaxation of tensions. Such moves fostered the first summit meeting in a decade of Western and Soviet leaders in 1955.

Recognizing how close each side had come to the brink of war in the Cuban confrontation, the White House in 1963 persuaded the Kremlin to embark on what President Kennedy called a "strategy of peace." Washington and Moscow sought and developed new ways to moderate and even transcend conflict. This led to several short-lived détentes in the 1960s and a more substantial but still fragile détente in 1972. In the late 1980s, however, the words and deeds of Soviet leader Mikhail Gorbachev, reciprocated by Presidents Ronald Reagan and George Bush, ended the Cold War.[20]

Psychologist Charles Osgood in 1962 called such processes "GRIT"—graduated reciprocation in initiatives for tension-reduction.[21] Whether or not top leaders read Osgood, many grasped the fundamentals of GRIT. Henry Kissinger and Zhou Enlai used such techniques to normalize U.S.-PRC relations in the 1970s.[22] Washington encouraged Taipei and Beijing, Seoul and Pyongyang, Islamabad and New Delhi, Athens and Ankara, Israel and its Arab neighbors to attempt their own versions of GRIT.[23] Starting in the late 1990s Iranian moderates attempted a GRIT-like strategy to reduce tensions with Washington.

Bitter rivals not only mitigated their conflicts but learned to trade goods and to exchange scientists, students, dancers, basketball teams, and wrestlers. They began to take action on common problems in environmental protection and other domains.

6. Arms and Arms Control as Twin Paths to Security

As the Cold War unfolded, the United States and the USSR built up their nuclear, conventional, and other forces. Washington sought a military posture that would deter the USSR and other rivals from attacking the United States or its allies. Washington and its NATO allies wanted conventional forces, buttressed with tactical nuclear weapons, able to stop a Soviet invasion of Europe without escalating into an all-out nuclear war. For a time the United States believed that it needed forces able to fight up to "two-and-one-half" major wars. As relations with China improved, this criterion was lowered to "one-and-one-half" major wars. After the USSR collapsed, the Pentagon sought forces able to fight and win two regional wars at the same time while conducting one peacekeeping or humanitarian action.

The U.S. nuclear triad—strategic forces on land, in the sea, and in the air—produced a highly credible deterrent to a first-strike by its foes. The size and quality of U.S. forces instilled confidence among America's allies. The long-reach, mobility, and comparative accuracy of U.S. forces was demonstrated often in the 1980s and 1990s. Their lead in applying new technologies helped them to fight against Iraq and Serbia and suffer very few casualties.

But the great powers also came to understand their shared security dilemma: More "defense" might provoke the other side to take steps that aggravate "security." The United States was blind to this idea at the 1899 and 1907 Hague peace conferences, but promoted it at the 1921–1922 Washington Naval Conference and again in its 1946 proposals for the international control of atomic energy. These initiatives disappointed or failed, but some U.S. leaders grasped that security might be enhanced by arms control. They came to see arms control as a means to strategic stability—a way not only to save money but to make war less likely or, if it erupted, less destructive.

Starting in the late 1950s, these assumptions led to arms control in specific domains—Antarctica, nuclear testing, orbiting of space weapons. By 1972 the goal of enhancing strategic stability was incorporated in SALT 1 and the treaty limiting antiballistic missile (ABM) defenses against ICBM (intercontinental ballistic missile) attack. Washington and Moscow agreed that it was wiser to count on mutual restraint than on unbridled arms competition.[24]

When the Brezhnev regime ignored the security dilemma and deployed hundreds of intermediate-range ballistic missiles (IRBMs) against Europe and Asia, the United States countered with its own IRBM deployment. In 1987 Mikhail Gorbachev agreed to Ronald Reagan's "zero option" and both sides destroyed their intermediate-range nuclear missiles—the first significant disarmament treaty of the century, one that not only reduced but eliminated entire classes of up-to-date weapons. The two sides pulled back tactical nuclear weapons; they and their allies pared conventional forces; they persuaded China to join in some efforts to curb nuclear spread. The end of the Cold War opened opportunities for much larger reductions in U.S. and Russian nuclear arsenals.[25]

Four heavily armed nuclear powers emerged from the USSR—the Russian Federation, Ukraine, Belarus, and Kazakstan—each with a larger arsenal than France, the UK, China, or Israel. Moscow and Washington agreed to continue their own arms reductions, and Washington persuaded Ukraine, Belarus, and Kazakstan to destroy or transfer their arsenals to Russia. The U.S. Defense and Energy Departments provided money and technical expertise to facilitate disarmament in the former USSR. America invested $3 billion on "cooperative threat reduction" in the 1990s and planned to provide another $5 billion between 2000 and 2004. These were bargain prices, for the former Soviet republics deactivated nearly 5,000 warheads in the 1990s and planned to deactivate a total of 8,515 by 2005. Only 160 former Soviet submarine-launched ballistic missiles were destroyed in the 1990s, but this number was to rise to 652 by 2005.[26]

The United States failed to stop the USSR, France, China, Israel, South Africa, India, and Pakistan from joining the nuclear club. But U.S. policies succeeded in limiting the "horizontal" spread of nuclear weapons. The main tools were the Nuclear Nonproliferation Treaty (NPT), inspection by the International Atomic Energy Agency, and satellite reconnaissance. But Washington also utilized

India and Pakistan did not welcome advice from outsiders.

other incentives. Its system of "extended deterrence" convinced some states they did not need their own deterrent. Washington also applied pressure against friendly states such as South Korea, Taiwan, Brazil, and Argentina. It sponsored intrusive inspection in Iraq and destruction of its weapons of mass destruction. The United States threatened North Korea but, with Japan and South Korea, persuaded North Korea to forgo nuclear arms in return for an energy package worth $5 billion—cheap at the price.

As a new century began there were less than ten nuclear-armed states—far fewer than the dozens widely predicted in the 1960s. When India and Pakistan started to deploy their own nuclear weapons in 1999, however, they did not like hearing from President Clinton and others that their decades-old confrontation over Kashmir had become more dangerous. Indian had long demanded that the established nuclear powers disarm and level the playing field.

7. Mediation and Peacemaking: Honest Brokering

Throughout the twentieth century U.S. diplomats and private citizens often acted as an honest brokers to help mediate others' disputes. Sometimes they merely used their "good offices" to bring disputants to the negotiating table. Sometimes they contributed ideas on how the dispute could be settled to mutual advantage. On occasion they sought not just to facilitate but to cajole, pressure, or compensate financially; sometimes they offered to provide military power to make the peace work; on occasion they threatened to oppose the side that proved intransigent. But the prerequisite for success was deep knowledge of the issues and needs of each party—essential for creating solutions acceptable to each side.

One of the most effective U.S. mediators was President Theodore Roosevelt. He won the Nobel Prize in 1905 for inviting Russian and Japanese diplomats to Portsmouth, New Hampshire, and pushing them toward a treaty ending the Russo-Japanese war. The next year he called the Algeciras Conference, which, with some backstage work by Roosevelt, quelled tensions between Germany and France over Morocco.

Another American, Ralph Bunche, brokered peace between Israel and its neighbors in 1948–1949, an achievement for which, in 1950, he became the first Afro-American to win the Nobel Peace Prize (followed by Martin Luther King in 1964, a man who brokered peace between races). A generation later, Henry Kissinger— then President Richard Nixon's special assistant for national security—shuttled back and forth between Israel and various Arab capitals seeking to broker more stable arrangements after the 1973 war. Kissinger, too, received a Nobel Peace Prize—sharing it with Le Duc Tho in 1973—not for mediating but for negotiating an end to war between Washington and Hanoi.

In 1978–1979 President Jimmy Carter combined knowledge, diplomatic skill, pressure, persuasive power, and promises of gigantic economic support (some $3 billion per year for Israel and $2 billion for Egypt) to induce Israel and Egypt to accept the Camp David framework agreement in 1978 and to sign a peace treaty in 1979.

The Clinton White House gave its blessing to the 1993 Oslo Accord between Israel and the Palestinian Liberation Organization, mediated by Norwegian scholars and diplomats.[29] The Clinton team tried to promote implementation of those accords but was stymied when the hard-line Likud party gained power in Israel. The U.S. State Department said it was doing all that was humanely possible to encourage Israeli compliance, but many observers thought Washington feared to offend a sacred cow.

Box 1.1 Ralph Bunche on Enlightened Self-Interest

Ralph Bunche was for years the second most powerful official in the United Nations, but at times he could not get a room in the best hotels in the still segregated U.S. South. The only black to graduate from the University of California, Los Angeles in 1927, Bunche was class valedictorian, and later earned a Ph.D. in government at Harvard University (the first black to do so). He led in building black consciousness in the 1930s and 1940s. He understood well that "there could be no national security without civil rights, and there could be no international peace without human rights."[27] As the key UN official dealing with international crises he practically invented "UN peacekeeping."

Speaking on "The International Significance of Human Relations" in 1951, Bunche expressed one of the theses of this book: "That people inevitably think in terms of their self-interest is something very little can be done about. But is it not equally tenable that a great deal can be done about influencing people to think and act in terms of their *true* self-interest? In this dangerous international age, notions of exalted and exaggerated nationalism, national egocentrism and isolationism, of chauvinism, of group superiority and master race, of group exclusiveness, of national self-righteousness, of special privilege, are in the interest of neither the world nor of any particular group in it. They are false views of self-interest and carry us all toward the disaster of war." Lincoln's Day Address, Springfield, Illinois, February 12, 1951.

When the Labor Party defeated Likud in Israel's 1999 elections, U.S. mediators resumed their active role in Middle Eastern affairs, pressing both sides to implement the Oslo Accord. Also, the White House invited both Syria and Israel to Washington and to a retreat in West Virginia, where Secretary of State Madeleine Albright and President Clinton proposed draft solutions and discussed material support for another "land for peace" deal similar to that mediated by Carter at Camp David a generation before.

Private U.S. citizens, including former President Carter, helped in the 1990s to broker the package deal that eased U.S. tensions with North Korea. Carter also helped mediate accords in Haiti and several other trouble spots.

The Clinton White House had reservations about Carter's freewheeling approach, but Clinton gave full support to former Senator George Mitchell as he mediated differences between the many

Box 1.2 How Americans Viewed Camp David in 1985

Asked to evaluate five recent foreign policy situations on a scale of one (poorest) to ten (the best), the U.S. public in February 1985 gave the Camp David negotiations the highest ranking—6.45. But a coercive action, the 1983 intervention in Grenada by the Reagan administration, placed second—at 5.86. The public gave a grade of just 4.95 to Carter's handling of the Iranian hostage crisis when U.S. diplomats were held captive for 14 months and released just as Reagan took office. Analysts had expected a lower grade for the Iranian share of Carter's legacy, because it implied U.S. impotence. One analyst surmised that the public was pleased that "it all turned out fine." But the public gave even lower ratings to two other developments on Reagan's watch in 1983: the bombings of the U.S. embassy in Lebanon (4.18) and the U.S. response to the Soviet shooting down of a South Korean airliner (3.96).

Camp David elicited nearly the same level of approval by respondents who voted to reelect Ronald Reagan in 1984 and those who voted for his Democratic rival, Walter Mondale—6.50 versus 6.56. But Grenada divided them sharply. Respondents who voted for President Reagan in 1984 marked the Grenada intervention at 6.63 while Mondale backers scored it much lower—4.1.

An earlier survey, taken in October 1984, showed that Camp David got roughly equally high ratings from liberals and conservatives and from men and women. College graduates and military veterans, however, were among its strongest supporters, while Camp David received somewhat lower ratings from younger people (aged 18 to 22) and from blacks.

Reagan's handling of Grenada elicited stronger divisions. Men rated it at 6.45; women, at 4.92. Those 65 and older marked it at 6.15 while 18- to 22-year olds graded it 5.10. Whites rated it 5.85 while blacks gave it 4.44. Southerners rated it at 6.06 and residents of the Northeast at 5.00.

Carter's handling of the Iranian hostage situation was graded by men at 4.59 and women at 5.28. Those with family incomes under $12,500 rated it at 5.43 while those over $50,000 graded it 4.09. But there were no appreciable differences related to party affiliation, liberal or conservative outlook, or race.

Even though Carter's mediation at Camp David drew the highest rating, the 1985 poll showed that 49 percent of the public approved Reagan's handling of foreign policy and 34 percent disapproved. Viewing the findings as a whole, Stanford political scientist Richard A. Brody observed: "The public remembers most fondly successes that don't use troops, that posed no great threat, and which have proven to be enduring."[28]

More than half a century of mediation and negotiation, however, left Palestinians and Israelis with divergent perspectives on the Holy Land.

groups concerned with the fate of Northern Ireland.[30] Indeed, Clinton risked alienating both the UK government and Irish-American voters when he pressed all parties to the Northern Ireland conflict for an accommodation. In 1994 the United States gave a visa to Gerry Adams, leader of Sinn Fein, the political wing of the Provisional Irish Republican Army (IRA). By 1998 Mitchell brokered the "Good Friday" agreement signed by most of the parties to the peace talks. David Trimble, leader of the Ulster Unionist Party, and John Hume, leader of the largest Irish nationalist party, the Social Democratic and Labour Party, won the Nobel Peace Prize that year for their role in the negotiations. But all concerned acknowledged the crucial roles played by Mitchell and Clinton. The Good Friday agreement broke down in 1999 but came to life again in 2000.

The dissolution of Yugoslavia in the early 1990s elicited mediation efforts by the United Nations and European Union. When the UN and EU efforts got nowhere, the United States intervened forcefully in 1995. U.S. mediator Richard Holbrooke induced the many South-Slav combatants to sign the Dayton Peace Accord.[31] U.S. forces then led an International Force—"IFOR" (later called Stabi-

The peace process in Northern Ireland required Gerry Adams, leader of Irish nationalist party Sinn Fein, to persuade the Irish Republican Army to decommission its weapons and renounce violence, but many IRA militants refused to do so.

lization Force—"SFOR") to uphold the Dayton agreements. A few years after Dayton, the United States led diplomatic and military efforts to secure autonomy for Kosovo from Serbia.

American troops were also stationed in Macedonia with other foreign forces to thwart cross-border violence between Serbia and Macedonia.

When the Balkans were relatively calm, Holbrooke also turned up south of Belgrade to dissuade Greece and Turkey from fighting over disputed islands and other problems. Having become U.S. ambassador to the United Nations, Holbrooke in 2000 began to push the world toward action to curb the AIDS epidemic in Africa and halt the fighting in and near the Congo.

8. Promoting Free Trade and Economic Development

Long before the twentieth century, Americans demanded access to the markets of Europe, North Africa, Japan, China, and the rest of the world. Starting in the nineteenth century the United States sought an open door to trade with Japan, China, Liberia and other parts of the world. Succeeding Theodore Roosevelt as president in 1912, William Howard Taft trusted that dollar diplomacy—commerce and investment—could promote U.S. objectives in the world as well as or better than military force. Substituting dollars for bullets, he said, appealed alike to humanitarian sentiments, to the dictates of sound policy, and to legitimate commercial aims.[32]

As Adam Smith predicted, the wealth of nations has been multiplied by free trade of the goods and services that each country produces best—international commerce unhampered by government restrictions or tariffs. To be sure, the development of the U.S. and other economies benefited from various forms of protectionism, industrial policy, and strategic trade—especially for infant industries. Granted also that free trade exposes inefficient producers to severe competition, autarky is not an optimal road to development—witness Albania.

Starting in the 1930s, Washington pushed the world to lower trade barriers. In 1944 U.S. and UK planners constructed the Bretton Woods system—including the World Bank and International Monetary Fund and other institutions—to promote freer trade and orderly financial transfers. Like Great Britain in the nineteenth century, the United States after World War II served as a stabilizing force in world commerce. President Nixon jettisoned parts of the Bretton Woods system in 1971, but Washington continued to support trade liberalization. It labored to expand the scope of the General Agreement on Tariffs and Trade (a multilateral forum launched in 1947, eventually joining more than 125 countries) and to found its more powerful successor, the World Trade Organization (WTO) in 1995.[33] The Clinton administration also helped establish the 1994 North American Free Trade Agreement (NAFTA) with Canada and Mexico. That same year Clinton and his Secretary of the Treasury arranged a rescue package for the Mexican peso—at no cost to the U.S. taxpayer.[34] At the turn of the century the Clinton White House put to Congress its African and Caribbean Basin trade initiatives.

Serving as the "buyer of last resort" in the late 1990s, the United States propped up the global economy, even though the U.S. trade imbalance ballooned.[35] But U.S. negotiators tried to batter down the tariffs and nontariff barriers by which Japan, China, and some other countries limited penetration of foreign goods, services, and investment.

Clinton's final State of the Union address called for a new consensus on trade—one that saw it as a way to lift Americans' living standards and values but never tolerating abusive child labor or a race to the bottom on the environment and worker protection. He contended that "open markets and rules-based trade are the best engines we know for raising living standards, reducing global poverty and environmental destruction, and assuring the free flow of ideas."

Washington's support for free trade did not apply to its Cold War enemies or, later, to "rogue states" such as Iraq. The United States sought to curtail not only the sale of militarily useful technology but also credits and investment from Western countries. In the late 1990s Washington was torn between those who would liberalize trade with China, Iran, and Cuba to nudge them toward liberal change, and those who counted on the leverage of denial. Judging by the complaints from Havana, Tehran, and Baghdad, however, U.S. sanctions hurt them (as well as U.S. and other Western economic interests). North Korea seemed to soften its military policies to gain access to Western technology and trade.

In the late 1990s Beijing pledged to open its economy and the Clinton administration agreed to press for China's admission to the WTO and to delink trade from China's human rights performance. In 2000 Clinton plus several ex-presidents and teams of business lobbyists persuaded Congress to approve the Permanent Normal Trade Relations agreement with China. If measured by White House priorities, this was a major victory. Its long-term effects remained to be seen.

The United States treated foreign aid as an auxiliary tool to promote economic development. Buoyed by the success of the Marshall Plan and goaded by rivalry with the USSR, Washington decided in the early 1950s that the United States could and should assist less developed countries (LDCs) onto the road to economic takeoff. If the Marshall Plan approach succeeded in India, America's grants and loans would be repaid by Indian purchases from the United States and by cordial relations.

It is hard to measure the success of foreign aid to the LDCs for many reasons. For starters, the amounts given were tiny on a per capita basis relative to the aid received by Europeans under the Marshall Plan. The only LDC to receive large volumes of U.S. assistance—private and official—on a per capita basis was Israel, which made the

Report Says Nike Workers in Vietnam Paid Starvation Wages and
Suffer Corporal Punishment and Forced Running Inflicted by Managers

*American labor unions said that "free trade" meant that other countries
could produce goods with cheap labor for U.S. markets. The poster on
the factory wall shows a photo of a Vietnamese child burned and crying
during the Indochina War.*

desert bloom and for decades devoted more than one-fifth of its economic resources to defense.

Free trade and direct foreign investment came to play a much
larger role than foreign aid in promoting economic development in
many less developed countries (LDCs). In the mid-1990s foreign aid
made up only one-third the net flow of resources to LDCs from the
rich countries. The other two-thirds came from trade and investment. In the 1990s official development assistance for China and
India amounted to less than one percent of their GDP. Official U.S.
aid (much of it for military purposes) amounted to about $12 bil-
lion per year in the 1990s. But the U.S. trade deficit with Latin
America, Asia, and Africa—omitting oil imports—exceeded $80 bil-
lion per year. In the 1990s the United States spent 0.1 percent of
GDP on foreign aid to the whole world—compared to about 2.5
percent for Europe under the Marshall Plan. Foreign *economic* aid

cost each U.S. taxpayer on average less than $15 per year in the 1990s.[36]

9. A Model of Democratic and Liberal Market Development

"Globalization," President Clinton declared in January 2000, "is about more than economics." America's "purpose must be to bring the world together around democracy, freedom, and peace, and to oppose those who would tear it apart."

Material and political achievements within the United States were a source of power and influence abroad. The more developed the country's economy and social cohesion, the greater the assets available for projects in the global arena. If U.S. values and ways appealed to others, this would redound to America's soft power—the ability to persuade and coopt others to behaviors congruent with U.S. policies. The greater the shared values among countries, the less potential for friction.

America's example attracted others more than its preaching. Throughout the twentieth century the United States generated the world's largest and most creative economy—producing and consuming more than one-fifth the world's goods and services (nearly one-half after World War II, a share that declined as other countries rebuilt and regained their prewar trajectories). Economic growth bolstered overall U.S. fitness—prosperity at home and influence abroad. American productivity was a crucial factor helping the United States and its allies win two world wars and the Cold War. Economic growth permitted the United States to make large investments in education, science, and technology with civilian as well as military applications. The U.S. economy also provided a foundation for influence in peacetime. Its success inspired other countries—even Communist states—to shift from state-dominated economies toward more market economies.

Americans attempted to encourage and even to teach democracy and its techniques.[37] The Central Intelligence Agency endeavored to promote anti-Communist parties and cultural movements in Europe and the Third World. It sought to match and surpass the exploits of Soviet operatives and front organizations. Radio Liberty, Radio Free Europe, and the Voice of America helped undermine tyranny in the Soviet empire. Later, the National Endowment for Democracy received bipartisan support from Congress and worked with partners in many countries.

The team of Adam Smith and Thomas Jefferson roundly defeated Karl Marx and V. I. Lenin. By 1989, when the Wall came down, there was no other universally appealing ideology to contest what prevailed in the West. Even statist Europe, except for France, drifted toward the U.S. model. In the 1990s the Labour and Socialist parties of Europe were adopting a "Third Way," the market-based pragmatism of the Clinton administration. Instead of being "exceptional," the U.S. approach to politics and economics was becoming the norm among industrial democracies.[38]

The Economist asked: "What is the point of 'Europe,' if Europe is turning out to be just another United States?" Its reply: This could be a "fate devoutly to be wished"—and not just by global financiers. A stiff dose of American competition, innovation, and enterprise would benefit Europeans in terms of jobs and a higher standard of living, though this could also mean less economic security.[39]

Many French people spurned the U.S. model, including those who had their own interpretation of the Marxist slogan, "From each according to his abilities, to each according to his needs."

Acceptance of and convergence with American ways redounded to U.S. influence. In A.D. 2000 the U.S. dollar was the preferred means of exchange in many places from Moscow to Quito.

10. Fostering Human Rights

According to former Secretary of State Dean Acheson, America's basic goal in foreign affairs should be to create "as spacious an environment as possible in which free states might exist and flourish."[40] Most U.S. presidents, at least since World War II, concurred with this view.

The first modern democracy, the United States helped to keep alive and spread ideals of freedom—political, economic, cultural, religious—and human rights. Setbacks occurred and could be expected in the future, but waves of democracy swept the world in the twentieth century—especially after World War II. An ever larger percentage of the world's people lived under governments that could be considered "free."

Eleanor Roosevelt helped persuade most members of the United Nations to endorse the Universal Declaration of Human Rights. President Jimmy Carter, to the chagrin of many realists, put human rights near the top of his foreign policy priorities. Congress made human rights observance a condition for U.S. foreign aid and required the State Department to produce annual reports on human rights developments in every country.

There were practical benefits to the spread of democracy and greater respect for human rights. Established democracies seldom if ever make war against other democracies. Governments that respect their own citizens' rights are less likely to violate those of others.[41] Authoritarian dictatorships started and lost the major wars of the twentieth century. Fighting back after attack by dictatorships, democracies always prevailed.[42]

As the veteran realist Henry Kissinger acknowledged: "It is above all to the drumbeat of Wilsonian idealism that American foreign policy has marched since his watershed presidency and continues to march to this day."[43] Americans' pursuit of these ideals changed the rules and the game of international politics in the twentieth century.[44]

11. Fostering International Understanding

Knowledge, like material wealth, can be hoarded for private good or shared to create values. America's record is far from pure, but the United States for most of its history has been a major force for openness in all realms—including science, culture, and communications.

Many experts see educational exchange as one of the greatest successes of U.S. foreign policy after 1945—much cheaper than the Marshall Plan and with far fewer risks than, say, trying to manage the Berlin or Cuban crises. Advances in education are cheap compared to building bridges or destroying them with cruise missiles.

For millennia small numbers of itinerant scholars crossed borders in quest of insight and knowledge. But educational exchange got a major boost after World War II from the Fulbright Act (1946) which supported student and teacher exchanges by tapping some of the monies owed to the United States by other governments. The expanded Fulbright-Hays Act (1961) provided direct support by Congress for a variety of exchange programs. In Fiscal Year 1998 Congress appropriated nearly $100 million for the programs, which were administered by the U.S. Information Agency. Foreign governments contributed another $23 million that year.

In the late 1990s some 4,500 new Fulbright grants were awarded each year. By century's end approximately 225,000 "Fulbrighters" had taught or studied in another country—84,000 Americans abroad and 141,000 foreigners in the United States.

As the English historian Arnold J. Toynbee put it: "Along with the Marshall Plan, the Fulbright program is one of the really generous and imaginative things . . . done in the world since World War II."

"The essence of intercultural education," Senator Fulbright wrote in 1989, "is the acquisition of empathy—the ability to see the world as others see it, and to allow for the possibility that others may see something that we have failed to see, or may see it more accurately."

The Fulbright exchanges may well be the "most successful international educational exchange program in human history"—a life-changing, mind-expanding experience for participants. The program also changed the nature of university education and U.S. relations with the rest of the world.[45]

The Fulbright program's success sparked many other educational exchange programs in the United States and elsewhere. Over time U.S. educational and scientific institutions drew more and more students and researchers from all over the world, most of whom paid their own bills. The United States benefited from this influx in many ways—in mutual understanding, wider appreciation of U.S. culture and institutions, the scientific, medical, and cultural contributions of visitors and immigrants, and material benefits for U.S. educational institutions and society. In the late 1990s there were hundreds of American professors teaching abroad under the Fulbright program, even in outlying provinces of China and Russia.

The U.S. Information Agency operated hundreds of libraries abroad until this program was radically cut back in the 1990s. The USIA helped foreign "VIPs" to meet their counterparts in the United States. It dispatched U.S. experts to lecture and hold seminars on all kinds of topics in foreign countries, paying their expenses and modest honoraria. Unlike comparable programs operated by the USSR, U.S. programs generally allowed participants the freedom to say and do what they wished.

Seeking to promote economic and cultural development, Peace Corps volunteers also contributed to and gained international understanding.

While citizen diplomacy can be expensive for an ordinary student or academic or other citizen, the cost is a trifle compared to most governmental outlays for foreign affairs.

12. Establishing a Reputation for Dependability

Most achievements in U.S. foreign policy required that Americans and their government have a reputation for dependability. After refusing to join the League of Nations in the 1920s–1930s, the United States behaved as a loyal ally to its partners in World War II. In the post–1945 era Washington proved relatively steadfast toward its friends and allies.

For the United States to develop a long-range posture in foreign affairs and hold to it is difficult. While the public cares little for most nuances of foreign policy, there is endless competition between political parties and a tendency within government for each branch to go its own way. Despite such difficulties, the United States maintained large military forces in Europe and Asia, and rebuffed any

Appendix 1.1 U.S. Military Personnel in Foreign Areas at end of Fiscal Year (in thousands)

	FY 88	FY 89	FY 90	FY 91	FY 92	FY 93	FY 94	FY 95	FY 96	FY 97	FY 98	FY 99
Germany	249	249	228	203	134	105	88	73	49	60	70	66
Other Europe	74	71	64	62	54	44	41	37	62	48	42	40
Europe, Afloat	33	21	18	20	17	17	9	8	4	3	4	4
South Korea	46	44	41	40	36	35	37	36	37	36	37	36
Japan	50	50	47	45	46	46	45	39	43	41	40	40
Other Pacific	17	16	15	9	3	1	1	1	1	1	1	1
Pacific Afloat (including Southeast Asia)	28	25	16	11	13	17	15	13	15	14	18	21
Latin America/ Caribbean	15	21	20	19	18	18	36	17	12	8	11	8
Miscellaneous	29	13	160	39	23	25	15	14	17	15	37	32
Total	541	510	609	448	344	308	287	238	240	226	260	247

Source: http://www.dtic.mil/execsec/adr2000/appc2.html

threat to West Germany, Turkey, Japan, or South Korea. It supplied and defended West Berlin despite its Communist encirclement. It backed Israel despite pressures from oil interests, the Arab world, and the USSR. It stood by Taiwan even though this risked conflict with mainland China.

Let us now analyze the other side of these coins—America's failures in the twentieth century world.

Notes

1. Barry M. Blechman and Stephen S. Kaplan et al., *Force Without War: U.S. Armed Forces as a Political Instrument* (Washington, D.C.: Brookings Institution, 1978); for a broader survey and a rich bibliography, see Allan R. Millett, "The Parameters of Peacekeeping: U.S. Interventions Abroad, 1798–1999," *Strategic Review*, 28, 2 (Spring 2000), pp. 28–38.

2. Alexander George, *Forceful Persuasion: Coercive Diplomacy as an Alternative to War* (Washington, D.C.: United States Institute of Peace Press, 1991) and bibliography, pp. 89–92.

3. Walter LaFeber, *The American Age: U.S. Foreign Policy at Home and Abroad* (2d ed.; New York: W. W. Norton, 1994), p. 261.

4. The texts of most treaties discussed here are in *Disarmament and Security: A Collection of Documents, 1919–55* (Washington, D.C.: U.S. Government Printing Office, 1956).

5. Walter C. Clemens, Jr., "American Policy and the Origins of the Cold War in Central Europe, 1945–1947," in Peter J. Potichnyj and Jane P. Shapiro, eds., *From the Cold War to Detente* (New York: Praeger, 1976), pp. 3–25.

6. George Bush and Brent Scowcroft, *A World Transformed* (New York: Vintage, 1998).

7. On the cat-and-mouse game in 1997–1998, see United Nations Association of the United States of America, *A Global Agenda: Issues Before the 53rd General Assembly of the United Nations* (Lanham, Md.: Rowman & Littlefield, 1998), pp. 84–88.

8. Walter C. Clemens, Jr., "The European Alliance Systems: Exploitation or Mutual Aid?" in Charles Gati, ed., *The International Politics of Eastern Europe* (New York: Praeger, 1976), pp. 217–238.

9. Philip H. Gordon, ed., *NATO's Transformation: The Changing Shape of the Atlantic Alliance* (Lanham, Md.: Rowman & Littlefield, 1997).

10. Richard Holbrooke, *To End a War* (New York: Random House, 1998).

11. Since NATO bombs were targeting not just Serbian military forces but also Serbian power stations and, in the fog of war, killing civilians and depriving them of basic needs (for example, power and water), some observers stated that Western leaders should also be indicted.

12. Dr. Joffe is the Harvard-educated foreign affairs editor of the *Süddeutsche Zeitung* published in Munich. His views are taken from the 1987 survey.

13. For comparisons, see the special issue on "Military Government," *The Annals of the American Academy of Political and Social Science,*" 267 (January 1950).

14. Alexis de Tocqueville, *Democracy in America* (New York: New American Library, 1956), especially Part Two, Book III; Zbigniew Brzezinski and Samuel P. Huntington, *Political Power: USA/USSR* (New York: Viking, 1964).

15. LaFeber, *The American Age,* p. 688.

16. State of the Union address, January 27, 2000.

17. For a "postrevisionist" interpretation, see John Lewis Gaddis, *We Now Know: Rethinking Cold War History* (New York: Oxford University Press, 1997; for facts without theory, see Jack F. Matlock, Jr. *Autopsy on an Empire: The American Ambassador's Account of the Collapse of the Soviet Union* (New York: Random House, 1995); also Robert Strayer, *Why Did the Soviet Union Collapse? Understanding Historical Change* (Armonk, N.Y.: M. E. Sharpe, 1998; for bad sovietology blended with bad social science, see Jerry F. Hough, *Democratization and Revolution in the USSR, 1985–1991* (Washington, D.C.: Brookings Institution Press, 1997).

18. For analysis based on recent sources, see Graham Allison and Philip Zelikow, *Essence of Decision; Explaining the Cuban Missile Crisis* (2d ed.; New York: Longman, 1999).

19. Seeking to understand cooperation cum competition, U.S. scholars pioneered the study of game theory and conflict resolution—among the few advances in international studies since Thucydides. These scholars included John von Neumann, Oskar Morgenstern, Thomas C. Schelling, Anatol Rapoport, Steven J. Brams, Robert Axelrod, and Frank Zagare. The *Journal of Conflict Resolution,* initially based at the University of Michigan and later at Yale, published many of their findings, as did *World Politics,* based at Princeton.

20. On "Actions Louder Than Words: Doing the Unthinkable," see Walter C. Clemens, Jr., *Can Russia Change? The USSR Confronts Global Interdependence* (Boston: Unwin Hyman, 1990), chapter 8.

21. At tense moments in the Cold War some Westerners called for unilateral disarmament. Their slogan: "Better Red than dead." But no Western government seriously considered this option. Charles Os-

good hoped to break the impasse. See Osgood, *An Alternative to War or Surrender* (Urbana: University of Illinois Press, 1962); also Amitai Etzioni, *The Hard Way to Peace: A New Strategy* (New York: Crowell-Collier, 1962).

22. Henry Kissinger, *White House Years* (Boston: Little, Brown, 1979), pp. 173, 187–88, 191–92. This and other cases are analyzed in Walter C. Clemens, Jr., *Dynamics of International Relations: Conflict and Mutual Gain in an Era of Global Interdependence* (Lanham, Md.: Rowman & Littlefield, 1998), chapter 7.

23. Jun Zhan, *Ending the Chinese Civil War: Power, Commerce and Conciliation between Beijing and Taipei* (New York: St. Martin's, 1993).

24. See entries in Richard D. Burns, ed., *Encyclopedia of Arms Control and Disarmament* (3 vols., New York: Scribner's, 1993); see the periodicals *Arms Control Today* and *Bulletin of the Atomic Scientists;* also the web sites of the Arms Control Association and the Federation of American Scientists.

25. For zigs and zags in Russian policy, see Clemens, *Can Russia Change?* chapters 4 and 9.

26. *Strategic Survey 1999/2000* (London: International Institute for Strategic Studies, 2000), p. 50.

27. Charles P. Henry, "Civil Rights and National Security: The Case of Ralph Bunche," in Benjamin Rivlin, ed., *Ralph Bunche: The Man and His Times* (New York: Holmes & Meier, 1990), pp. 50–66 at 63. The other essays examine Bunche as "scholar activist," "Africanist and decolonizer," and "world statesman."

28. Each survey was based on telephone interviews with from 1,253 to 1,533 voters around the United States, the numbers chosen by a computer from a complete list of exchanges in the country to represent each region in proportion to its population, with the results weighted to take account of household size and variations related to race, sex, age, and education. See Adam Clymer, "Camp David at Top in U.S. Policy Poll," *The New York Times,* April 1, 1985, p. A6.

29. Uri Savir, *The Process: 1,100 Days That Changed the Middle East* (New York: Random House, 1998).

30. George J. Mitchell, *Making Peace* (New York: A. A. Knopf, 1999).

31. Holbrooke, *To End a War.*

32. Thomas Jefferson in Paris employed most-favored-nations treatment to win recognition of the United States by European princes.

33. The multilateral trade agreement known as GATT rested on three principles: nondiscriminatory treatment of all signatories in trade matters; the reduction and eventual elimination of barriers to trade through periodic negotiation—"rounds"; and resolution of conflicts by consultation—not by any international forum, as provided by the World Trade Organization.

34. When Congress turned down a support package for Mexico, Clinton used his executive authority to take money from the Exchange Stabilization Fund—a loan that Mexico soon repaid.

35. On behalf of free trade, see Jagdish Bhagwati, *The World Trading System at Risk* (Princeton, N.J.: Princeton University Press, 1991); for criticism of free trade and the World Trade Organization, see Eric Alterman, *Who Speaks for America? Why Democracy Matters in Foreign Policy* (Ithaca, N.Y.: Cornell University Press, 1998), chapters 4 and 5; for neo-mercantilist advocacy, see Edward N. Luttwak, *The Endangered American Dream: How to Stop the United States from Becoming a Third-World Country and How to Win the Geo-Economic Struggle for Industrial Supremacy* (New York: Simon & Schuster, 1993).

36. See World Bank and other studies cited in Clemens, *Dynamics of International Relations,* pp. 356–361.

37. As part of the U.S. occupation policy of denazification and democratization, William E. Griffith—later a professor at MIT—lectured in German to prospective German leaders on democratic theory and practice. His syllabi contained references to Kant and other German thinkers as well as to Locke, Rousseau, Jefferson, and de Tocqueville.

38. Seymour Martin Lipset, "Still the Exceptional Nation?" *Wilson Quarterly,* 24, 1 (Winter 2000), pp. 31–45.

39. "What is Europe?" *The Economist,* February 12, 2000, p. 15.

40. Dean Acheson, *Present at the Creation* (New York: Signet, 1970), p. 923.

41. For essays by Michael W. Doyle, Bruce Russett, Edward D. Mansfield and Jack Snyder, and others, see Michael E. Brown et al., eds., *Debating the Democratic Peace: An International Security Reader* (Cambridge, Ma.: The MIT Press, 1996).

42. Washington was not compelled to fight North Vietnam, but chose to do so, and lost. The United States did not perceive North Vietnam as a democracy but as an expansionist Communist dictatorship.

43. Henry Kissinger, *Diplomacy* (New York: Simon & Schuster, 1994), p. 30

44. Robert A. Pastor, "Divided by a Revolutionary Vision," in Pastor, ed., *A Century's Journey: How the Great Powers Shape the World* (New York: Perseus, 1999), pp. 191–238 at 238.

45. Harriet Mayor Fulbright in a speech in Washington, D.C. for Phi Beta Delta on April 3, 1997.

2.

Failures of United States Foreign Policy, 1898–2000

The United States erred both by omission and commission—by attempted detachment from world affairs and by messianic crusading to change how others think and act. Its greatest blunders arose from pressures to choose between the Scylla of nonintervention and the Charybdis of excessive intervention. The right balance, of course, was difficult to find. Faced with the bitter results of detachment or activism, Americans often pushed in the opposite direction.

American foreign policy often failed in the same spheres where it succeeded. Successes and failures often overlapped and fed one another.

1. Force: Washington sometimes resorted to force too early—without good cause—or too late. America's Indochina adventure became its greatest debacle in world affairs. But a stronger U.S. stance might well have prevented or limited some wars.
2. Governance: Washington undermined the League of Nations and did much to weaken the United Nations and international law.
3. Interdependence: Stalin's USSR and Boris Yeltsin's post - Soviet Russia did not join the First World.
4. Containment: The strategy to contain Soviet expansion became a global crusade against leftists or nationalists posing little challenge to U.S. interests.
5. Conflict control: Washington failed to explore some opportunities to reduce tensions with Moscow, Beijing, Tehran, and other adversaries.

6. Arms and arms control: U.S. and Russian overkill out-paced arms control.
7. Mediation and peacekeeping: Washington should have acted earlier and more forcefully to curtail conflicts in the Middle East, the Balkans, Northern Ireland, and elsewhere.
8. Free trade and economic development: America's trade and aid policies did little to help Third World development.
9. Modeling a Third Way: A rising GDP and stock market left the United States with severe domestic problems.
10. Human rights: Many American policies hurt liberty at home and abroad.
11. International understanding: Most Americans remained apathetic to the world, while many U.S. cultural exports gave an unbalanced picture of American life.
12. Dependability: Some U.S. leaders weakened the country's reputation for honesty, integrity, and dependability.

Not all people who liked Magna Macs also embraced the Magna Carta. As the century ended, many peoples and countries were determined to resist Americanization and U.S. hegemony.

1. Force: Often Too Early or Too Late

Force can be used to "continue" policy when other means do not succeed. Even without resort to war, a show or threat of force may persuade other actors to change their behavior. But the United States often resorted to arms too early—without good cause—or demonstrated its will to fight too late.

From 1898 to World War II

Spain's oppressive rule in Cuba was already on its last legs when the United States declared war on Spain in 1898. Indeed, authorities in Madrid were seeking ways to accommodate U.S. demands.

The United States quickly defeated Spain—in the Philippines as well as in Cuba. But Americans then lost the peace, for their war booty—or white man's burden, as Kipling put it—generated problems that endured more than a century. Washington turned Cuba into a virtual U.S. protectorate, breeding conditions for deep anti-Yankee resentment, while American forces in the Philippines waged a three-year war to suppress Filipinos seeking self-determination. The Philippines then became a U.S. dependency with naval and air bases that attracted a Japanese attack in 1941.

Having routed Spain with relative ease, the United States began to intervene elsewhere—even in China, helping to repress the Boxers in 1900. But most U.S. interventions took place "south of the border"—in Cuba, Panama, Haiti, Nicaragua, the Dominican Republic, and Mexico.

After the Bolsheviks took power in Russia in 1917, the U.S. government found more reasons to worry about the Caribbean and Latin America. Washington treated leftist or nationalist challenges to the status quo as "Bolshevist" threats. One U.S. diplomat warned in 1926: "By basing our policy with Latin America upon a fear of Bolshevism, we not only destroy our influence and prestige with Latin America, but we give great encouragement to the Bolshevists."[1]

American imperialism, like its European antecedents, often benefited some investors in overseas markets and boosted career opportunities for naval officers and missionaries. But it achieved little for most Americans who could have cheap bananas and sugar regardless who owned the plantations. Few interventions did much to promote avowed U.S. objectives of local self-government and economic stability. The most that Washington could claim was that, when U.S. forces withdrew, the local leader was "an S.O.B., but he is our S.O.B."

Force Without War as a Political Instrument

As the Cold War unfolded both Moscow and Washington often used force for political ends, trying to remain below the threshold where any party would consider a nuclear riposte. In the half- century after World War II the United States used military force as a political instrument without war hundreds of times in efforts to intimidate others. A Brookings Institution study sponsored by the U.S. Defense Department identified 215 incidents between 1946 and 1976—23 percent of them in Central America or the Caribbean (half of which targeted Cuba); 20 percent in Europe; 19 percent in Southeast Asia; 18 percent in the Middle East; 9 percent in East Asia; and 11 percent elsewhere, for example, Africa and South America.[2] The USSR also used force as a political instrument, especially in Eastern Europe, but at a lower rate than the United States.[3]

The Brookings study did not question the *wisdom* of U.S. shows of force but only whether they achieved their goals. Examining 33 cases in depth, investigators found that in the short-run some three-fourths of the outcomes were favorable, but that, three years after the initial show of force, the success rate dropped to less than one-half. Beyond the initial success, American policy failed to achieve its goals in nearly two-thirds of the incidents.

To illustrate: America's diplomacy of force in 1962–1963, reinforced in 1970, succeeded in removing and keeping Soviet offensive weapons out of Cuba. But U.S. efforts to dissuade Hanoi from intervening in Laos, South Vietnam, and Cambodia got nowhere. B-52 flights over Laos in 1973 encouraged Prince Souvanna Phouma and Meo tribesmen but did not stop North Vietnam and the Pathet Lao from taking over the country.

Demonstrations of U.S. might often bought time for diplomacy to achieve a more lasting remedy, but the kind of remedy desired by Washington seldom took shape. The most common outcome was the initial achievement of U.S. aims followed by long-term failure. For example, the United States intervened more than once in the Dominican Republic and in Lebanon only to feel compelled to intervene again. After the 1960s, to be sure, Washington was content with developments in the Dominican Republic but not in Lebanon—which continued as an unstable battleground for Syria, Iran, Hezbollah, and Israel into the twenty-first century.

The pattern and record of U.S. interventions in the last quarter of the twentieth century did not differ substantially from the 1946–1976 period studied by the Brookings Institution. In Grenada, for example, U.S. objectives were fully achieved. But there were also conspicuous failures, as in Lebanon and Somalia; initial victories with long-term problems, as in Haiti; and very mixed results in Iraq, Kosovo, and elsewhere.

Cuba.   Seeking to destroy the Castro regime in Cuba, U.S. agents trained and dispatched anti-Castro forces who landed at the Bay of Pigs in 1961, where most were killed or captured. Both the Bay of

Pigs invasion and the follow-on Operation Mongoose were cases of too little or too much force—insufficient to overthrow Castro but enough to bolster his reasons for accepting Soviet missiles.[4] Robert S. McNamara later said the United States had not planned, before the missile crisis, to invade Cuba. Still, he could understand how U.S. maneuvers might have given a different impression.

Indochina.   Despite its repeated missteps in Cuba, the Kennedy administration soon launched another intervention with far worse consequences. Starting with 15,000 advisers in 1963, U.S. military forces in Indochina reached half a million by 1968. Kennedy's campaign was expanded by President Johnson and continued under President Nixon. The United States fought for nearly a decade in Indochina and lost—probably the greatest debacle ever suffered by Americans on the world stage.[5]

The costs for caring for U.S. veterans of the Vietnam War exceeded U.S. outlays for the fighting, but many veterans felt that their sacrifices were not appreciated and complained that their illnesses caused by use of defoliants were not even officially acknowledged.

Sexual Perversity in Afghanistan

Afghanistan. When the USSR invaded Afghanistan in 1979, the United States supplied the anti-Soviet resistance with weapons that helped them contain Soviet forces and, after nine years, oust them. But American aid may have been unnecessary and undesirable. Without it, the *mujahideen* would probably have continued to resist and tie down Soviet forces. When Soviet forces withdrew, many Afghan fighters turned their weapons not only against one another but also against the United States, despised by many of them for a variety of reasons.

By the late 1990s the Taleban movement controlled most of Afghanistan and imposed its own interpretation of Islamic morality.

The Costs of Passivity

But Americans often remained aloof from world affairs even though their basic interests were threatened. Had Americans signaled their determination to fight potential aggressors, several serious wars— from 1914 through the 1990s—might have been averted or curtailed.

The World Wars. The United States should have done more to prepare for, prevent, or curtail World Wars I and II. Had Washington followed a realist policy of balancing power, it would have thrown its weight on the side of Britain and France before or at the onset of each world war. Only when attacked did the United States enter each fray. Then, angry and self-righteous, Americans crusaded to destroy the regimes that struck them. By the time the United States joined the fighting, much damage had been done and the aggressors had gained much headway. Victory was far more costly because Americans watched and waited for so long. World War I continued for so long that four major empires collapsed, leaving instabilities that conduced to World War II.

Realists also say that Wilson's messianic approach made peace harder to achieve and make last. To be sure, Woodrow Wilson tempered his crusade by calls for a peace without indemnities or annexations. But at the 1919 Paris Peace Conference he could not deliver on this offer, because the other victor states demanded reparations and territories from the vanquished. The contradiction between Wilson's offer of a magnanimous peace and the 1919 Versailles Treaty, presented on a take-it-or-suffer basis to the German delegation, helped cultivate German determination to undo the new world order.

America's crusading spirit was even stronger after Pearl Harbor than in 1917. U.S. demands for unconditional surrender probably stiffened resistance in Germany and Japan and discouraged efforts to topple Hitler and Tojo.

Failure to Anticipate Soviet Expansion. The United States cooperated effectively with its allies during World War II to defeat the aggressors. But President Franklin D. Roosevelt did little to prepare for the possibility that the victors might fall out among themselves. He seemed to worry more that Great Britain might reestablish its empire than that the USSR would expand its realm.[7]

The forward sweep of the Red Army permitted the USSR to occupy most of Eastern Europe and a great deal of Germany—a set of facts difficult to alter.[8] But if the United States could not prevent a divided Berlin from being located in the Soviet occupation zone of Germany, at a minimum Washington in 1944–1945 should have negotiated secure access rights to West Berlin. But it did not—setting the stage for one crisis after another beginning with the Berlin blockade in 1948–1949.

Box 2.1 How Realistic Are the Latter-day Critiques?

Arguing against power balancing, some historians contend that the United States should not have permitted itself to be drawn into World War I. Had Americans wished to be neutral, Washington should not have insisted on the right to send cargo ships to England, for these shipments were bound to provoke attacks by German U-boats.

But the retrospective critiques of U.S. policies toward World Wars I and II are somewhat ivory-tower. They demand that Americans and their political system be something different from what they were. Democracies are loath to prepare for war, as de Tocqueville forecast in the 1830s. Democracies seldom launch preventive or preemptive wars. Once engaged, however, a country with the values and attitudes of Americans would tend to go all-out. The awful lessons of the post–Versailles decades had to be absorbed before the next set of victorious governments could consider magnanimity, as did the Americans and Europeans who rebuilt Europe after 1945.

Many critics claim that the United States did not need to drop even one nuclear bomb—much less two—on Japan to end the war.[6] But this criticism also ignores how things looked at the time and the momentum that had developed.

Roosevelt's words to Stalin at Tehran in 1943 and Yalta in 1945 suggested that he saw imposition of Soviet rule in the Baltic republics and in Poland as inevitable. He asked Stalin only for a fig leaf to help Democrats in U.S. elections.[9] Though Roosevelt's successor, Harry S. Truman, was far more skeptical of Stalin's intentions, he capitulated to domestic pressures to "bring the boys home" when the fighting stopped.[10]

From Korea to Kabul to Kuwait and Beyond.   Despite U.S. pledges in 1946–1947 to "contain" Communist expansion, the United States often looked irresolute to Communist and other aggressive leaders, tempting them to bold moves. Washington's failure to take a strong stance invited North Korean aggression in 1950; tempted Nikita Khrushchev's Cuban missile gambit in 1962; and removed any Kremlin inhibition about invading Czechoslovakia in 1968 or Afghanistan in 1979.

In the 1990s an irresolute American posture probably encouraged Iraq's invasion of Kuwait; ethnic warfare in the Balkans and

The Russians Enter Grozny

Russia's 1999 campaign against Chechnya, directed by then acting President V. V. Putin, razed the capital Grozny.

Rwanda; massacres in East Timor; and two Russian military campaigns in Chechnya.

2. Governance: Weakening International Organization and Law

Having led the campaign to found the League of Nations, the United States refused to join it—delivering a death blow at birth to the world's first major attempt to organize collective security.

Neutrality

Standing apart from the League of Nations, America counted heavily on geography and legalisms to shield it from external dangers. U.S. Secretary of State Frank B. Kellogg and French Foreign Minister Aristide Briand in 1928 offered the world a treaty banning war as an instrument of policy—the Kellogg-Briand Pact, followed in 1932 by the Stimson Doctrine refusing to recognize political and territorial change by conquest. The pact and the doctrine won wide approval, but they provided no more than what Chinese call "spears of straw." When legal barriers failed to stop the march of aggression, Congress in 1935, 1936, 1937, and 1939 proclaimed American's intention to be neutral in any war that might erupt.

American detachment had unfortunate consequences—not just in Tokyo and Berlin but also in Moscow. Warning that "peace is indivisible," Soviet Foreign Commissar Maxim Litvinov sought in the mid-1930s to make the League of Nations into a stronger tool for collective security. When Litvinov and the League failed, he was replaced and the USSR signed nonaggression treaties with Germany and later with Japan.

The Dis-United Nations

The United States led in founding the United Nations, a second effort at organized collective security. As conditions changed, however, the United States did much to weaken this organization as well.

From 1945 until the mid-1950s, U.S. officials were usually pleased with the United Nations. Washington had a built-in majority in most UN organs thanks to its European and Latin American partners. Except for the USSR and its allies, most UN members usually voted with the U.S. delegation. Even when the USSR vetoed a Security Council resolution, the United States won points in the Cold War, because the Soviet delegate showed himself the odd-man-out. The Uniting for Peace Resolution, as noted in chapter 1, empowered the General Assembly to act on threats to security if the Security Council were hamstrung. This device helped keep the United Nations viable, but flouted the spirit—and some said the letter—of the UN Charter.

Beginning in 1955, waves of newly independent countries joined the United Nations. Since many of the new states claimed to be "nonaligned," the United States lost the nearly automatic majority it enjoyed in the first decade of the United Nations.

In the 1960s and 1970s many UN delegations from the Third World denounced Israel—whatever it did—for "Zionism." Many delegations sided with oil-producing countries against both Israel and the United States. Many seeded the UN Secretariat and other UN agencies with unskilled political appointees, making for higher budgets and less efficiency. Many demanded a New International

Economic Order (NIEO), further antagonizing Washington, which saw the NIEO as another scheme to expropriate the haves and weaken the West.

Expecting wide disapproval of its role in Vietnam, U.S. diplomats kept the Indochina War off the UN agenda. This course prevented a bruising fight at the United Nations, but left the world body sidelined in the most important military contest since World War II.

President Ronald Reagan's administration withdrew U.S. membership from the UN Educational, Scientific, and Cultural Organization (UNESCO) because it joined the NIEO campaign and wasted money on cronyism. The United Kingdom and Singapore also withdrew from UNESCO in 1984.

Seeking to reshape the United Nations by exerting America's financial leverage, Congress in the 1980s and 1990s refused to pay some UN assessments. The United States in 1999 owed more than $1 billion to the United Nations—making it by far the UN's biggest debtor and severely cramping the UN capacity for peacekeeping and other tasks. Washington was so far in arrears that it risked losing its vote in the General Assembly. At this juncture Congress promised to pay most of the assessed debts, but conditioned payments on future reforms. U.S. debts to the UN rose to $1.6 billion in 2000.

Rise and Fall of a New World Order

President George Bush expressed hope for a "new world order" in September 1990 as the USSR voted in the Security Council endorsing U.S. policies to press Iraq from Kuwait (the Chinese delegation either concurring or abstaining on the relevant votes). Addressing the American people on September 11, Bush said he hoped for a new world order "free from the threat of terror, stronger in the pursuit of justice, and more secure in the quest for peace. An era in which the nations of the world, East and West, North and South, can prosper and live in harmony."

But Washington and London soon found themselves facing opposition from Moscow, Beijing, and even Paris on Iraq and other issues. Moscow did not like Western policies in Bosnia and liked them even less in Kosovo. Washington and its European partners could not count on Russian or Chinese acquiescence in a campaign to oust Serbian forces from Kosovo. So NATO in 1998–1999 bypassed the

France and Russia blocked U.S.-UK efforts to maintain a tight regime of arms inspections and economic sanctions on Iraq. France wanted Iraqi oil and business contracts; Russia, for starters, wanted to be repaid for previous arms deliveries.

United Nations and ignored Russian objections as NATO forces threatened and then blasted Serbian targets. Meanwhile, Washington and London acted without specific UN approval as their warplanes regularly flew over Iraq, attacking Iraqi targets whenever Iraqi radars turned on or interceptors rose to challenge them.

Washington versus International Law

As a seafaring power with far-flung commercial interests, the United States from its early years sought to utilize the international law of the sea and neutrality to advance its interests. In the nineteenth century it became a strong supporter of third-party adjudication of international disputes. When Mexico nationalized property owned by U.S. interests, Washington sought compensation under international law. The United States did not join the Permanent Court of International Justice set up in conjunction with the League of Nations, but a legalist outlook gripped both the State

Department and Congress—witness the 1928 pact to outlaw war and the 1930s neutrality acts.

Reducing its traditional defense of national sovereignty, the United States accepted the compulsory jurisdiction of the International Court of Justice set up in 1945—except for matters "essentially" within U.S. domestic jurisdiction. Washington gladly took its complaints against Iran to the World Court in 1980.

In the 1980s and 1990s, however, the United States pulled back from its traditional support for international law. The Reagan administration renounced U.S. acceptance of the World Court's "compulsory jurisdiction" when Nicaragua charged the United States with warlike actions in 1986. The court look the case and ruled against the United States anyway, whereupon Washington flouted the ruling (as it did also in 1916, when the Central American Court ruled for Costa Rica against the United States).

The Reagan administration also refused to ratify the Law of the Sea—negotiated over nine years (1973–1982) with active U.S. participation. The treaty dealt with navigation, fishing, and other matters important to the United States, but the Reagan White House rejected the entire package because of its provisions on deep seabed mining. By A.D. 2000 more than 130 states were parties to the convention, including the European Community and all important maritime states except the United States. The Clinton White House transmitted the convention to the Senate for approval in 1994, but six years later the Senate Foreign Relations Committee headed by Senator Jesse Helms had still not scheduled hearings!

For its part, the Clinton administration refused to endorse the treaty banning land mines, claiming they were needed in Korea. As we shall see below, Washington also labored to narrow the scope of its human rights obligations and to avoid or weaken some arms control obligations.

Virtually all U.S. moves against world order were short-sighted, for law tends to favor the strong. Haves benefit from stability; only those who challenge the existing order can profit from chaos.

3. Interdependence: Could Russia Be One with the West?

The United States tried but failed to keep Russia as a partner after World War II. Later, even after the fall of Soviet Communism,

Land mines in Vietnam, Angola, Mozambique, and elsewhere killed and maimed years after they were planted.

Washington and its allies failed in the 1990s to integrate Russia with the West. The main reason for these failures lay not in the United States but in Russia—in a political culture deeply suspicious of outsiders, prone to authoritarian solutions, and unable to cope with the complexities of freedom; and, in the Marshall Plan era, in the character of the greatest demicidist (murderer of one's people) of all times, Josef Stalin.

The Soviet leadership declared in 1917–1921 that it intended to overthrow capitalism, beginning in the West. So, if the Kremlin offered concessions, Washington feared a trick. Alternatively, U.S. officials interpreted such offerings as a sign that the Soviet regime was crumbling. Either way, Washington found reason to reject Soviet overtures. By treating the Soviets as inveterately hostile, however, American suspicions served as a self-fulfilling prophecy.

President Wilson refused to meet with Soviet emissaries during the 1919 Paris Peace Conference. He dispatched U.S. troops to join

Box 2.2 *Limits to Interdependence:*
Russian Political Culture

Is Russia part of Europe? If not, can it be? These questions have lingered since the tenth century when Kyiv partnered with Constantinople. In time Hanseatic traders acquired a base in Novgorod. European architects, artisans, and admirals worked for the tsars. But Russia played no part in the Renaissance or the Reformation. The individualism and literacy fostered by Lutheranism percolated no farther east than Sweden's Baltic provinces. The empress Catherine the Great, however, welcomed the Enlightenment. And when Russian diplomat Vasilii Malinovskii in 1803 published a plan for world government, he presumed Russia to be a European power—an assumption echoed in the Holy Alliance proposed by Tsar Alexander in 1815.

In the nineteenth century French capital financed railroads linking Russia with Europe. By the early twentieth century Russia's economy grew faster than any in Europe. St. Petersburg aligned with Paris and London before World War I, but Tsar Nicholas II still wrote to his cousin the German Kaiser in English.

The Bolshevik Revolution in October 1917, however, underscored again Russia's uniqueness. The poet Aleksandr Blok declared: "We are Scythians"—marching against Europe. Lenin and his followers assumed that Soviet Russia would spark the transformation of bourgeois Europe. When that did not happen, the Soviets began to think of themselves as superior to Communists elsewhere—big brothers and teachers of would-be revolutionaries from Germany to China. The USSR became the "socialist fatherland."

with or keep tabs on French, British, Czech, and Japanese troops intervening in Russia's Civil War between Reds and Whites. The memory of American participation in these events undercut much of the goodwill produced by the famine relief organized by Herbert Hoover. In 1921 the State Department spurned a Soviet request to take part in the Washington Conference, saying that the U.S. delegation would uphold the interests of the Russian people in the deliberations. Indeed, the Americans won a Japanese pledge to withdraw from Siberia, but—having refused Soviet representation in Washington—got no thanks in Moscow. Washington did not recognize the USSR until 1933, even though U.S. firms such as Ford and International Harvester helped organize Soviet industry in the 1920s.

Hoping to overcome a troubled past, the Roosevelt administration during World War II gave Stalin the benefit of the doubt. FDR hoped he could win Stalin's confidence in face-to-face contact. When Roosevelt and Truman met Stalin, however, they faced a leader who expected betrayal. So doubtful was Stalin of his own "comrades" that he purged—killed—most of the Soviet officer corps and most top Communist Party officials in the late 1930s. Suspicious of England and France, Stalin in 1939 partnered with Hitler; betrayed by Hitler in 1941, he aligned with England and America to defeat Hitler. Could such a person become a long-term partner with the democratic West?

Why Did the USSR Not Welcome the Marshall Plan?

Following Roosevelt's death, U.S. officials became alarmed by signs—in Poland, Turkey, Iran, and elsewhere—that Stalin meant to expand the Soviet sphere as far as he could reach.

No doubt the United States could have done more to assuage Soviet suspicions about Western intentions. Early in 1947 the "Truman Doctrine" expressed U.S. determination to contain Soviet expansion. Still, the Iron Curtain was not yet firmly in place.

Despite growing concerns about Soviet intentions, Washington in 1946–1947 offered Moscow three platforms to continue their partnership: a mutual security treaty to prevent renewed German or Japanese aggression; the Baruch Plan to eliminate nuclear weapons; and the Marshall Plan. But Moscow spurned all three.

The Kremlin objected to the first two proposals on security grounds. It conditioned an alliance on Germany's "industrial disarmament." It turned down international control of atomic energy unless the United States first destroyed its nuclear monopoly. But why would the Kremlin turn down U.S. aid to rebuild the war-ravaged Soviet economy?

Secretary of State George C. Marshall invited participation by the USSR and the states of Eastern Europe as well as Western Europe in the European Recovery Program (ERP). In late June 1947 Soviet Foreign Minister Viacheslav M. Molotov traveled to a meeting in Paris to look this gift horse in the mouth, but he pronounced it unfit and returned to Moscow. When Molotov said "*nyet*," Western officials breathed a sigh of relief, for the Soviets could have sabotaged an already difficult undertaking. Pressured by Moscow, Czechoslovakia and Poland also kept away from the ERP.[11]

Molotov asserted that the U.S. plan would enslave European states and destroy their independence. The whole scheme, he said, was designed to save the *American* economy.[12] But there were deeper problems, which Moscow did not express in public. The ERP required transparency. Stalin would not willingly expose to outsiders the damage the USSR suffered in World War II or reveal his gulag archipelago in which millions of Soviets slaved until they perished of starvation and cold.

Once the Soviets rejected the ERP and the Kremlin proclaimed that the world was divided into "two camps," American officials tended to discount Soviet peace campaigns as empty propaganda aimed only at undermining Western unity. If Moscow smiled, Washington frowned.

A pendulum had swung in Washington. In the 1950s the United States sought to bargain from strength, but when the Kremlin suggested ways to deal with divided Germany or disarmament, Washington usually pulled away and sought still more bargaining power. The West did not explore Soviet overtures, initiated in 1952, for a reunified German state to be lightly armed and nonaligned—something like the status conferred on Austria in 1955. The West gave a cold shoulder to Soviet and Polish proposals for a nuclear-free zone in East Central Europe, along with a thinning out of foreign troops in the region.

U.S. Secretary of State John Foster Dulles and German Chancellor Konrad Adenauer feared that all such proposals were tricks to derail West German entry into NATO (accomplished in 1955) and rearmament. Bolder leaders might have seen the Soviet overtures as a possible avenue to liberate East Germans and weaken Moscow's hold on Eastern Europe.

The United States would neither negotiate seriously with Moscow to liberate Eastern Europe nor back East European rebels except with promises. Dulles called for "rolling back" the Iron Curtain, but Washington did nothing to help East Europeans when they rebelled against Soviet domination in 1953 and 1956. The U.S. Congress paid homage to the "Captive Nations," but the executive branch—White House, State Department, and Pentagon—treated

Eastern Europe and the Soviet border republics as off-limits under a Soviet-sphere Monroe Doctrine. This pattern continued in 1968 when Czechoslovakia tried to go its own way and endured as late as 1991. President Bush tried not to rock Gorbachev's foundering boat.[13]

Post-Soviet Russia and the West

A new set of opportunities arose when the Communist dictatorship fell in 1991. Washington and its European partners sought to help Russia become a democratic polity with a market economy playing a constructive role in world affairs. Many Russian as well as Western leaders hoped Russia would promptly join the West, but they were soon disappointed.

Faced with the complexities of freedom, Russian life turned in the 1990s from rigid order to chaos. Russian males—many of them despondent and seeking solace in vodka—lived on average five years less than in the 1980s. Corruption pervaded business and politics. Challenged in parliament, President Boris Yeltsin shelled the Duma in 1993 and then rewrote the constitution to expand the president's powers. Despite the Kremlin's dominion over key news outlets, anti-Yeltsin Communists still won the most seats in the 1994 and 1999 Duma elections. Yeltsin appointed a series of prime ministers in the 1990s—two of them spy masters and one the head of the Ministry of Internal Affairs. Yeltsin resigned at the end of the century and named V. V. Putin acting president. Exploiting that position, Putin then won the presidential election in 2000 and proceeded to institute what he called a "dictatorship of law."

American money helped Russia to disarm, as noted in the previous chapter. But other Western aid to Russia backfired or registered little positive effect. Rebuilding the Russian economy and promoting democracy was bound to be an uphill struggle. Western economists dispensed advice as if Russia were no different from Germany or Chile or Poland. Unlike Germany in the 1950s, Russia in the 1990s was ill-prepared for capitalism and self-rule; it was not an occupied country. Indeed, many former *aparatchiki* still filled major posts. The West gave Russia much less aid than Europe received under the ERP. Apart from the Soros Foundation, few outsiders invested in efforts to reshape Russia's educational system.

But Clinton's foreign policies—too soft on Chechnya, too tough on other dimensions—aggravated an already difficult and dangerous situation. The Clinton team delivered only mild tut-tuts to the brutal Russian invasions of Chechnya in 1994–1996 and 1999, but it provoked Russians—not just hard-liners but liberals—by expanding NATO eastward, attacking Serbia, and pressing to loosen restraints on antiballistic missile (ABM) defenses.

Enlarging NATO worsened relations with Moscow needlessly, for Russia in the 1990s had lost its erstwhile potential to bully its western neighbors. NATO's inclusion in 1999 of Poland, Hungary, and the Czech Republic—each a former Soviet ally—seemed to draw a line once again between the West and Russia. George F. Kennan, Michael Mandelbaum, and many other experts on Russia warned that this was a potentially disastrous course of action. If Russia's will and ability to threaten Europe reemerged, there would be time to take countermeasures.

Enlarging NATO added vulnerabilities. The new members were militarily weak and had much Soviet-era equipment different from any NATO standard. Still, the alliance agreed to defend its new members even without stationing outside forces on their territories. Congress approved NATO expansion with very little debate and with no solid estimates of costs for U.S. taxpayers or those in the new member states. Clinton sold out U.S. interests to gain votes in Chicago and Pittsburgh and elicit donations from Lockheed and other arms manufacturers hoping to expand sales to Eastern European markets.

NATO threw Russia a bone by giving Moscow a consultative voice in Brussels. But when push came to shove in Kosovo, NATO dismissed Russian objections and proceeded to attack Serbia.

Concurrent with these threats on the ground, the Clinton administration, hard pressed by Republicans, explored new ways to shoot down missiles. To accommodate expanded U.S. defenses, Washington asked Moscow to relax the 1972–1974 ABM treaty. But Moscow, like Beijing, worried that a nationwide defense for the United States could degrade its deterrent, while many Europeans feared it could precipitate a U.S. withdrawal to "Fortress America."

Adding to other insults and injuries, Americans weaned Kazakstan and Azerbaijan away from Russia to collaborate with U.S. oil firms and to send Caspian oil and gas westward without crossing either Russia or Iran. Though Kazakstan and Ukraine did not belong to NATO, the United States demonstrated its ability to assist these former Soviet republics. American paratroopers flew nonstop from

North Carolina and jumped into Kazakstan. Making a similar point, NATO forces conducted maneuvers with Ukrainians near the Simferopl base—part of "Russia's soft underbelly"—attacked by British and French forces in 1854.

Did Washington "lose" post-Soviet Russia in the 1990s? No, but it certainly did not "save" Russia. Many Western policies rekindled both the authoritarian and anti-Western strains within Russian political culture.

4. Containment: Universal Scope, Unlimited Means

The United States was correct in 1946–1947 to develop a long-term strategy to contain expansion by the USSR, the world's largest country and leading totalitarian dictatorship. American and Soviet leaders treated the world as a chessboard where any piece lost by one side, the other gained.

To combat the USSR the United States adopted a global strategy with few holds barred. Washington utilized nearly every means it could muster and opposed any political force that *might* be an instrument of Soviet policy, whether directly or indirectly. Since the USSR utilized the black arts and propaganda to weaken and overcome its opponents, the United States did too.

Washington saw most nationalist and leftist movements as tools of Soviet expansion. Only in Belgrade did Americans perceive that a Communist government could also be truly nationalist and determined to resist Soviet domination. The United States aided Marshal Tito's Yugoslavia after it broke with Moscow in 1948. Elsewhere, however, American agents shored up right-wing forces and discouraged or opposed those struggling for social and economic reforms. Washington acted as though independence and the New Deal were fine for Americans but not for Asians and Africans.

Intervention Hubris

Americans contracted intervention hubris. As we saw earlier this chapter, the United States often used force and shows of force to shape behavior around the world. But Washington also exploited a wide range of nonmilitary methods and instruments to advance its goals.

The United States subsidized the Christian Democratic Party in Italy to help it defeat Communists; backed a coup to overthrow a nationalist government in Iran in 1953 and in Guatemala in 1954; endeavored to overthrow, assassinate, or undermine Fidel Castro from 1959 into the twenty-first century; supported a deadly coup against South Vietnam's president in 1963; invaded the Dominican Republic in 1965; backed a deadly coup against Chile's democratically elected president in 1973; armed and financed the Contras in Nicaragua and invaded Grenada and Panama in the 1980s.

Many of these adventures succeeded in their immediate objectives, but most proved to be phyrric victories whose consequences haunted the United States for decades. Thus, when Iranians seized the U.S. embassy in 1979, they denounced the Great Satan for having reinstalled the Shah in 1953 and having backed him thereafter. The right-wing government in Guatemala set up with U.S. aid in 1954 committed horrendous human rights abuses for decades, killing even Americans who got in its way.

Even good ideas could be spoiled by their sponsorship. The journals *Encounter* and *Der Monat* served as vibrant forums for anti-Communist intellectuals, but lost credibility when their CIA subventions were revealed. Ditto the U.S. National Student Association, supported by a CIA front in a global struggle against Communist youth organizations based in Prague and Moscow. Radio Free Europe and Radio Liberty did excellent work, but why could they not be funded openly instead of covertly?

Alienating and Antagonizing Potential Partners

Americans violated their own ideals and wasted their assets in unnecessary contests that turned potential partners into determined adversaries. The words of Franklin Roosevelt, like those of Woodrow Wilson a generation before, led people everywhere after World War II to count on Washington to champion progressive reform and national self-determination. Instead, the United States generally behaved like a gendarme of reaction. It soon alienated Hanoi and, as we shall see in the next section, Beijing. Determined to enlist France in the anti-Soviet cause, Washington did not even reply to requests from nationalist Communists in Vietnam to help them resist France's efforts to reimpose its colonial rule. Washington appeased the dictatorship in Lisbon because it wanted to secure long-term leases to bases in Portugal's Canary Islands. Virtually the only place where the United States actively opposed the reimposition of European colonial rule was in Indonesia, where American oil men had their own interests.

Consider the consequences if the United States had not become an adversary of Hanoi and Beijing! Americans would not have fought in Indochina. Vietnamese and Chinese Communists might not have been drawn into the Soviet camp. Even the Korean War might have been avoided if Mao Zedong had not given his reluctant approval. If the USSR had possessed no putative allies in Asia, perhaps it would have mellowed more quickly. Instead, N. S. Khrushchev and Mao Zedong tried to outdo one another promoting world revolution.

The Foibles of Pactomania

The 1950s witnessed a global U.S. campaign to form security treaties against Communist expansion. John Foster Dulles, Secretary of State from 1953 to 1959, railed against "neutrality" and "nonalignment" and wanted every country to take a stand against Communism. He organized two multilateral alliances that backfired for Washington and their members—CENTO and SEATO. Critics said Dulles suffered from "pactomania." Winston Churchill coined the progression "Dull, duller, Dulles."

As Hanoi's troops drove the French from Vietnam, Dulles cobbled together in 1954 the Southeast Asia Treaty Organization (SEATO) as an Asian counterpart to NATO. SEATO members included Australia, France, New Zealand, Pakistan, the Philippines, Thailand, the United Kingdom, and United States. Unlike NATO, SEATO members lacked geographic and cultural cohesion, consensus on threats, and a shared command structure. It did not oblige members to fight if one was attacked. SEATO encouraged the United States to subsidize Pakistan's military governments, a trend that weakened democracy in Pakistan and helped inflame tensions between Islamabad and New Delhi. SEATO collapsed and dissolved between 1972 and 1977.

After the first Soviet arms shipments reached Egypt in 1955, Dulles put together the Baghdad Pact, later known as the Central

Treaty Organization (CENTO), to thwart Soviet expansion in the Middle East. The original members were Iran, Iraq, Pakistan, Turkey, and the United Kingdom, with the United States only an observer (though it had bilateral agreements to cooperate with Iraq, Pakistan, and Turkey). The pact's name changed to CENTO after Baghdad withdrew in 1959. Iran pulled out in 1979, soon followed by Pakistan and Turkey. CENTO did not curtail Soviet expansion in the Middle East, but U.S. policies toward Egypt and Washington's alignment with Israel helped push Egypt's President Gamal Abdal Nasser further into Khrushchev's embrace.

Both SEATO and CENTO gave an illusion of security and cohesion. Neither embraced the principle "one for all, all for one," as NATO did. Instead, members were required only to consult. Each "organization" existed only on paper and did nothing to check its intended adversaries. Each grouping antagonized other countries and even member-states.

In Africa, as in Asia, the United States did nothing to assist nationalist movements against European imperialists. When anti-imperialist forces became strong, Washington backed those who claimed to oppose groups favored by Moscow or Beijing. The upshot was that the Americans helped to install and keep in power a bevy of monstrosities such as President Mobuto Sese Seko in Zaire. Only when white rule in Zimbabwe and South Africa neared the breaking point did Washington and London switch to favoring majority-rule there. The Americans, however, could not decide whether to emphasize sanctions against the white government or "constructive engagement" or both.

In Latin America, too, the United States generally collaborated with right-wing forces—conservative or military juntas against leftists and Indians. The major exception to this pattern was President Jimmy Carter, who campaigned for human rights in Latin America and elsewhere, though with little visible effect. His successor, President Reagan, aided by Oliver North and other loose cannons, did all he could to help putative anti-Communists from Nicaragua to Afghanistan. For his part, President Clinton promoted a $1.6 billion program to help the Colombian government wipe out its opponents in a civil war that had raged for more than three decades, though many experts thought the money could be better used reducing demand for drugs in the United States.

5. Conflict Control: Missed Opportunities

Washington often pursued a hard line toward its adversaries when conciliation might have proved fruitful. The United States missed many opportunities for cooperation or conflict reduction and stumbled into or provoked many conflicts that could have been avoided. As noted earlier, U.S. policy sometimes multiplied tensions and deepened wounds with Moscow. Here we review the U.S. record with the People's Republic of China (PRC) and Iran.

China

As with the Soviet Union, the United States was sometimes conciliatory toward the PRC leadership when it should have been firm. But Washington lost a major opportunity to establish normal if not cordial relations with the Chinese Communists in 1949 when they won power, compelling the Nationalists to retreat to Taiwan. To be sure, the top U.S. leadership had long favored the Nationalists (against the advice of many "old China hands"), but so had Stalin. Mao Zedong and his comrades had far more reason to resent Soviet interference in China's domestic affairs than American. United States educators in the nineteenth and early twentieth centuries had established a reservoir of good will in China toward the United States. The founder of modern China, Sun Yat-sen, had learned about democracy when he studied at a missionary school in Honolulu.

The Chinese Communists in Beijing expressed hope for good relations with the United States and other Western governments. Still, America's historic tilt toward the Nationalists convinced Mao Zedong that he must ally with the Kremlin. China and the USSR signed a treaty of mutual assistance on Valentine's Day 1950. Any Chinese hope for reconciliation with the United States disappeared in the Korean War as General Douglas MacArthur's advances triggered Chinese intervention and the U.S. Navy started to protect Taiwan.

The Korean Armistice in 1953 opened new possibilities. Chinese Premier Zhou Enlai in April 1955 called for negotiations with Washington on Taiwan. In July 1955 Beijing released eleven U.S. airmen imprisoned in China and again suggested talks with Washington. PRC and U.S. ambassadors then met in Geneva. They scored no breakthroughs but developed a format used in later ambassadorial talks.

The United States did not formally recognize political realities in mainland China from 1949 until the 1970s. Washington claimed to worry about the advancing "monolithic" Communist bloc, but did little to exploit the tensions evident or suspected between and among Beijing, Moscow, Hanoi, and Pyongyang. Instead, the United States attacked North Vietnam (just as Soviet Premier Aleksei Kosygin visited Hanoi in 1965), thereby pushing the Communist regimes together, even though each depicted the other as a miscreant.

Not until PRC and Soviet troops fought on their disputed border did the Americans seriously approach Beijing. The Nixon-Kissinger team hoped to use China as a lever against the USSR and vice versa. This "triangular diplomacy" achieved few dividends, but Washington did finally normalize relations with Beijing.

From the 1970s through the 1990s the United States succeeded in "engaging" China. To do so, however, the United States made substantial concessions. Washington terminated its alliance with Taiwan and withdrew diplomatic recognition, though Congress preserved many ties by passing the Taiwan Relations Act in 1979. In the last decades of the century Washington approved the transfer of much dual-use technology to China, thereby strengthening PRC military capabilities. Beijing made some gestures toward arms control, but continued to proliferate advanced weapons and technology. It built structures on two disputed islands in the South China Sea, and threatened Taiwan with hundreds of missiles. Chinese agents, perhaps abetted by Americans, filched U.S. technology.

In the 1990s the Chinese Communist Party interfered less in private life but tightened its hold on power. PRC judges gave long jail sentences to pro-democracy dissidents. Beijing signed two UN human rights covenants, but China continued to inundate Tibet and Xinjiang with Han settlers and to repress Tibetans and Uighurs seeking greater religious, cultural, or political freedoms. Washington complained about China's repression of human rights and treatment of ethnic minorities. But not even the 1989 Tiananmen Square massacre or the later crackdowns on democratic activists and the *Falun Gong* movement seriously disrupted business between the United States and China.

By 2000 the balance sheet was mixed. Presidents Clinton and Jiang Zemin had exchanged visits and promises. Buffeted by Asia's economic crises in the late 1990s, China liberalized less than Washington hoped and the U.S. trade deficit with China widened. Still,

Both presidents—Clinton and Jiang Zemin—wanted to separate human rights issues from U.S. trade with China.

hoping to shape a better future, Clinton backed PRC entry into the World Trade Organization and got Congress to delink trade from China's human rights practices. Some analysts praised Washington for maintaining businesslike if not cordial relations with the world's most populous country. Others called for a tougher line analogous to the containment policy earlier mounted against the USSR.

Iran

Washington's support for Shah Mohammed Reza Pahlevi from 1953 until his departure in 1979 also undermined an historically grounded reservoir of goodwill toward the United States. In the first half of the twentieth century Americans had helped Iran in many ways, from regularizing its finances to documenting its cultural riches. In 1946 the United States led the diplomatic campaign to remove Soviet troops from northern Iran.

Ignoring how U.S. ties with the Shah had antagonized many Iranians, Americans became mesmerized by Iran's theocracy. Washington seemed to forget that Iran, no matter who ruled it, was the largest and potentially the strongest power in the Middle East. Not only could Tehran help contain the USSR, but—a non-Arab and a Shi'i Islamic country—Iran could weaken the united front of Sunni Muslim countries against Israel.

Instead, when Saddam Hussein attacked Iran in 1980, Washington backed Iraq—a dictatorship with no saving graces, not even a serious claim to religion. Washington stood by Iraq throughout an eight-year war that killed two million. When Iraqi missiles hit a U.S. frigate ("by mistake"), Washington barely complained. When a U.S. warship shot down an Iranian Airbus, Washington scarcely apologized and later gave medals to the ship's commanders!

U.S. officials hardly acknowledged the calls of President Mohammad Khatami, elected in 1997, for a dialogue between civilizations. Iran's new president said that he wanted to promote civil society in Iran and better relations with the American "people." When Iranian wrestlers arrived in the United States for what could have been détente-through-sport in 1998, they were fingerprinted at

A Show of Hands

One of Elian Gonzales' Lesser Known Grandmas Arrives at U.S.Customs

Cuban Prime Minister Fidel Castro took a great interest in the well-being of Elian. First he dispatched the boy's two grandmothers; then his father; and then . . .

the Chicago airport. Congress funded a radio station hostile to the Iranian regime. As with Cuba, Washington persisted in a tough line that harmed American interests as well as those of the target country. Petulance and pettiness outweighed grand strategy.

Washington and Tehran wanted to neutralize Saddam Hussein and stabilize Afghanistan. Both also shared an interest in developing Iran's oil reserves and getting them to Western markets. But Washington maintained its ban on investment and commerce with Iran—even by non-U.S. firms. Instead of directing Kazak oil across Iran, Washington tried to bypass Iran by subsidizing a pipeline under the entire Caspian Sea—an expensive and environmentally dangerous enterprise.

By what logic did the White House decide to engage China but to ostracize Iran and Cuba? By what logic did Washington object to Castro's dictatorship while winking at unsavory regimes in Azerbaijan and Kazakstan so long as they cooperated with U.S. firms and avoided contact with Iran? Was it that a combination of the pro-Chinese business lobby, the pro-Israeli constituency, and the anti-Castro vote in Florida had more clout than the oil business or strategic logic?

Washington waited to see whether liberals or conservatives prevailed in Tehran. When liberal forces (in the Iranian context) won control of the Iranian parliament in 2000, however, U.S. words and deeds suggested movement in the Clinton administration (though not in Congress) toward GRIT.

In 2000 there was also some improvement in U.S.-Cuban relations as Washington moved to return a waif found at sea to his father in Cuba even though this meant antagonizing much of the Cuban community in Florida. Economics also played a role; American farmers wanted to sell their goods to Cuba as well as to embargoed Iraq.

6. Arms and Arms Control:
Strategic Overkill, Conventional Weakness

Strategic arms outpaced arms control. U.S. arms control policy pursued three goals: To reduce the danger of war; to limit damage if war occurs; and to curb the costs of arms competition. Each goal was partially met, leaving serious shortfalls. The United States avoided an all-out war after 1945 but several times came close to the brink. If a major war occurred, the consequences would be horrific—perhaps ending all life in a "nuclear winter." The U.S. economy managed the financial burdens of arms competition but the opportunity costs were high. What if the money and brains devoted to producing multiple warheads and Stealth bombers had gone into more constructive pursuits?

Americans sought strategic stability by means of a capacity for Mutual and Assured Destruction—a doctrine nicknamed MAD. The United States and USSR built far more weapons than needed to deter each other. Washington and Moscow agreed to and implemented many arms controls, but each side's power to destroy outpaced all efforts to moderate the competition.

The U.S.-Soviet arms competition started slowly and then picked up speed. Usually the Soviets played catch-up, but the USSR tested the world's first space satellite and ICBM in 1957. In 1961 the Kennedy team accelerated the U.S. strategic buildup even after it grasped that the much discussed "bomber gap" and "missile gap" favored the West—not the USSR. Self-righteousness blinded Washington to how its military deployments might appear to Moscow and how Soviets might feel entitled to a force in Cuba analogous to that which the United States fielded in Turkey.

While the United States was first to deploy submarine-launched ballistic missiles and multiple warheads, the Soviets brandished whatever weapons they built readily or well—for example, large thermonuclear warheads and intermediate-range ballistic missiles.

In the early 1960s serious analysts thought that each of the two nuclear rivals might need a deterrent of several hundred nuclear weapons. By the 1980s, however, both Washington and Moscow had well over 20,000 strategic nuclear weapons, plus thousands of tactical nuclears—arsenals much larger than required to deter attack by any combination of nuclear rivals. START 2 called on the United States and Russia to cut their respective forces to no more than 3,500 strategic nuclear weapons by 2003—a deadline later extended to 2007. After Putin became President, the Russian Duma finally ratified START 2 but conditioned its implementation on strict observance of the ABM treaty, which Washington wanted to revise if not abrogate.

Ever since President Reagan called for a Strategic Defense Initiative, the Kremlin had denounced U.S. plans to alter the balance between offensive and defensive weapons. The Clinton administration asked Moscow to revise the treaty to accommodate a defense useful against a small-scale attack from a "rogue" state, and even offered to share defense technology with Russia, but the Kremlin was cool to opening a new arena of military competition that could degrade its deterrent.

Critics pointed out that, even if an ABM system intercepted *most* incoming missiles, the few that got through could inflict "unacceptable" damage. Russia and China might choose to beef up their offensive forces to assure their ability to intimidate the United States. An ABM defense would not stop "suitcase" bombs or those delivered by low-flying cruise missiles; it might well be evaded also by airplanes.

Starting in 1985, the Pentagon spent about $3 billion a year on RDT&E (research, development, testing, and evaluation) of ballistic missile defenses against "theater" as well as "strategic" weapons. By A.D. 2000 these efforts consumed more than $60 billion. But the Pentagon had still not successfully conducted even one realistic test of an ABM defense against even one incoming ICBM—much less dozens or hundreds or thousands. Those who hoped for security through ABM defenses were probably barking up the wrong tree.

Ignorance contributed to complacency and confusion. Surveys conducted by Boston University students from the 1970s into the twenty-first century revealed that most Americans believed their country *already* possessed an ABM system able to shoot down at least 500 of 1,000 incoming ICBMs. Very few Americans—even professors of political science—remembered (if they ever knew) that President Nixon and Soviet leader Leonid Brezhnev had agreed in 1972 to limit ABM defenses.

So poorly did Americans—even on Capitol Hill—understand the dangers of nuclear spread that the Senate in 1999 rejected the Comprehensive Nuclear Test Ban Treaty.

The spread of nuclear weapons amounted to a failure of U.S. carrots and sticks. Starting in 1946, the United States tried and failed to halt the spread of nuclear weapons beyond the United Kingdom, which, with Canada, had helped the Manhattan Project. In time the USSR, France, China, Israel, South Africa, India, and Pakistan joined the nuclear club, while North Korea, Iraq, and Iran also sought admission. Washington had tried to assuage the security concerns of India and Pakistan, but failed. India complained that the 1968 Nuclear Nonproliferation Treaty presumed U.S. and Soviet nuclear arms reductions. By 1999, however, Washington and Moscow had more weapons than in 1968. Meanwhile, China had gone its own way, creating a nuclear threat to India. If China increased its arsenal to break through an American ABM, the chain reaction would probably reach India and then Pakistan. South Africa set an example to the others: It dismantled its nuclear weapons.[14]

Table 2.1 tracks the size of the nuclear weapons stockpiles in the five permanent members of the UN Security Council. It includes the years when each broke into the nuclear weapons club. The total number of weapons peaked in 1986. The arsenals of the other nuclear powers would not add significantly to these totals. U.S. and Russian totals after 1986 include many weapons held in reserve or awaiting dismantlement.

Nuclear overkill paired with shortcomings in other domains. The United States maintained large, well-equipped conventional forces and urged its NATO allies to do the same. But allied forces were weak relative to the huge missions they faced. Despite much U.S. urging, most European NATO members did not contribute their fair shares. Could combined NATO forces have stopped a Soviet push toward Hamburg and Paris without resorting to tactical or other nuclear arms? Doubtful. Weakening NATO forces still further, the United States shifted many of it best units from Europe to Vietnam, where they failed to stop Hanoi's expansion.

Table 2.1 Nuclear Weapons, 1945–2000

Year	USA	Russia/ USSR	UK	France	China	Total
1945	2	0	0	0	0	2
1949	169	1	0	0	0	170
1953	1,161	120	1	0	0	1,282
1964	31,600	5,100	310	4	1	37,015
1976	26,700	25,800	350	212	190	53,252
1986	23,400	45,000	300	355	423	69,478
2000	10,500	20,000	185	450	400	31,535

Source: Robert S. Norris and William M. Arkin, "Global Nuclear Stockpiles, 1945–2000," *Bulletin of the Atomic Scientists* (March/April 2000), p. 79.

In the 1990s the Pentagon sought the ability to prevail in two regional wars fought nearly simultaneously (for example, against North Korea and Iraq) while conducting significant humanitarian or peacekeeping operations. By the end of the century U.S. conventional forces were stretched very thin—a large fraction of them in Bosnia and Kosovo, neither a vital interest of the United States.

But Washington's greatest security failure was that, in more than a half century since Hiroshima, the United States failed to eliminate the threat of catastrophic war by weapons of mass destruction—nuclear, biological, chemical—by governments or by terrorists. Barring a revolution in ABM defenses, there was no prospect of radical change. The United States sought only to modify the status quo. The former head of U.S. strategic forces, General George L. Butler, advocated complete nuclear disarmament. But radical shifts were barely discussed by officials in Washington or elsewhere. As the millennium began, even de-alerting of U.S. and Russian forces had stalled. Many thousands of strategic warheads—

the equivalent of 100,000 Hiroshima bombs—were poised for "launch on warning," even if by a false signal, or by a cabal of Russian generals or by a temper tantrum.[15]

7. Mediation and Peacekeeping

Here, as in other domains, the United States sometimes did too little or endeavored to do too much. Washington should have acted earlier and with greater force to curtail disputes in the Middle East, Northern Ireland, the Balkans, and elsewhere.

American mediators since the late 1940s tried to broker peace in the Middle East. Conflicts between Arabs and Israelis were profound—not easy to resolve. But U.S. mediators were weakened by their reluctance to lean hard on Israelis. When Jimmy Carter finally brokered the Camp David framework accords, he failed to push Israeli Primer Minister Menachem Begin to halt settlements in Israeli-occupied territory. Begin promised Carter only to "think about" halting settlements longer than the three-month period before a treaty with Egypt was to be formalized. Yasser Arafat rejected the Camp David provisions for Palestinian autonomy as too modest while other Arab governments denounced President Sadat's compromises. Egypt was left isolated in the Arab world. Despised by some of his own subjects, Sadat was assassinated in 1981. Nor did Camp David come cheap for the United States. Critics asked: Why should the United States each year have to pay $3 billion to Israel and $2 billion to Egypt to entice them not to shoot one another? The bill from 1979 to 1999 totaled some $100 billion—nearly twice the Pentagon's outlays for ABM defense research since the mid-1980s!

Respect for another ally, the United Kingdom, led Washington to sit silently and watch as Northern Ireland and some sites in London exploded, starting in 1969. Not till the Clinton administration showed some respect for Sinn Fein leader Gerry Adams did Unionists, Republicans, and 10 Downing Street begin to talk. Not till George J. Mitchell sat with them did they reach any accord.

In the early 1990s George Bush's White House, followed by Bill Clinton's, watched as the European Union and United Nations sought to pacify the warring tribes of the erstwhile Yugoslavia. (Asked why the United States sat on its hands, a U.S. ambassador in Europe told me in 1992: "We are waiting for the Europeans to re-

Serbs Stone US KFOR Troops

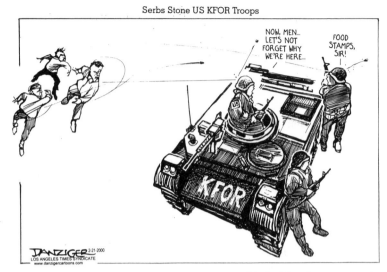

The NATO-led Kosovo Force (KFOR) was established by the UN Security Council on June 10, 1999 to establish security in Kosovo. But when OSCE members sent too few police, KFOR found itself trying to keep the peace between Serb-speakers and Albanian-speakers in Kosovo. The expense of such missions was high for the Pentagon, but the pay for U.S. troops was so low that the families of many soldiers qualified for food stamps.

alize they can't do much without us.") After TV showed American audiences images of civilians killed in the streets of Sarajevo, the Clinton team decided on action. It moved decisively in 1995 to mediate and impose the Dayton Accords on the contenders for Bosnia. NATO troops enforced the peace but did little to help victims of "ethnic cleansing" return home. Only on rare occasions did the troops arrest indicted war criminals—usually of low or middle rank.

The American-led NATO intervention in Kosovo in 1999 was even more problematic. The Western governments demanded a great deal of Serbia and then, when Belgrade balked, attacked Serbia with no veneer of UN approval. Striving to coerce Belgrade into submission, NATO struck bridges, power plants, and buildings far from Kosovo. Inevitably, civilians died—both Serbs and Kosovars. Fortunately for NATO, Belgrade buckled when Moscow signaled that Russia would not help if NATO invaded with ground troops.

Box 2.3 Mediators between Rocks and Hard Places

Mediation is seldom easy. Even with knowledge, goodwill, power, and time, U.S. federal authorities in the 1970s–1980s could not broker a compromise deal acceptable to Hopis and Navajos seeking to use if not own the same lands. Failing to reach a settlement, the authorities decided that some 10,000 Navajos had to move and offered them material incentives to do so. Many refused. Many who did move became lost souls, separated from their traditional way of life.

In 1982 Secretary of State Alexander M. Haig tried but failed to prevent war between Argentina and the United Kingdom over the Malvinas/Falkland Islands. When push came to shove, Washington helped London with intelligence about Argentine military movements.

Moscow's efforts at mediation were less successful than Washington's. The Kremlin failed to arrange a durable peace between India and Pakistan in 1966; between Somalia and Ethiopia in 1977–1978; and between Armenia and Azerbaijan over Nagorno-Karabakh in the 1980s–1990s.

NATO policy was incoherent. NATO wanted to halt Serbian repression of Kosovars but insisted that Kosovo remain within Serbia. The West wanted to protect all ethnic groups in Kosovo. But the Organization for Security and Cooperation in Europe could not muster half the 6,000 policemen needed to do the job. If NATO troops had to perform police duties, however, they risked looking like brutes or like wimps.

The Kosovo intervention worsened U.S. relations with China and Russia. They complained that NATO bypassed the Security Council and ignored Moscow's voice in Brussels. Beijing doubted that U.S. bombs struck the PRC embassy in Belgrade by mistake. Russians suspected that NATO intended to occupy Yugoslavia as part of its enlargement eastward. When Russia attacked Chechnya later in the year, Moscow claimed that its tactics mirrored NATO's in Serbia.

Was America again doing too little and too late—or attempting too much? Some critics said the United States should curtail its "social work" abroad—humanitarian relief, peacekeeping, defense of human rights. The Balkans may have been a Class C threat to U.S. security, but Haiti was in Class D. Rwanda, however terrible the genocide there, was even more remote from the United States than Haiti. To deal with such problems effectively required high level, concentrated attention, and diverted military resources from higher priorities. Social work made it harder for America to focus on Class B threats such as Iraq and North Korea and potential Class A problems such as Russia and China.

Social work also risked "mission creep." Thus, Americans went to Somalia trying to avert starvation, but soon found themselves fighting warlords. Failed and failing states cropped up in many places in the 1990s. America could not save them all. Nor could the United Nations, which had no material assets except those its members provided.

8. Free Trade and Economic Development

The United States did not retreat from the world in the 1920s but sought rather to restructure global affairs. Americans tried to make the dollar the foundation of the new structure, on which they piled the treaties of Washington, Locarno, Geneva, and Kellogg-Briand. The structure aimed to serve the needs of Americans and their individualism (Herbert Hoover's term) as they circled a globe now shaped by new technology, industry, and national hatreds. Many Americans believed that the world was becoming so open, so integrated, and so Americanized that another major war was impossible. But the dollar collapsed and with it the delicate structure of the 1920s treaties.[16]

Congress passed the Smoot-Hawley Tariff in 1931 to protect America's sinking economy from foreign imports. But this act cut world trade and aggravated the Great Depression worldwide and in the United States.

After a few years of protectionism, however, Congress endorsed the Roosevelt administration's support for freer trade (by means of reciprocal trade agreements) as an engine for U.S. and global development. But overlapping crises swept away the foundations of economic and political stability laid in the 1920s. Not American individualism but Fascism changed the world's structure.

As World War II ended, Washington again placed its faith in free trade. Experience showed that this was a good wager in some but not all respects. As the century ended, statistics showed that world trade increased at a faster rate than world GDP. Free trade brought cheap consumer goods to Americans and permitted U.S. firms and investors to penetrate foreign markets.

But there were also many problems. First, special interests often persuaded Congress to protect certain industries. Second, Japan and other countries defied U.S. pressures to open their economies by a variety of nontariff barriers. Third, the tendency of Americans to consume more and save less than many other peoples contributed to a huge imbalance in U.S. exports and imports. Fourth, many of the benefits that freer trade brought to the United States and other developed economies did not percolate to the less developed economies—especially to those dependent on one or two commodities and those with infant industries trying to compete in global markets.

No presidency pushed harder for free trade than the Clinton White House. Clinton argued that free trade provided a fundamental tool for realizing the full possibilities of the global economy. But American labor, environmental, and other groups worried about the

Not every U.S. export was healthful. Increasingly fettered at home, the U.S. tobacco industry looked to China and other distant markets.

byproducts of freer trade and investment—from sweat shops on the U.S.-Mexican border to Chinese prison factories. U.S. trade unions worried that NAFTA and the WTO threatened their jobs and wages. Environmental groups complained that the WTO pressured the United States to weaken its Green laws.

Clinton in 1999–2000 warned foreign governments and business leaders that labor and environmental concerns had to be addressed if Americans were to accept expanded free trade. Clinton's final State of the Union address declared that a win-win outcome was possible. But Clinton's hope did not win over U.S. or foreign critics of the WTO. Mexican President Ernesto Zedillo objected to what he saw as Washington's efforts to make the WTO an enforcer of U.S. labor and environmental laws.

Contrary to the high hopes invested in foreign aid by Washington and other governments in the 1950s and 1960s, outside assistance did little for most LDCs. To be sure, emergency food and medical relief saved lives, as did public health campaigns to wipe out smallpox (mounted by the World Health Organization, at the initiative of a Soviet doctor) and some other endemic ailments. U.S. Peace Corps volunteers introduced appropriate technology—for example, water pumps powered by bicycle parts. Nongovernmental agencies promoted literacy and women's rights.

But talk of a "Marshall Plan" for LDCs (or the former Soviet Union) was unrealistic. After World War II Europeans were *rebuilding* structures and a way of life that most LDCs had never experienced—with far more aid per capita than the West and Japan would ever deliver to LDCs (or to the former Soviet republics). From 1979 into the twenty-first century Israel and Egypt got the lion's share of official U.S. aid. Egypt received nearly as much as Israel but for a population many times larger. By the end of the century Colombia became number three for disbursements of U.S. aid, most of which went to the military campaign against drug interests.

Second, some forms of aid undermined incentives. American food grants, for example, disrupted markets and discouraged LDC farmers.

Third, aid fed corruption, siphoned for private gain and influence.

Fourth, much aid went to projects ill suited for local needs—often to large projects that employed U.S. firms and were meant to look good next to those funded by the USSR. Most U.S. aid programs required recipients to "buy American." An exception to this rule, Israel could buy wherever it wished and got what it needed at the best price.

The "Green Revolution" based on hybrid seeds permitted India to become self-reliant in grains and helped some farmers become rich. But the resolution's demands for water and chemical fertilizers put many small farms out of business. High dams and large irrigation projects displaced still more people and often left irrigated lands glistening with salt deposits and rich with the parasites that bring schistosomiasis ("snail fever") to farmers through their bare feet.

While foreign aid amounted to only one percent of India's GDP in the 1990s, foreign aid to many African countries exceeded their GDPs. Still, most of sub-Saharan Africa was no richer per capita in 1999 than twenty or thirty years before. The same factors that kept Africa poor also discouraged foreign investment. Africa received only one percent of foreign direct investment (FDI) in 1999. While Singapore and other "tigers" profited from the global economic system, UN Secretary-General Kofi Annan warned that the system was not working for many LDCs. AIDS made everything worse.

There was no simple formula. Europe and the United States took centuries to develop modern economies; Japan, less than a century; Singapore and Taiwan, a few decades—building on habits accumulated over many centuries. The United States, Singapore, and Taiwan all benefited from foreign investment. But each depended ultimately on its own boot straps.

Washington sought to limit trade and technology transfer that might benefit its foes. But economic pressures and sanctions seldom bent the will of determined foes and sometimes backfired. The Carter administration barred additional commitments of U.S. grain to Soviet buyers to punish the USSR for invading Afghanistan, but Moscow bought what it needed in Australia and elsewhere, leaving U.S. farmers the poorer. The Reagan administration tried to persuade Europeans not to invest in or become dependent on Soviet natural gas exports, but the Europeans rejected U.S. advice. Washington antagonized many other Western states by its efforts to sanction Cuba, Iran, Iraq, and other states. Saddam Hussein defied U.S. and UN pressures throughout the 1990s even though Iraq's public health and economy deteriorated.

Dual-use technology was hard to control. In the 1990s Washington permitted the sale of supercomputers to China and Russia for weather forecasting and other civilian purposes, but found that

France in Oil Deal With Iran and Libya Over US Objections

French Prime Minister Lionel Jospin was not a staunch backer of U.S. efforts to sanction Iran and Libya for their support of terrorism.

Chinese and Russian customers found ways to divert their purchases for military applications. If the United States barred export of advanced encryption devices, foreign firms gained.

9. Modeling a "Third Way": Between Statism and Anarchy

Despite strong GDP growth and some positive social trends, such as lower infant mortality, the American model of development had serious shortcomings. But to the extent that the United States became richer and stronger, these achievements inspired not just admiration and emulation but also fear and envy.

Many Americans embraced short-term, materialistic perspectives. About 4 percent of humanity, Americans consumed many times their share of the world's resources. Their factories, autos, airplanes, and life-style were leading sources of greenhouse gases and many other environmental problems. To be sure, Americans also led in developing lead-free gasoline and alternatives to ozone-depleting coolants. But they were reluctant to alter a way of life that endangered the biosphere.

If some aspects of American life attracted foreigners, outsiders could try to pick and choose. Lenin, for example, urged his comrades to emulate "Taylorism"—efficiency in mass production. Chinese could have the world's largest emporium for Magna Macs without embracing the Magna Carta or other institutions of limited government. A library of religious texts in Iran's "sacred city" of Qum employed the latest in U.S. and European computer technology but, when I visited there in 1998, permitted women to use the library just one day a week. Many societies sought to tap Western innovations without imbibing U.S. or other Western values.

Britain's Labour Party and Germany's Social Democrats discarded socialist dogmas for Clintonian pragmatism. But governments in Russia, China, and France did not jump on the American bandwagon. They endeavored—each in its own way—to preserve their respective values and balance against the threat of U.S. domination. To rival American arms makers, European governments and manufacturers endeavored in the late 1990s to form and service a common market for armaments. Airbus Industrie began to act more like a firm and less like a consortium of national companies. In 1999 it took more orders for new planes than Boeing.

10. Limiting Human Rights

Racism, "red scares," and the doctrine of "state's rights" limited human rights within the United States and weakened U.S. influence abroad. American interference in the domestic affairs of other countries limited human rights elsewhere.

Despite the Founding Fathers' affirmation that "all men are created equal," the U.S. Constitution allowed for slavery. Not till 1863 did the Constitution ban slavery—later than in the British, French, or Tsarist Russian realms. The U.S. armed forces were still racially segregated in World War II. Racial discrimination was practiced even in voting booths until the Civil Rights legislation of the 1960s. In the 1990s policemen in Los Angeles, New York, Chicago, and elsewhere were accused of treating blacks worse than whites.

U.S. immigration laws in the twentieth century generally welcomed immigrants from northern and central Europe and limited or excluded those from southern Europe, Asia, Latin America, and elsewhere. Whatever the laws stated, however, many Americans discriminated against ethnic and religious groups different from themselves. Japanese-Americans in California were interned during World War II. The civil rights of all Americans, even whites, were constricted by the Alien and Sedition Acts, the suspension of many rights during America's Civil War and two world wars, harassment of "anarchists" before and after World War I, and anti-Communist purges in the Cold War.

The United States sponsored many human rights conventions at the United Nations but was slow to ratify them or added killer reservations when it did so. Sometimes a Southern senator would explain that "states' rights" limit the treaty-making authority of the federal government; at other times U.S. leaders seemed to worry that their country would be indicted for its treatment of Native Americans, blacks, and other minorities. Thus, the United States endorsed the Genocide Convention in 1948 but did not ratify it until 1988—and then with five "reservations" so sweeping that Greece, Italy, Ireland, and Mexico called them "invalid" because they violated the "object and purpose" of the convention.

A strong movement took shape in the 1990s to establish a permanent International Criminal Court (ICC) to try those accused of genocide, war crimes (including rape), and other crimes against humanity when national judicial systems failed to do so. The United States worried that other states might "frivolously" charge U.S. peacekeepers with war crimes. Washington wanted to subordinate the court to the Security Council. Senator Jesse Helms, chairman of the Senate Foreign Relations Committee, vowed in March 1998 that the tribunal would be "dead on arrival" in the Senate unless the United States had veto power over the cases that came before it. So the United States did not join the ICC even though Washington endorsed the ad hoc tribunals dealing with crimes in the former Yugoslavia and in Rwanda.

The United Nations adopted a Convention on the Political Rights of Women in 1952. It asserted that women were entitled to vote in all elections on equal terms with men and to hold public office on terms equal with men. However, the U.S. Senate did not assent to this mild commitment until 1976.

In 1979 the UN General Assembly adopted the Convention on the Elimination of All Forms of Discrimination Against Women, which entered force in 1981. The treaty banned any gender-based distinction impairing women's "human rights and fundamental freedoms" in any field. The United States signed it in 1980 but then did not ratify it.

Beginning in the mid-1970s the Department of State issued a yearly survey on human rights worldwide—*Country Reports on Human Rights Practices*. In the Reagan-Bush years these reports were soft on Latin American dictators, China, and America's European allies. In the 1990s, however, the *Country Reports* became more objective, and exceeded 1,000 pages—filled with facts both positive and negative.[17]

Starting in 1984 Congress required that the *Country Reports* contain information on workers' rights in countries benefiting from duty-free access to the U.S. market. The yearly surveys detailed policies by Indonesia, Taiwan, and other friendly countries to block collective bargaining. Beginning in 1992 Congress also demanded that the *Country Reports* provide more information on (1) children, (2)

Truth in Labeling

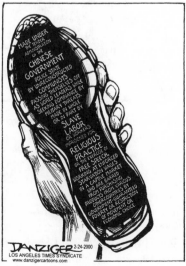

indigenous peoples, and (3)—for recipients of U.S. aid—data on their efforts to curtail military expenditures.

Despite detailed accounts in *Country Reports* of human rights abuses in China, in 1994 the Clinton administration uncoupled its trade policy from human rights, lifting this source of leverage on Beijing.

Meanwhile, the United States lagged behind most other industrial democracies in adopting international human rights obligations.[18] Would Americans suffer if all human rights conventions became the law of their land? If the United States were implementing the broadest standards of human rights, would race riots convulse U.S. cities from time to time?

Taking Mr. Putin to See the Queen

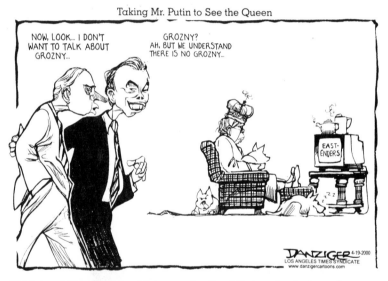

UK Prime Minister Tony Blair was the first Western leader to welcome V. V. Putin to high society. Bill Clinton was among the first to make the pilgrimage to Moscow to meet the new leader.

If human rights guided U.S. foreign policy, would the United States have intervened to oppose leftist forces in Greece, Italy, Iran, Guatemala, the Dominican Republic, Chile, and other countries? Would it have coddled Spain and Portugal under right-wing dictators? Patronized Suharto and Saddam Hussein—butchers of their own subjects? Would it shake the hand of V. V. Putin, exterminator of Chechens? And if the United States had let human rights steer it away from these actions, would its material power and security be weaker or greater? Individual cases can be debated, but in most cases respect for human rights would have enhanced U.S. security and influence.

11. International Understanding

Despite jet travel and all manner of exchange programs, despite or because of improved electronic access, most Americans remained ignorant of world geography, history, and current events. Many Americans were well traveled, curious, and informed. But many more were indifferent and ignorant.[19]

A growing number of students and professionals came to the United States—a plus for international understanding, but many stayed. The brain drain harmed economic development in many LDCs, though a small reverse migration to India took place in the 1990s.

Many U.S. cultural exports gave a sordid and unbalanced picture of American life. Did the United States gain or lose soft power if foreigners enjoyed "Dallas" family feuds or "Bay Watch" capers? What happened when new technology was grafted with popular values? Would the ability to listen lovingly to music be supplanted by insistence on high velocity gratification at download speed?[20]

Was the American mainstream good for humanity's blood stream?

12. Dependability

Some U.S. leaders weakened the country's reputation for honesty, integrity, and dependability. Relations with adversaries are also easier to manage if U.S. commitments are credible.

America's credibility suffered greatly when Woodrow Wilson could not win Senate approval for the Versailles Treaty and—eighty years later—when William J. Clinton failed to win Senate approval for a comprehensive ban on nuclear testing.

President Dwight D. Eisenhower did Americans a major disservice when he lied about the nature of the U-2 plane shot down in the USSR in 1960, only to be exposed by Soviets who had captured the pilot alive.

In 1964 the Johnson administration deceived Congress about an incident in the Gulf of Tonkin to get a free hand against North Vietnam. For the next decade U.S. officials deceived one another and the public about body counts and other aspects of the Indochina War.

The Iran-Contra affair was a major failure for the Reagan administration—found to be violating its own embargo on trade with Iran and a U.S. law forbidding military shipments to the Contras.[21]

The United States usually honored arms control agreements, but may have violated the ABM treaty in two ways: by tests undertaken for the Strategic Defense Initiative and by U.S. radars built in the Aleutians, Greenland, Fylingdales Moor in the United Kingdom. None of these actions violated the treaty so blatantly as the radar the Soviets started to build near Krasnoyarsk until, when Washington protested, M. S. Gorbachev had it dismantled. The Clinton administration may also have violated the ABM treaty by building the "Have Stare" radar in Norway just 40 miles from Murmansk.[22] Per-

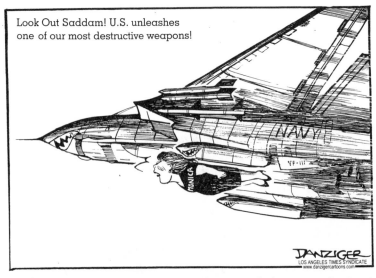

The president's disavowal of "sexual relations with that woman" was a powerful weapon—against himself and his country.

haps the greatest threat to America's reputation as a negotiating partner was the cavalier way that the Reagan and Clinton administrations were prepared to junk what Moscow and many other capitals saw as a cornerstone for security and trust.

Some leaders in Taipei felt let down when Washington shifted diplomatic recognition to Beijing in 1979 and later, when the United States refused to sell certain weapons to Taiwan. PRC leaders, for their part, often complained that U.S. arms sales to Taiwan violated Washington's undertakings to Beijing.

The words of "slick Willy" lost credibility everywhere. Not just the president but many officers in his cabinet became renowned sophists on NATO expansion and other matters. Meanwhile, politicians from both parties nearly perjured themselves when explaining how their campaigns were funded.

A Balance Sheet

The big picture after World War II was that the United States did well in its relations with Europe, and not badly with Communist countries, but poorly in much of the Third World.[23]

Both achievement and failure are often Janus-faced. Most successes have a dark side; few are pure. Many failures, in turn, have a bright aspect. The same event may be seen as a victory and as a failure. Some gains rapidly go up in flames. Many victories arise from failures, and many failures from victories. Some policy outcomes endure for years; some are short-lived. Some change the world; others pass with little effect.

Let us review the successes outlined in chapter 1 and place them next to the failures discussed in this chapter. Here is the record in summary form:

America's achievements probably surpassed its failures, even though the table lists both under the same headings.[24] For example, America's victory in two world wars and in most other conflicts outweighed its defeat in Indochina—a serious failure from which the country bounced back.

The United States did much to undermine global governance, but it also served as the driving force behind creation of the United Nations—an international organization far greater in scope and power than any in history, and with great future potential.

Table 2.2 Successes and Failures of U.S. Foreign Policy, 1898–2000

Successes	*Failures*
1. Force: The United States and its partners prevailed in both world wars and drove aggressors from South Korea and Kuwait.	1. Force: Washington sometimes resorted to force too early—without good cause—or too late. America's Indochina adventure became its greatest debacle in world affairs. But a stronger U.S. stance might well have prevented or limited some wars.
2. Governance: Americans helped forge institutions and habits of collective security and strengthened world order.	2. Governance: Washington undermined the League of Nations and did much to weaken the United Nations and international law.
3. Interdependence: The U.S. helped rebuild Europe and Japan and form a trilateral community for trade and security.	3. Interdependence: Stalin's USSR and Boris Yeltsin's post-Soviet Russia did not join the West and Japan.
4. Containment: The U.S. won the Cold War without a U.S.-Soviet hot war and coped with crises such as the Cuban confrontation without suffering a defeat or a major loss of life.	4. Containment: The strategy to contain Soviet expansion became a global crusade against leftists or nationalists posing little challenge to U.S. interests.
5. Conflict control: The U.S. learned, with the USSR and Communist China, how adversaries can mitigate conflict and collaborate for parallel objectives.	5. Conflict control: Washington failed to explore some opportunities to reduce tensions with Moscow, Beijing, Tehran, and other adversaries.
6. Arms and arms control: The U.S. developed the world's most powerful armed forces but also made arms control an integral part of security planning.	6. Arms and arms control: U.S. and Russian overkill outpaced arms control. Nuclear weapons spread. In the twenty-first century humanity could self-destruct.
7. Peacemaking: Americans mediated the peaceful settlement of others' disputes and contrib-	7. Peacemaking: Washington should have acted earlier and more force- fully to curtail conflicts in the

(continues)

Table 2.2 *(continued)*

Successes	*Failures*
uted to peacekeeping and to peace enforcement.	Middle East, the Balkans, Northern Ireland, and elsewhere.
8. Free trade and economic development: The U.S. promoted free trade and institutions fostering economic development and financial stability.	8. Free trade and economic development: Many Americans worried about job losses and the environmental consequences of free trade. Neither trade nor aid did much to help many less developed countries.
9. Modeling a Third Way: The market-based liberal democracy of the U.S. served as a model not just for many former Communists but also for statists in Japan and Europe.	9. Modeling a Third Way: A rising GDP left Americans with severe domestic problems. Their production and consumption was a major source of pollution and global warming. U.S. wealth and power inspired fear and envy as well as emulation.
10. Human rights: Americans kept alive and spread the ideals of freedom and promoted human rights—political, economic, cultural, religious.	10. Human rights: Many American policies undercut human rights at home and abroad.
11. International understanding: The U.S. promoted international exchanges—in science, in culture, and other realms—and open communications.	11. International understanding: Most Americans remained apathetic to the world, while many U.S. cultural exports gave an unbalanced picture of American life.
12. Dependability: Americans forged a strong reputation for reliability as allies.	12. Dependability: Some U.S. leaders weakened the country's reputation for honesty, integrity, and dependability.

To forge a security community with most of Europe and Japan was a greater gain for America than failing to integrate Russia, which stayed outside mainly for its own reasons. Containment of the USSR succeeded, though at great cost and with many excesses.

Americans honed the arts of conflict control, arms control, and third-party mediation. They practiced these arts too little and often too late, but some achievements were unprecedented, such as the 1987 intermediate-range nuclear forces treaty requiring Moscow and Washington to destroy two classes of their most modern missiles.

Efforts to liberalize trade and promote economic development encountered many obstacles. But world trade increased even faster than world GDP, and most governments wished to jump onto the WTO bandwagon. Many countries remained less developed, but most of them wanted *freer* trade. If nothing else, LDCs showed that they prized global trade talks as a mechanism for exerting leverage on the rich north.[25] Mexican President Ernesto Zedillo, like many other Third World leaders, expressed contempt for Westerners "determined to save developing countries from development."[26] Many people were doing something right, because living standards and life expectancy in most countries shot up sharply in the second half of the century. In 1975 only one rural Thai in six had access to safe drinking water; in 1999 it was four out of five.

As Paul Krugman noted: "Much of the twentieth century was dominated by a search for perfection. Panglossian advocates of laissez faire claimed markets always got it right, then were discredited by the Great Depression; idealistic revolutionaries promised utopia, and delivered the Soviet Union." As the new millennium began, one could "say of capitalism what Churchill said of democracy: It is the worst system we know, except for all the others that have been tried."[27]

America's Third Way embodied deep inconsistencies and explosive fault lines. At century's end, however, it offered more hope than other approaches.

U.S. support for human rights was inconsistent at home and worldwide. Despite clashes of civilizations, however, most governments pledged to back a wide range of specific human rights. International law began to accept the idea that outsiders might have a duty as well as a right to intervene to stop genocide and other heinous abuses of human rights.

International understanding, though imperfect, improved greatly in the second half of the century. The Fulbright and other exchange programs contributed to experiences far deeper than achieved by tourism, television, or the Internet.

U.S. leadership, though imperfect, was seen by many as an anchor in a sea of potential storms. No country wanted to shake its partnership with the United States. Most former Soviet allies sought to join NATO.

Let us now consider the sources of both achievements and failures.

Notes

1. Walter LaFeber, *The American Age: U.S. Foreign Policy at Home and Abroad* (2d ed.; New York: W. W. Norton, 1994), p. 361.
2. Barry M. Blechman and Stephen S. Kaplan with others, *Force Without War: U.S. Armed Forces as a Political Instrument* (Washington, D.C.: Brookings Institution, 1978), p. 556.
3. See Stephen S. Kaplan et al., *Diplomacy of Power: Soviet Armed Forces as a Political Instrument* (Washington, D.C.: Brookings Institution, 1981).
4. The Bay of Pigs landing did not provoke an uprising against Fidel, and President Kennedy refused to provide it air cover. The Bay of Pigs fiasco notwithstanding, the CIA's "Operation Mongoose" continued to infiltrate Cuba with saboteurs and would-be assassins and to train Cuban exiles for another landing. The Pentagon prepared contingency plans for an invasion by U.S. forces. In April 1962, however, Kennedy told a key exile leader that he would not commit U.S. troops to back up a revolt in Cuba even if one occurred. See Graham Allison and Philip Zelikow, *Essence of Decision: Explaining the Cuban Missile Crisis* (2d ed.; New York: Longman, 1999), p. 84.
5. The Indochina adventure produced battlefield defeat and serious social unrest combined with inflation at home. The war killed many Americans and left many veterans with psychological as well as physical wounds. It killed or crippled far larger numbers of Vietnamese; wasted their lands; hardened the dictatorship in Hanoi and extended its grasp. The war spread to Cambodia and destabilized that country, leading to demicide. The Vietnam syndrome weakened America's will and capacity in the 1970s to resist Soviet expansion in the Middle East, Africa, and even the Caribbean.
6. For a survey of the literature, see J. Samuel Walker, "The Decision to Use the Bomb: A Historical Update," in Michael J. Hogan, ed., *America in the World: The Historiography of American Foreign Relations Since 1941* (Cambridge, UK: Cambridge University Press, 1995), pp. 206–233.

7. Stalin's long-term intentions were not evident during World War II. Some of his words and deeds suggested that he hoped the Grand Alliance with the West would continue into the post–world war world. Thus, the Kremlin in 1943 dissolved the Communist International. But history should have put Western leaders on guard that the USSR after Hitler's defeat might continue the expansionist policies of the tsars combined with the totalitarian and bloody techniques Stalin had already used against internal foes for decades. Winston Churchill worried about such possibilities, but he was overruled by a U.S. president confident he could charm Uncle Joe into changing his ways and those of Russia.

8. In early 1945 the United States welcomed Red Army advances that relieved German pressure at Ardennes and the promise of a Soviet attack that would shorten the war against Japan.

9. See Walter C. Clemens, Jr., *Baltic Independence and Russian Empire* (New York: St. Martin's, 1991), pp. 297–298.

10. Truman pulled back U.S. troops from Czechoslovakia in 1945 without negotiating in advance a comparable Soviet withdrawal. When Truman asked Stalin, however, the Kremlin soon withdrew most Soviet forces from Czechoslovakia.

11. What Czech sources told the U.S. ambassador in Prague is reported in Laurence Steinhardt to George C. Marshall, July 10, 1947, in *Foreign Relations of the United States 1947* (Washington: Government Printing Office, 1972), 3, 319–20. For Molotov's recollections on this point, see *Sto corok besed c Molotovym: Iz dnevnika F. Chueva* (Moscow: Terra, 1991), pp. 88–89.

12. V. M. Molotov, *Problems of Foreign Policy* (Moscow, 1949), p. 466; see also Scott D. Parrish and Mikhail M. Narinsky, "New Evidence on the Soviet Rejection of the Marshall Plan, 1947: Two Reports," *Working Paper No. 9*, Cold War International History Project (Washington, D.C.: Woodrow Wilson International Center for Scholars, March 1994).

13. When Bush visited Kyiv, however, he and his entourage treated Ukraine as sovereign and made sure that only Ukrainian and English were used. See Jack F. Matlock, Jr., *Autopsy on an Empire: The American Ambassador's Account of the Collapse of the Soviet Union* (New York: Random House, 1995), pp. 564–571.

14. Joseph Cirincione, ed., *Repairing the Regime: Preventing the Spread of Weapons of Mass Destruction* (Washington: Routledge, 2000).

15. Harold A. Feiveson, ed., *The Nuclear Turning Point: A Blueprint for Deep Cuts and De-alerting of Nuclear Weapons* (Washington, D.C.: Brookings Institution Press, 1999), p. 113.

16. LaFeber, *American Age*, p. 362.

17. Thus, the 1993 report said of one friendly country: "A wide range of individual freedom is provided for by the Mexican Constitution and honored in practice." But the State Department also reported "the use of torture," "extrajudicial killings," and "electoral flaws" in Mexico. *Country Reports on Human Rights Practices for 1992: Report to the Committee on Foreign Relations of the U.S. Senate and the Committee on Foreign Affairs, U.S. House of Representatives by the Department of State* (Washington, D.C.: U.S. Government Printing Office, 1993), pp. 440–451.

18. Washington is legally bound by several antislavery conventions; the 1949 Geneva conventions on treatment of prisoners and civilians in wartime; by the refugee protection convention; by the UN Convention on Political Rights for Women; and the Genocide Convention; by the ban on racial discrimination; and by the ban on torture. The United States ratified the International Covenant on Civil and Political Rights in 1992, but President Bush (and the U.S. Senate) reserved the right of U.S. states to execute juveniles and to protect hate speech. As of 1997 the United States had signed but not ratified the covenant on economic rights; the ban on discrimination against women; the convention on the rights of the child; and the American Convention on Human Rights. Washington refused to sign the 1948 Convention on the Right to Organize, the 1949 Convention on the Right to Bargain Collectively, and the 1950 Convention to Suppress Prostitution.

19. When I returned from Austria in 1953, many friends asked me how I liked the South Pacific (Australia). When they learned in the 1990s that I studied the Baltics, they asked what's it like in Yugoslavia (the Balkans).

20. Pianist Russell Sherman interviewed on "The Connection," radio station WBUR, February 25, 2000.

21. See *The Tower Commission Report: Full Text of the President's Special Review Board* (New York: Bantam Books and Times Books, 1987).

22. See four articles in *Bulletin of the Atomic Scientists,* 56, 2 (March-April 2000), pp. 22–41.

23. These distinctions were suggested to the author in 1999 by Bruce Cumings, Department of History, University of Chicago.

24. Three other caveats apply to table 2.1, First, it omits or downplays important factors. For example, the U.S. impact on the global environment gathers weight cumulatively and may well become more salient in the twenty-first century.

   Second, the table's headings are not necessarily listed by their importance. To be sure, surviving and winning two world wars was a precondition for most other accomplishments. But the relative importance of other successes can be debated.

Finally, the list includes outcomes that serve as means as well as ends. Economic development and a reputation for dependability, for example, are potential stepping stones to other achievements.

25. Delegates to the UN Trade and Development Organization meeting in Bangkok commended trade and economic integration as the path for future development and a way to bridge the north-south divide. See William Barnes, "Poor nations assert place in global trade," *Financial Times,* February 21, 2000, p. 6.

26. Quoted in Paul Krugman, "Reckonings," *The New York Times,* February 16, 2000, p. A29.

27. Paul Krugman, "Unleashing the Millennium," *Fortune.* 141, 5 (March 6, 2000), pp. F-16 to 20 at 20.

3.

Sources of Success and Failure

Levels of Action and Analysis

To explain U.S. accomplishments and failures on the world stage is not easy. What succeeds in one situation may fail in another. As in sports, there are many near-misses. Circumstances of time and place can be crucial. So, it seems, can luck—what Machiavelli called *fortuna*.

For every success and failure in foreign policy there are usually multiple causes. Lacking a controlled laboratory setting, we cannot conduct scientific experiments to establish causal relationships and sort out the incidental from the essential. But we can order the inquiry by examining forces on each level—international, societal, individual—that may have contributed to policy outcomes:

Figure 3.1

Action Levels Shaping Foreign Policy Formulation and Implementation

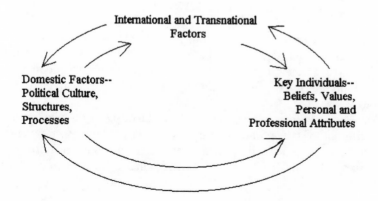

International and Transnational
Factors

Domestic Factors--
Political Culture,
Structures,
Processes

Key Individuals--
Beliefs, Values,
Personal and
Professional Attributes

Analyzing each level we shall note explanations suggested by major historians and policy analysts, including the experts whose opinions were surveyed for this book. We shall ask to what extent the record confirms the hypotheses set out in the introduction regarding fitness, mutual gain, and openness.

Each level conditions the others. None reigns supreme over the others. But there was far more variation in level 3 than in levels 1 and 2. For most of the twentieth century America's power position in the world and the domestic context of U.S. policy varied much less than the individuals who shaped and implemented it.[1]

International and Transnational Factors

Global politics remained basically anarchic throughout the twentieth century. Despite the growth of international organizations, there was no supranational government. Despite an efflorescence of transnational nongovernmental agencies and businesses, there was no sure system of global governance. Still, a certain order was imparted by the key actors, the hierarchy of power and influence among them, their policies, the norms to which they claimed to subscribe, and their adaptation and use of new technologies. This combination of structure and norms permitted, encouraged, and curbed certain behaviors.

Even as empires fell and new nations arose, America's position on the world stage grew stronger. Hard power permitted (but did not require) the United States to coerce and compel; soft power, to persuade and coopt; conversion power, to translate hard and soft power into influence and fitness. Table 3.1 traces the parameters of power from 1776 through the 1990s.[2]

Basic Resources.   Relative to other great powers, the United States in 1776 ranked high only in basic resources: But two hundred and more years later America's location, climate, size, shape, and mineral and food resources remained among the most favorable in the world.

Economic Power.   From the 1880s to the onset of the twenty-first century, the United States had the world's largest and most dynamic economy. To be sure, other countries and regions rebounded or rose up after World War II, but the United States continued to produce

Table 3.1

Parameters of Power, 1776-1990

(H = high; M = medium; L = low strength)

	Actor	Basic Resources	Economic Power	Political Cohesion	Military Power	Brain Power	Universal Culture	International Institutions	Fitness at Home	External Fitness
1776 U.S. Declaration of Independence	USA	H	L	M	L	M	M	L	M	L
	Russia	H	L	L	M	L	L	M	L	M
	Prussia	M	L	M	M	M	M	M	M	M
	Britain	M	H	M	H	H	H	H	M	H
	Japan	L	L	M	L	L	L	L	L	L
	China	M	L	L	L	L	L	L	L	L
	Ottoman Empire	H	M	L	M	L	M	M	L	L
1914 Eve of World War I	USA	H	H	M	L	H	H	M	M	M
	Russia	H	M	L	M	M	M	M	L	M
	Germany	M	H	H	H	H	M	M	H	H
	Britain	M	H	M	H	H	H	H	M	H
	Japan	L	M	H	M	M	L	L	M	M
	China	M	L	L	L	L	L	L	L	L
	Ottoman Empire	M	L	L	M	L	L	L	L	L

1939 **Eve of** **World War II**	USA	H	M	M	M	H	M	M	M
	USSR	H	M	L	M	H	M	M	M
	Germany	M	H	H	H	H	M	H	H
	Britain	M	M	M	M	H	H	M	M
	Japan	M	M	H	M	H	L	M	M
	China	M	L	L	L	M	L	L	L
1962 **Cuban Crisis**	USA	H	H	H	H	H	H	H	H
	USSR	H	M	M	M	M	M	M	H
	European Community	M	M	M	M	M	H	M	M
	Japan	L	M	H	L	M	L	M	L
	China	M	L	M	M	L	L	L	L
1976 **After the** **Vietnam War**	USA	H	H	M	H	H	H	M	H
	USSR	H	M	H	M	M	L	M	H
	European Community	M	H	M	M	H	H	H	M
	Japan	L	M	H	L	M	L	M	L
	China	M	L	M	M	L	L	L	L
1990 **After the** **Afghan War**	USA	H	H	H	H	H	H	M	H
	USSR	H	L	L	M	M	M	L	M
	European Community	H	H	M	M	H	H	H	M
	Japan	L	H	H	L	M	M	H	M
	China	M	M	M	L	M	L	L	M

2000 After the Gulf War									
USA	H	H	M	H	H	H	H	M	H
Russian Federation	H	L	L	M	M	M	M	L	M
European Union	H	H	M	M	H	H	H	M	M
Japan	L	H	H	M	H	M	M	H	M
China	M	M	M	M	M	L	L	L	M

more than one-fifth of the world's GDP, as it had since before World War I.

Political Cohesion. All other components of power come to naught unless the body politic holds together—even under stress. Americans fought each other in their Civil War. Their cohesion suffered during their wars with England, Mexico, Spain, the two world wars, and the Indochina War. It suffered from slavery and its aftermath; from ethnic and religious discrimination; from labor-management conflict; from regional differences; and from ideological and other conflicts between political movements. Still, the country's cohesion remained at least medium-strong in the twentieth century except in the peak years of the Indochina War. Although dictatorships often look more cohesive than pluralistic democracies, history shows that authoritarian governments started and lost most of the century's major wars.

Military Power. The United States was the richest country in the world by 1885, but it had weak armed forces and little influence abroad. Why? It had a weak central government. Not until the late nineteenth century, when power shifted from states to Washington, and from Congress to the executive branch, did U.S. presidents have the means to muster American strengths and project them onto the world stage. As this happened, the United States became more assertive. Between 1865 and 1889 U.S. policymakers perceived 22 serious opportunities to expand, but acted in less than one-third—for example, by purchasing Alaska and acquiring base rights in Samoa. From 1889 to 1908, however, the United States seized 25 of 32 such opportunities, for example, in Panama. The United States did not expand against strong states threatening American security but largely against weak areas where expansion could be accomplished at low cost.[3]

Starting in the 1890s, the federal government gradually acquired the means to mobilize the country's material and human resources to shape world affairs. Even so, Americans often *chose* detachment. Their armed forces were comparatively puny even in 1917 and 1941. The United States did not seriously mobilize its resources for military purposes until hard pressed to enter World Wars I and II. Following a brief retrenchment after World War II, however, the United States became a military superpower—at parity with its Soviet rival—and with no military equal after the Soviet Union collapsed.

Brain Power. Brain power is key to unleashing all other power. Brain power helps societies to avoid both stagnation and chaos, while adapting to complexity. America's intellectual resources were always high, even before 1776.

Universal Culture. If a country's way of life and values seem legitimate to others, this is soft power to persuade and coopt. America gained influence in the Cold War competition because its path, charted by Adam Smith and John Locke, had more worldwide appeal than the Communist ways endorsed by Marx and Lenin. America gained also because Coke, Levis, and Hollywood had greater allure than Stolichnaya vodka, fur hats, or the Bolshoi Ballet. But the appeal of Western culture can be superficial. Deeper down the clash of civilizations remained.

International Institutions. The structure and policies of international institutions are shaped by the dominant actors. The United States gained in the Cold War because the world's major economic institutions—the World Bank, International Monetary Fund, and the General Agreement on Trade and Tariffs—harmonized with U.S. preferences for free markets and free trade.[4] States whose values conflicted with prevailing institutions had to struggle harder just to hold on.

Perceptions of Power. While the relative weight of the U.S. economy changed little throughout the century, *perceptions* of material reality fluctuated wildly and often proved wrong. In the 1930s many people believed that the freewheeling U.S. economy was lost and that the future belonged to the command economies of Mussolini, Hitler, and Stalin. From the 1950s through the 1980s various observers bet on a variety of top-down systems—Soviet planning, Maoist mobilization, French guidance, Germany's marriage of finance with industry, or the wisdom of Japan's Ministry of International Trade and Industry (MITI)—to overtake the more demand-driven U.S. economy. By the end of the century, however, most major economies were striving to become more like the American model.

When leaders and publics believed that the systems headed by Josef Stalin, Adolf Hitler, Nikita Khrushchev, Mao Zedong, or MITI were besting the United States, their perceptions reduced America's influence in global affairs. The words and silences of U.S. leaders sometimes reinforced beliefs about the strengths of America's foreign rivals. President Eisenhower did little to calm public fears in the late 1950s that the USSR led the United States in bombers, missiles, and science.

Still, the United States retained vast stores of persuasive and cooptive power throughout the century. When the country's leaders offered to mediate others' disputes or launched a crusade for human rights, other governments and peoples listened. America's ideals coexisted with material wealth and technological innovations. Often America's foreign overtures seemed selfless. Many U.S. initiatives did nothing to generate material gain for Americans. This too caught foreigners' attention.

Since America's share of the world's hard and soft power remained relatively constant for most of the century, neither Marxist nor neorealist ("structuralist") theories go far toward explaining the ups and downs of U.S. foreign policy. America's achievements and failures in the world derived more from fluctuations in U.S. conversion power—the capacity to utilize hard and soft assets to enhance national fitness and to influence others.

Along with conversion power, however, comes the question of *will*. Even though the United States had the means to play a major role in the world, many Americans preferred to remain unentangled.

Also, some Americans wished to relate to other peoples across borders—not as objects to be influenced, but as fellow humans with whom they might pool resources for common goals.[5]

To assess changes in conversion power, will power, and popular concerns we look next at the domestic context of U.S. foreign policy and then at the key individuals shaping it.

The Domestic Context: Rational Consensus versus Divergent Interests and Beliefs

The Myth of a Monolith.   History books or newspapers may say that "the United States embarked upon another bout of imperial expansion" or that "the country turned inward again in the 1970s." But this is shorthand, for no country acts like a monolith. Each is divided by political affiliation and outlook, age, sex, education, economics, ethnicity, religion, and region. No country systematically pursues its "vital national interests," because individuals and groups disagree on how to define those interests. An authoritarian regime as in Saddam Hussein's Iraq may repress differences but cannot entirely extinguish them. Given a chance, they may explode. In a democratic country such as the United States these differences contend, often in the open, and push policy in one direction or another.

America's ability to mount a unified and farsighted foreign policy suffered many handicaps. The problems that Alexis de Tocqueville perceived in the 1830s never disappeared.[6] Rivalry between political parties, combined with the demands of diverse interest groups, diluted any sense of shared national purpose. The American public was literate but not deeply interested in world affairs.

Given the many groups seeking to shape America's foreign policy, U.S. decision makers had great difficulty in formulating a rational policy to maximize "America's vital interests." Indeed, they had trouble adopting any consistent policy and sticking to it for long periods.

The rational-actor "RAM" model of foreign policy, however, is a straw man easy to push over. It brings together two quite different variables under one heading—rationality and the image of monolithic unity within a country. A government could rationally pursue its perceived interest even without monolithic unity; a country could be unified and yet behave irrationally.

Let us examine in more detail some of the factors that divide Americans and their government on foreign policy. One or another of these factors were highlighted by nearly all the experts whose opinions were consulted for this book.

A Contradictory Political Culture.   American political culture embodied a wealth of contradictions. The twentieth century generated much evidence that "Americans" were:

- Religious and puritanical but also materialistic and hedonistic;
- Generous but obsessed with material wealth;

- A country of immigrants disinterested in other civilizations;
- Ready to fight only in self-defense but practiced in military interventions from the "halls of Montezuma to the shores of Tripoli";
- Determined to maintain a "Fortress America" and untrammeled sovereignty, but also dedicated to collective security and world order;
- Isolationist and internationalist. Not till after World War II did Americans often use the term "isolationist" to describe one strain of their political culture. Only when they looked back to the 1920s and 1930s did they wonder how some Americans might have thought their country could prosper "apart from the main."[7] Historian Walter McDougall, as we see below, contends that so-called isolationism was usually a form of unilateralism.

These rifts in political culture fed on and contributed to debates about what doctrines should guide U.S. foreign policy. For hundreds of years Americans agreed that theirs was a "promised land." In the twentieth century they debated whether it should also be a crusader state.

Should the United States merely defend its liberties and trading rights, keep Europeans from retaking the Americas, fill in its continent, and set an example to others? Or should it expand and intervene abroad to promote the blessings of liberty, thwart aggression, and meliorate the world's ills? Before 1898 Americans were more content to set an example; for much of the twentieth century they behaved like gendarmes or crusaders. As Walter McDougall depicts it, their Old Testament fundamentals became overlaid with a set of New Testament rules, as summarized in box 3.1.[8]

Shaped by a multiplicity of doctrines, America's policies in the twentieth century became more complex and contradictory than in the late eighteenth and nineteenth centuries. Confusion about doctrines led to hesitation and to inconsistent behavior. Americans did not lack principles; they had too many. Like Athenians, they had many gods. "A democracy of many religious and secular faiths ... is constantly at war with itself over matters of right and wrong, prudence and folly."[9] Critics asked: Could the country act like a Crusader State and still remain a Promised Land?

Box 3.1 America's Foreign Policy Bible

The Old Testament (prevailed from 1770s through the 1890s)

1. Liberty, or Exceptionalism (so called)
2. Unilateralism, or Isolationism (so called)
3. The American System of States, or the Monroe Doctrine (so called)
4. Expansionism, or Manifest Destiny (so called)

The New Testament of the Twentieth Century Crusader State

5. Progressive Imperialism
6. Wilsonianism, or Liberal Internationalism (so called)
7. Containment
8. Global Meliorism

These divisions in political culture and foreign policy doctrine deepened cleavages within the structure of political power.

Separation of Powers. For starters, the Constitution separates governmental powers. This separation can be a plus or a minus for foreign policy. It prevents tyranny by any one branch of government but often obstructs action.

The Senate, which must approve treaties for the president to ratify them, spurned the League of Nations and later the comprehensive nuclear test ban—delivering major setbacks not just to the Wilson and Clinton administrations but probably also to U.S. and world security. Congress balked at funding a support package for Mexico in 1994, spurring Clinton to utilize the Exchange Stabilization Fund; Congress then retaliated by placing new restrictions on the ESF making it difficult for the White House to react to the Asian financial crisis in 1998–1999.

The Constitution says that the president is commander-in-chief but that Congress declares war and controls the purse strings. President Truman exploited the Constitution's ambiguities to send large forces to fight in Korea, where U.S. troops remained for more than half a century, both intimidating and provoking North Korea. But President Johnson extracted a blank check from Congress (the

Tonkin Gulf Resolution) and sent even larger forces to Vietnam, where they fought for a decade and lost. If we regard the Korean "police action" as a success, the Constitution's flexibility was an asset. If we see the Vietnam War and other U.S. military interventions as mistaken or unnecessary, then the Constitution's ambiguities opened the door to blunders and even disasters.

Interventionists want to keep the door ajar for rapid military action; noninterventionists prefer to keep it under lock and key.

Politics, Interest Groups, and Money.   Political competition encourages individuals and groups to place their partisan and ideological differences ahead of any hypothetical national interest (usually defined differently in each party's platform). Citing their opposition to abortion, members of Congress withheld major funding for UN agencies in the 1990s. Defying the Clinton White House, the chairman of the Senate Foreign Relations Committee refused even to hold hearings on nominees for dozens of ambassadorships, including China, where the United States had no ambassador for more than a year.

In A.D. 2000 New Hampshire Republican Judd Gregg used his position as chairman of the Senate Appropriations Subcommittee to block $328 million for UN peacekeeping missions in East Timor, Sierra Leone, and Congo. In May, however, he released his hold on $40 million for a UN peacekeeping mission in Kosovo.

Partisan politics meant that almost any major foreign policy initiative required a major effort. In 2000 there were only ten members still in the House of Representatives who had voted a consistent internationalist line in the 1990s—one Republican from the suburbs of Washington, D.C.; two Democrats from Washington State, which exported Boeing aircraft to the world; and several Democrats from the south, who faced no labor union critics. Only when local business interests pushed Republicans to vote "yea" in 2000 did Clinton secure one of his major foreign policy successes—a bill normalizing U.S. trade with China.[10]

Competition between parties sometimes made foreign policy an exercise in maneuvering as various groups vied to put a wrinkle on this or that policy. The frequency of national elections contributed to short-term perspectives, reinforced by the two-term limit for presidents. Dependency on donors to finance political campaigns tempted politicians to curry the favor of certain interests—"prolife" groups; the lobbies for Taiwan, Israel, Greece; anti-Castro forces; labor unions; environmental groups; and many more. Of

Some critics said that Clinton and Gore had become lap dogs of PRC and other foreign donors to their campaign chests.

course some lobbies were better financed and more determined than others—and more influential.

These factors led the Clinton administration into two courses of action—eastward enlargement of NATO and accelerated movement to deploy nationwide missile defenses—that antagonized Russians for no good reason. Would the Clinton administration have stumped to expand NATO had it not lusted for donations from airplane and tank manufacturers and support from voters of East European descent living in Chicago, Cleveland, and Pittsburgh? Would the Clinton team have rushed preparations to test and deploy a national missile defense if Republicans were not accusing Democrats of neglecting the U.S. security? Clinton, in 1999, pledged a deployment decision in 2000 even though no missile defense system was evident; and the proposed system would do nothing to stop "suitcase bombs" or cruise missiles. If defensive missiles were deployed, the Clinton team opted to build a site in Alaska rather than in Grand Forks, North Dakota, as permitted by 1972–7974 understandings with Moscow. Why did Clinton favor a site that riled the Russians and would cost billions more to build and operate than one in North Dakota, given an Alaskan climate that made the western prairies look mild? To mollify Alaska Republican Ted Stevens, who chaired the Senate Appropriations Subcommittee on Defense, and who might resist the North Dakota site because its reach would not protect several thousand of his constituents living in the westernmost Aleutian Islands. Clinton also sought the support of Hawaiian Senator Daniel Inouye, ranking Democrat on the subcommittee, who might object that Grand Forks could not shield two uninhabited Hawaiian Islands.

Bureaucracy. Besides the basic three-fold separation of powers in Washington, even the executive branch and its vast bureaucracy was fragmented. Many agencies played major roles in foreign policy—not just the Departments of State and Defense but also Commerce, Energy, Treasury, the Environmental Protection Agency, and others. Besides the Central Intelligence Agency, other agencies also gathered and interpreted intelligence. Aerial surveillance of Cuba was delayed in 1962 while the Air Force and the CIA quarreled over whether a uniformed military officer or a CIA pilot should fly the plane.

The National Security Council, located physically close to the Oval Office, was supposed to help the president make sense of the inputs from the foreign policy hydra. Headed by such strong personalities as McGeorge Bundy, Henry Kissinger, and Zbigniew Brzezinski, the NSC often disagreed on some points with the Secretary of State and other agencies.[11] Battles for turf and influence ensued. President Nixon and his National Security Assistant Henry Kissinger kept Secretary of State William Rogers in the dark about their efforts to establish face-to-face contacts with top Chinese leaders. Reflecting later on Nixon's choice of Rogers, Kissinger wrote: "Few Secretaries of State can have been selected because of their President's confidence in their ignorance of foreign policy."[12]

The voice of Secretary of State Madeleine K. Albright counted for less in the Clinton White House than that of Special Assistant Samuel R. Berger. How could it be otherwise when she was in the air, meeting with foreign dignitaries, or coping with jet lag while Berger remained a few steps from the Oval Office?

The President nominates the major officials responsible for foreign policy, but this does not assure unity—even within the cabinet. Consider the debate about trade with China in the 1990s. The State Department wanted to use trade as a lever to promote human rights; the Defense Department opposed the sale of supercomputers and other

Mrs. Albright Explains Our Bosnia Policy

U.S. forces played a leading role in the International Force—"IFOR" (later called Stabilization Force—"SFOR") maintaining the Dayton Accords in Bosnia. Secretary of State Madeleine Albright was said to be more ready to deploy U.S. military forces than the Pentagon. The peace enforcement mission, however, probably weakened the war-fighting capacity of U.S. forces. The president, though he occupied the driver's seat, could not shake his reputation as a draft-dodger.

militarily useful high technology to China; the Commerce Department favored trade with China, no matter what. There were also frequent disagreements on when to use force. This divergence helped account for an uneven performance as U.S. forces attacked Serbia in 1999.

Even if the bureaucracies are not wrestling with each other, each has its own work habits—standard operating procedures—that may slow if not impede the overall policy thrust sought by the White House. Thus, in 1990 the Los Alamos National Weapons Laboratory set off an underground nuclear explosion just as Soviet leader Mikhail Gorbachev arrived in the United States for a visit. Did the White House wish to remind the visiting Soviet leader of U.S. power and underscore U.S. resistance to Gorbachev's calls for a ban on underground testing? Probably not. The White House by that time sought to coopt Gorbachev—not intimidate him. Most likely the weapons engineers were just following their schedule, left out of planning for Gorbachev's visit.

Secrecy.   Some parts of the body politic may not know what another is doing, even though they ostensibly strive for the same cause. Some leaders try to keep things secret—not only from the public but from other government officials. U.S. Senators got their first glimpse of the Versailles Treaty text from newspapers—not directly from President Wilson in Paris. In the 1940s the U.S. Army's *Project Verona* broke Soviet codes and gathered vast information on Soviet spies in the United States, but kept both their code breaking and what they discovered from President Truman![13] As Max Weber noted decades earlier: "Every bureaucracy seeks to increase the superiority of the professionally informed by keeping their knowledge and intentions secret."[14]

Public Opinion.   The swings of public opinion can shape foreign policy in many ways. Public moods cycle between demands for action and calls for consolidation.[15] Such tempers respond to many factors—the state of the economy and the world, stimuli from the media, the urgings of politicians and preachers, and the interplay of values and perceived interest. Segments of the public may call for a more active foreign policy, as in 1898, or for a lowered U.S. profile on the world stage, as in 1945–1946. Thus, when many Americans demanded "bring the boys home" after Germany's defeat, this gave President Truman little room to keep U.S. troops in Czechoslovakia even though he worried about Soviet designs for Eastern Europe. After America's defeat in Indochina, Congress and the public were reluctant to counter Soviet and Cuban adventures in Africa.

Individuals

Constitutions, structures, and large forces set the stage, but it is individuals who propose, tailor, implement, and refine policies. Conversion power in foreign policy ultimately depends upon individuals—leaders in government and other fields—and their ability to utilize assets in the world arena. But very different kinds of individuals have helped the United States achieve successes abroad. Two of the most successful—Harry Truman and Ronald Reagan—came from modest backgrounds. Some of the best-trained leaders and their advisers failed.

   The capacity of individuals to shape foreign policy depends first of all on their unique blend of mental, emotional, and physical traits. Their personal and professional qualities condition how they interact with domestic assets and restraints to deal with challenges abroad. Some waste riches, become complacent or arrogant, and buckle before difficulties; others exploit even limited assets and help their compatriots rise to challenges.

Does the record point to individual qualities that are both necessary and sufficient for policy success? No, because "success" in world affairs depends on trends and events in the domestic and global arena beyond the direct control of individual countries and their policymakers. Complex problems such as global warming cannot be resolved by any one country but require the cooperation of many actors.

No package of individual traits assures foreign policy success and none is absolutely essential, but the following traits are helpful:

Table 3.2 Individual Qualities Helpful in Foreign Policy

1. Knowledge of the players, the issues, the cultural context, and the languages being used
2. Domestic support from one's own government and society
3. Internal drive and commitment
4. Management skills to coordinate other players
5. Timing—the ability to wait, pull back, initiate, persist, and follow through when conditions are ripe
6. Communication skills in speech, writing, and gestures
7. Constructive imagination to identify or create mutual gain solutions
8. Leverage—carrots and sticks—to persuade
9. Toughness to stand pat, threaten, bluff, fight—balanced with:
10. Flexibility to accommodate when appropriate
11. Stamina and patience
12. Integrity to inspire trust
13. A winning personality
14. Empathy with all whose interests are at stake
15. Draftsmanship to produce treaty language that copes with differences either by precision or by creative ambiguity

But there is no magic formula. Some attributes may be more important than others. The package of traits that succeeds in one domestic or international setting may fail in another. To be effective a leader's personality must fit the situation.[16]

Even if a foreign policy maker possesses most of these attributes, success is not assured. One group of experts ranked Henry Kissinger "strong" in ten of these qualities; Jimmy Carter, in eight; Ronald Reagan, only in three—domestic support, communication skills, and a winning personality.[17] And yet Reagan's foreign policy achievements may well have surpassed those of the Kissinger-Nixon and the Carter administrations. Luck and circumstances favored the "teflon president" more than his predecessors.

Depending on what we regard as valuable, we can find positive and negative features in each president's foreign policy. If we believe the United States should try to make the world a better place, we may approve the policies of Woodrow Wilson and John F. Kennedy; if we think Americans should mind their own affairs, we may prefer those of Herbert Hoover and Dwight D. Eisenhower.

A Report Card for U.S. Presidents

Here is my report card on how leading presidents advanced or hurt U.S. interests in the world. In many cases it differs sharply from the rankings assigned by 58 historians asked by C-SPAN to evaluate U.S. presidents' handling of international relations. Their opinions are summarized in box 3.2 on page 131.

Woodrow Wilson.   His articulate support for liberal ideals helped him to become the most influential person in the world in 1919. But Wilson permitted his interactions with Senate Republicans to keep the United States out of the League of Nations. Given this ultimate failure, it is hard to agree with the C-SPAN historians that Wilson was the past century's fourth-most effective president in foreign affairs.

Franklin D. Roosevelt.   His administration promoted reciprocal trade agreements, the Good Neighbor Policy, an arms buildup to make the United States the "arsenal of democracy," and Lend-Lease. He steered the United States to victory in World War II while fostering the Bretton Woods economic system and the United Nations.

Perhaps for these reasons, the C-SPAN historians ranked FDR the most successful president in the entire history of U.S. foreign policy. Analysts of the Cold War, however, will fault him for failing to prepare for the possibility of an expansionist Soviet empire. Wilsonian idealists can hardly forgive him for discussing Poland and the Baltic states with Stalin as though they did not matter except for their impact on his re-election.

Harry S. Truman.   The Truman administration spurred the rebuilding of Europe and Japan, initiated containment of the USSR,

Box 3.2 C-SPAN *Survey of Presidential Leadership in International Relations*

Code: The first number is the rating in international relations among twentieth-century presidents. The number in parentheses is the rank in international relations among 41 U.S. presidents since George Washington, while the number in brackets is the president's overall rating since 1789 on ten dimensions.

1. Franklin Delano Roosevelt (1) [2]
2. Theodore Roosevelt (3) [4]
3. Harry S. Truman (5) [5]
4. Woodrow Wilson (6) [6]
5. Richard Nixon (8) [25]
6. Dwight D. Eisenhower (9) [9]
7. George Bush (12) [20]
8. John F. Kennedy (13) [8]
9. Ronald Reagan (14) [11]
10. William McKinley (17) [15]
11. Jimmy Carter (20) [22]
12. Bill Clinton (21) [21]
13. William Howard Taft (22) [24]
14. Gerald Ford (23) [23]
15. Herbert Hoover (25) [34]
16. Calvin Coolidge (30) [27]
17. Warren G. Harding (35) [38]
18. Lyndon Baines Johnson (36) [10]

Source: C-SPAN Survey of Presidential Leadership, released February 21, 2000

and galvanized the United Nations to repulse North Korean aggression. But the words and deeds of Truman's subordinates tempted North Korea to strike southward and provoked China to join the war.

The C-SPAN evaluations ranked Harry S. Truman as the fifth-most effective president in foreign policy. But I see him as number one—at least for the twentieth century.[18] His accomplishments were gigantic in the face of complex and unprecedented challenges. Never had the stakes been so high—a possible nuclear war. Never had the United States tried to lead a global coalition in a Cold War against a totalitarian empire under a cunning dictator. Never had the United States endeavored quickly to conciliate former foes and turn them into partners. These were challenges for which there was less precedent than fighting a world war; challenges more difficult than merely continuing the containment strategy, as Eisenhower and other presidents did; more taxing than watching the sunset of a decaying empire, as Reagan and Bush did later on.

Dwight D. Eisenhower.   The Eisenhower administration continued Truman's containment policy but also opened the way to détente, beginning with the Geneva Summit in 1955. But while "Ike" was a cautious military man, he gave the Dulles brothers, Allen and John Foster, wide rein for adventures that caused long-term problems. As head of the CIA, Allen Dulles organized coups d'état in Iran and Guatemala; as secretary of state, John Foster Dulles sabotaged détente, denounced "neutralism," and built a reputation for pactomania. Opposing the 1954 Geneva plan for a unified Vietnam, the Eisenhower administration sponsored a South Vietnamese client state.

The Eisenhower White House avoided catastrophic commitments. It did not "roll back" the Soviet empire, as John Foster Dulles once promised, and did not really try actively to do so. After eight years of Ike's presidency, one observer wrote that "nothing has been settled" but "nothing vital to the free world has been lost."[19] Compared to his immediate predecessors and those presidents who came after him, Ike presided over a quiet eight years. Despite the adventures of Allen and John Foster, the United States became involved in no wars. It suffered no deaths from major battles. Ike's grade of number nine by the C-SPAN historians is about right.

John F. Kennedy.   JFK and his associates performed well during the Cuban missile crisis, and did much to promote U.S.-Soviet accords on arms control and trade. But it was their missile buildup and support for Cuban exile invaders that helped bring on the Cuban confrontation. In another portentous move, the Kennedy team sent military advisers to South Vietnam and endorsed a coup d'état in Saigon.

Lyndon B. Johnson.   His administration oversaw the massive escalation of U.S. participation in the Indochina War, America's greatest débacle abroad. This earns him the lowest ranking of any president in the C-SPAN survey. Though Johnson failed tragically in Vietnam, he persuaded the USSR that arms control talks needed to consider defensive and offensive weapons at the same time. This set the stage for the ABM treaty negotiated in 1972.

Richard M. Nixon.   Nixon and his special assistant for national security, Henry Kissinger, played their cards close to the chest as they moved to normalize relations with China; stabilize the arms competition with the USSR; and destabilize Chile's leftist president, Salvador Allende. Having continued and widened the Indochina War for three fruitless years, the Nixon-Kissinger team accepted a treaty that North Vietnam promptly broke, occupying South Vietnam and Cambodia. Nixon and Kissinger also exaggerated their détente with Moscow, which promptly blew up as Israel repulsed Egypt in 1973.

Nixon and Kissinger erred on the side of secret diplomacy. The president's inferiority complex and Kissinger's superiority complex led them to keep others out of the loop—even the cabinet officers chosen by Nixon.

Kissinger had publicly warned that in a democracy obtaining public support was a statesman's "acid test," but he failed to do so himself. Why? He and Nixon "stepped outside the constraints imposed by the American political tradition without reshaping that tradition itself."[20]

Jimmy Carter.   He mediated Camp David and promoted human rights, but also presided over multiple disasters in Iran, Afghanistan, and the Horn of Africa. However he should not be ranked below McKinley, who spawned an empire that generated endless headaches.

Ronald Reagan.   This president signed far-reaching accords with Gorbachev, but his Star Wars ambitions played havoc with U.S. security interests. His Iran-Contra affair violated both U.S. and international law.

George Bush.   His team organized collective security against Iraq but then let the incipient new world order disintegrate in the Balkans.

Contrary to findings of the C-SPAN survey, both Reagan and Bush probably deserve to be ranked higher than Nixon, Eisenhower, or Kennedy. The century's last two Republican presidents may have been no more adept at steering a ship of state than Nixon, Ike, or JFK, but they sailed with more favorable winds and tides.

William J. Clinton.   Acting as CEO for the United States, Inc., he fostered free trade but needlessly antagonized Russia by expanding NATO, while debasing the presidency.

What Is the Role of Knowledge and Experience?

Let us review just one variable—the intellectual attainments of U.S. leaders—and see how it interacted with other traits to usher in successes or failure on the world stage. We shall see that knowledge by itself does not guarantee success in foreign affairs; is not always necessary for victory; and can even be harmful if blended with other traits, such as overconfidence. At times ignorance may be an asset: A leader might shrink from large tasks if the hurdles were fully known.

Most U.S. presidents and their top aides in foreign affairs were well educated and broadly traveled. Many attended prep schools and prestigious colleges; many went on to get law degrees or doctorates. But there were important exceptions: Harry S. Truman was the only twentieth-century president who did not attend college. Truman's mother, however, taught him to read—perhaps before age five. He attended night courses in law for two years but was largely self-taught—a history buff, with a predilection for the stories of great men. Two more exceptions: Neither Lyndon B. Johnson nor Ronald Reagan attended a famous college. Reagan showed little interest in book learning. LBJ, though a former teacher, trusted more in human contacts than in the printed page.

Theodore Roosevelt.   TR knew languages, science, history, as well as people and used them all to become a renowned mediator. In 1906 TR exploited his friendship with Germany's ambassador to Washington to extract concessions from Kaiser Wilhelm to end the Moroccan crisis.

William Howard Taft.   Born in Cincinnati, Taft came to know the world. He headed the commission governing the Philippines, traveled extensively in the Far East, and served as Roosevelt's secretary of war. A judge and a professor of law, his mind had a legalistic cast. His dogged backing of "dollar diplomacy" became a defense for American investments abroad rather than a support for broad U.S. interests. His policies helped to undo the Manchu empire and open China to Japanese and Russian penetration.

Woodrow Wilson.   The president with the most formal education failed to achieve his vision of America in the world. Wilson mobilized a team of experts to advise him at the Paris Peace Conference, but then ignored them. While teaching political science at Princeton, Wilson had analyzed the powers of Congress.[21] But as U.S. president—with League of Nations membership at stake—he tried to bulldoze the Republican majority in the Senate, and failed.[22]

Were Wilson's stubborn ways a psychological reaction to a domineering father, a physical response to stress, or a result of his Presbyterian upbringing? The experts disagree.[23] They concur, however, that Wilson's insistence that he was right and others wrong helped to destroy him and his vision of a world safe for democracy. Wilson was the wrong prophet even if his message was good.

Herbert Hoover.   Before serving as president from 1929 to 1933, Hoover acquired vast practical experience abroad. As a geologist and engineer he had built major projects on four continents; as a Quaker humanitarian he had organized famine relief across Europe and Russia after World War I; sensitive to history, he brought back wartime pamphlets and documents to launch the Hoover Library at Stanford University. As secretary of commerce in the early 1920s Hoover labored to make the world the oyster for American "individualism." He did not favor U.S. isolation but an "independent internationalism."

As U.S. president, Hoover named Henry L. Stimson his secretary of state. Stimson had seen the Indian wars, commanded a unit in World War I, served as an enlightened governor of the Philippines, and written a book about Nicaragua. Despite their great minds and vast experience, Hoover and Stimson did not integrate the United States with the world to stave off the Great Depression or Fascism. On their watch Congress passed the Smoot-Hawley Tariff that aggravated economic chaos.

Franklin D. Roosevelt.   Although he graduated from Harvard College and the Columbia Law School, FDR was not renowned for his mind but for his optimistic pragmatism. Still, as president he collected a "Brain Trust" to advise him in Washington. The ultimate in hubris, he counted on personal charm and intuition to negotiate with Stalin. Like Wilson in 1919, he paid too little heed to specialists on foreign affairs.

Harry S. Truman.   America's greatest successes abroad came under the president with the least formal education of any twentieth-century president. Like Lyndon Johnson later, Truman succeeded to the presidency following the death of a Harvard-educated, East coast millionaire. The short, self-educated haberdasher from Missouri radiated confidence. He welcomed and befriended the experienced advisers he inherited from FDR.

What was there about Truman and his aides—George C. Marshall, Dean Acheson, Douglas MacArthur, and others—that helped them to succeed in foreign affairs? The school of hard knocks may have helped. Their outlooks were molded in the crucible of their generation. Each served in government or the armed forces during World War I; lived through America's retreat from foreign affairs; observed Germany labor under the Versailles Treaty and finally reject it; watched as Nazi Germany and Japan challenged the world; and contributed to U.S. victories in World War II.[24]

Dwight D. Eisenhower.   His education and life experience were similar to those of George C. Marshall, but Ike was less bold. His caution, however, was more than compensated for by the Dulles brothers. Allen and John Foster had not experienced combat, but each had formal training in international affairs and long experience in espionage and/or diplomacy. Each knew a great deal about disarmament negotiations before and after World War II. Their crusader mentality, like that of Woodrow Wilson, probably owed something to their father, a Presbyterian minister. Dean Acheson's father was also a man of the cloth, but a British-born Episcopal bishop, married to a Canadian woman.

John F. Kennedy.   The youngest president sought the best and brightest for cabinet and other responsible positions. Many of their actions, however, helped no one. They sharpened conflicts with

---

Box 3.3 Generational Birds Flock Together: Does Age Bring Wisdom?

Age plus experience can sometimes generate wisdom. In the late 1940s Truman, Marshall, and MacArthur were in their 60s; the youngest key member of that team was Acheson, then in his 50s.

The Truman team was more mature than the others discussed here, and more successful. But there was no formula. The Dulles brothers— Allen and John Foster—were also in their 60s when their zeal and Manichean outlook took the Eisenhower foreign policy into troubled waters. They were roughly the same age as Marshall when he served as secretary of state.

When Ike stepped down at age 70, he was the oldest American to have held the highest office (before Reagan); he was replaced by the youngest, John F. Kennedy—then 43. Like JFK, most of his key advisers were in their 40s except for Dean Rusk, already in his mid-50s.

Still later, President Clinton also selected associates close to his own age. Most were in their 50s. They generally lacked the wisdom of the people around Truman and the dynamism of those close to Kennedy.

In 2000 only nine World War II veterans remained in the House of Representatives. Bob Dole's voice was gone from the Senate, where he urged his colleagues to back the White House when the president made a commitment. The Vietnam-era generation dominated Congress and refused to accept that "the president knows best." Worried about becoming involved in foreign quagmires, Congress passed resolutions demanding withdrawal of troops from Bosnia and Kosovo and delays in funding drug wars in Colombia. This Congress wanted a national missile defense but its upper house refused to approve the nuclear test ban treaty.

Moscow and Havana. They helped Kennedy and, later, Lyndon Johnson, plunge into the Indochina quagmire.[25] Why did the Kennedy team blunder? The Greeks had a name for it: *hubris*. They trusted excessively in their own minds and in technological fixes for human problems. While Truman's advisers tried to learn from their sobering experiences, Kennedy's aides acted as though they already knew whatever was needed. They had been renowned professors at MIT and Harvard; the head of the Rockefeller Foundation; the president of the Ford Motor Company—a graduate of the Harvard Business School with his train of "whiz kid" number crunchers.[26]

While still in college Kennedy had seen Europe from inside the U.S. embassy in London and turned his senior thesis at Harvard into a book, *Why England Slept* (1940). He also knew that war is not fun. As president he lived in near constant pain from his own wounds suffered 20 years earlier. He sought out associates who had also served in World War II. Robert McNamara, for example, had been an air force lieutenant colonel. McGeorge Bundy, a junior army officer, had landed at Normandy one day after D-Day.

Kennedy's entourage had experienced the shining victories of World War II and postwar reconstruction, but was too young to have suffered the disillusionments of the 1920s and 1930s. They knew Europe well—less so Asia or Russia, where the biggest troubles lay. When they read Nikita Khrushchev's January 1961 speech committing the USSR to assist wars of national liberation, they resolved to stop the Communist advance.[27] They pictured the Third World as the place to confront the Communists and defeat them militarily. They would use elite counterinsurgency forces backed by electronic gadgetry and helicopter gunships. If all else failed, McNamara considered building an electronic Maginot line to prevent North Vietnamese from moving into the South.

Lyndon B. Johnson. Like Truman, LBJ became president when a Harvard-educated easterner died. Most Kennedy aides stayed on for a while to assist LBJ. Johnson wanted to develop his Great Society program in the United States, but he also wanted to stop Communist aggression.[28] Determined to be as assertive on the world scene as JFK, Johnson relied on advisers left over from Camelot.[29]

Richard M. Nixon. This life-long politician built his career on anti-Communism, including his 1959 "kitchen debate" with Khrushchev. Despite his 1960 defeat by John F. Kennedy with his Ivy Leaguers, Nixon after his election in 1968 selected another Harvard professor, Henry Kissinger, to be his special assistant for national security. No U.S. foreign policy leader knew both the issues and the players better than Kissinger. His dissertation on the post-Napoleonic era, published as *A World Restored,* generated ideas that helped guide Kissinger's conservative realpolitik.[30] His address files bulged with the names of elites from around the world who attended the summer institutes he led at Harvard University. Before joining the Nixon team in 1969, Kissinger advised Republican Nelson Rockefeller in the 1950s and Democrat John F. Kennedy in the 1960s, even functioning as JFK's emissary to Chancellor Konrad Adenauer in Germany.

But knowledge is no guarantee of success. While Kissinger negotiated many deals, few of them stuck. His Vietnam peace treaty quickly gave way to Hanoi's takeover of the south and of Cambodia. His détente with the Brezhnev Kremlin gave way to a serious 1973 confrontation over the "Yom Kippur" War. His backing for Chile's generals led to decades of embarrassment.[31]

Jimmy Carter. He had studied engineering; commanded a submarine; served as governor of Georgia; and run a successful farm. Introduced to foreign policy circles by Columbia University professor Zbigniew Brzezinski, Carter convinced many at the Council on Foreign Relations that he could learn quickly about international affairs. His Baptist beliefs helped inspire his quest to understand and mediate conflicts in the Holy Land.[32]

Elected in 1976, Carter was probably the most intelligent president in half a century, but his mind then was ahistorical. He did not care about how the story turned out before. The president did not lack information or expert advice about the relevant past, but he was not inclined to take a longer, historical perspective. This mindset led him in 1977 to ignore an arms control understanding with Moscow reached by his predecessor, Gerald Ford, and to press for a radical disarmament plan the Soviets quickly rejected.[33]

Carter named Brzezinski to be his special assistant for national security, while Cyrus Vance, an international lawyer with years of government service, became secretary of state. But the result looked like a Russian troika. Brzezinski the veteran hard-liner pulled right; Vance the idealist leaned left. Between them was Carter. His idealism tilted him toward Vance, but his shock at the Soviet invasion of Afghanistan and the Iranian takeover of the U.S. embassy in Tehran pushed him toward Brzezinski. Had Carter listened to either adviser, the result would probably have been superior to a course that zigged and zagged.[34]

Ronald Reagan. Of all U.S. presidents in the twentieth century, Reagan was the least well read, the least traveled, the least curious about the real world. He preferred a good story to good analysis.

But Reagan's energies awoke for at least a few hours a day, helping him to make persuasive appearances at home and abroad.[35] Also, he had strong beliefs and principles, which his aides tried to advance. In all this he differed from two of his Soviet contemporaries.[36] Wife Nancy Reagan was active in selecting her husband's staff. Her astrologer also played a role. For example, Reagan's first official meeting with Gorbachev in Washington and their lunch were compressed on December 8, 1987 so that the INF Treaty could be signed at precisely 1:45 P.M.—the moment the astrologer deemed most propitious.[37]

Reagan chose knowledgeable, experienced persons to run the Department of State and National Security Council. One adviser, Harvard professor Richard Pipes, was a well-known hard-liner on things Soviet. A distinguished historian, he was known in Washington for his fanciful thesis that the USSR planned to launch and win a nuclear war.[38] But Reagan listened to his own drummer with regard to the "evil empire." Not long after Gorbachev became the top Communist in Moscow, Reagan concluded that—as Margaret Thatcher told him—the West could do business with the new Soviet leader, and Reagan's team began to search for arms control and other accords. Fortunately for the world, Gorbachev persisted in his efforts to come to terms with a man whose mind was more shaped by Hollywood memories than by briefing papers.[39]

George Bush. He had the most varied experiences in foreign affairs of any president—a naval aviator in World War II, an ambassador to China and to the United Nations, a director of the CIA, and a vice president to Reagan. His contacts help him to mobilize a grand coalition against Saddam Hussein—history's most successful case of collective security in action. Though Bush lacked what he called the "vision thing," he functioned well as team leader of a global coalition. His adviser on Soviet affairs, Condoleezza Rice, another exponent of realpolitik, was—like Wilson and the Dulles brothers—the child of a Presbyterian minister.[40]

William J. Clinton. A Rhodes scholar at Oxford, Bill Clinton and his advisers were well-educated men and women of the world. But Clinton permitted himself indulgences that weakened his moral authority.[41] His opportunism often overshadowed his vision. Clinton's old friend and major adviser on Russia, Strobe Talbott, knew Russian literature and arms control. But the former *Time* columnist offered sophist defenses both of NATO expansion and of Russia's right to defend its territorial integrity by fighting Chechens. While Talbott could speak to Russians in their language and empathize with them, Secretary of State Madeleine Albright could speak in Czech or Serbian to East Europeans. She sometimes veered right when Talbott cruised left, while Defense Secretary William S. Cohen—students of his poetry said—often circled on cloud nine. Like Jimmy Carter, Clinton had trouble moving in a straight line. For his entourage, truth was just another option.

Circumstances

Correlation need not imply causation. A given outcome may *correlate* with a certain leader and yet not be due to that leader. The makeup and actions of any president's administration may have only a modest impact on developments abroad.

The personal qualities and policies that succeed in one time and place may fail in another. If John Foster Dulles had called for a "roll-back" of the Iron Curtain in the 1980s instead of the 1950s, he might well have had more success.[42]

The Cold War ended on Reagan's watch and the USSR disappeared on that of George Bush. The fall of the Iron Curtain surely resulted from many factors besides Ronald Reagan and his policies. The "evil empire" suffered from many internal stresses accumulating decades before Reagan took office. The most we can claim is that Reagan and his policies did not prevent the Soviet breakup and may have contributed to it. Still, the friendly hand extended to Gorbachev by Reagan and Bush helped assure that the USSR disappeared not with a bang but a few whimpers. Like Kennedy after the Cuban crisis, Reagan and Bush did not gloat—at least not in public. Bush enlisted the USSR as a partner rather than a rival in organizing the campaign to oust Iraq from Kuwait.

Nor can we credit President Clinton with the long years of U.S. economic growth on his watch, because the expansion started before him and was sustained by many individuals and forces not controlled by the White House. We can be sure only that Clinton did not prevent economic expansion and may have helped it.

Coping with Complexity: What Works?

Let us shift our gaze from levels of action and review the policies themselves. What worked? The following table summarizes the major successes and failures already listed at the end of chapter 2, but table 3.3 (on p. 143) also provides a thumbnail sketch of their sources, drawing on this and the first two chapters.

U.S. foreign policy successes arose from the capacity of American society, guided by effective leaders, to cope with complexity. Sometimes there was experimentation, feedback, and adaptation. Winston Churchill remarked that Americans always do the right thing, but not until trying all the alternatives.

Successes such as the Marshall Plan, the broadening of free trade, and the Fulbright exchanges arose from a strategy aimed at creating values for all partners—and from open diplomacy. The more that participant societies resembled Kant's ideal, the greater the peace, prosperity, and mutual advantage created. But Americans also negotiated with rivals in Moscow and Beijing to mutual advantage. With Russians they limited the dangers of war and the costs of arms competition. With the Chinese they opened a dialogue in which many issues could be discussed. The greatest U.S. success abroad, the Marshall Plan, depended on U.S. leadership that fostered cooperation with others for mutual gain. Open diplomacy—open accords openly arrived at—worked better than secret diplomacy. America's greatest failure abroad, intervention in Indochina, was conceived in secret and promulgated with deception—from the Tonkin Gulf incident to claimed "body counts" to Kissinger's claims for the 1973 treaty he negotiated with Le Duc Tho in Paris.

How can it be that the Marshall Plan and Washington's handling of the missile crisis are both regarded as major achievements of U.S. foreign policy? Some differences were stark: The Marshall Plan was launched in the open with "carrots"; the Cuban blockade, with "sticks"—prepared in secret. The Marshall Plan sought and achieved mutual gain; it was proposed and implemented in the open. By contrast, the Kennedy team saw the missile crisis as part of a zero-sum struggle. Kennedy masked the U-2 discovery while preparing a firm response—a time and place when secrecy was probably essential.

Table 3.3 Summary Analysis of U.S. Successes and Failures

Successes	Sources	Failures	Sources
1. Win two world wars and drive aggressors from South Korea and Iraq	Mobilize U.S. human and material assets; excellent generalship; good coalition diplomacy	Too much or too little: fight without good cause in the Caribbean but fail to deter or limit major wars; enter and lose Indochina war	Naive isolationism alternating with excesses of crusading zeal
2. Promoting collective security and world order	Wilsonian vision; effective leadership and diplomacy	Abort League of Nations and weaken UN and international law	Isolationism and excessive concern to protect sovreignty
3. Reconciliation and reconstruction help form a U.S.-European-Japanese security community after 1945	Perceived interdependence with Japan and decision to promote mutual gain with bipartisan and popular support in the U.S.	Soviet bloc excluded from European Recovery Plan in 1947; post-Soviet Russia remained outside the First World in the 1990s	Russian/Soviet political culture combine with suspicions of Stalin and foibles of Yeltsin regime as West girds for Cold War and, in 1990s, enlarges NATO
4. Contain the USSR and win the Cold War without a U.S.-Soviet hot war; skillful coping with Cuban and other crises	Nurturing U.S. fitness at home and abroad; strong economic and scientific base; NATO; fear of escalation	Inappropriate applications of containment, from PRC to Cuba, push potential partners into the Soviet camp	Simplistic thinking, "pactomania" and indifference to national self-determination struggles
5. Conflict control and reduction: many détentes and normalizations starting in 1950s	Seek mutual gain with adversaries; learn from growing skill in conflict resolution	Possible missed opportunities to ease tensions in divided Germany and elsewhere	Blind momentum and self-righteousness, e.g., of John Foster Dulles; pressures from West German government
6. Developing both arms and arms control	Technological dynamism plus fear of war—deliberate or inadvertent; learn from game theory	Overkill; abet or permit excessive vertical and horizontal weapons proliferation;	Security dilemma: excessive trust in weapons and technological solutions; Soviet

(continues)

Table 3.3 (*continued*)

Successes	Sources	Failures	Sources
		weaken ABM regime	deception
7. Peacemaking by mediation and peacekeeping	Vision plus personal dedication and skill of T. Roosevelt, R. Bunche, J. C. Carter, R. Holbrooke, and others	Fail to act promptly in Balkans, Rwanda, and East Timor; weaken mediation capacity by perceived tilt	Isolationism; fatigue; indifference to Africa; influence of ethnic lobbies in the U.S.
8. Promoting trade and economic development by GATT, NAFTA, WTO	Belief in free trade and "invisible hand" of comparative advantage	Failure of trade and foreign aid to boost economic standards in most LDCs	Lack of peace and other preconditions for economic development in many LDCs
10. Promoting liberal democracy and liberal economics	Success of U.S. model vs. failures of autarky, central planning, mercantilism, and statism	Failure to promote democracy or liberal economics in much of the rest of the world	Weaknesses of U.S. model; limits to preaching in unfavorable conditions
10. Promoting human rights	Leaders such as Eleanor Roosevelt, M. L. King, and J. C. Carter, power of the Helsinki Process	Failure to promote human rights; ignoring them in places like East Timor	Racism, sexism, and concern for "states' rights" in the United States; resistance to Western ideas on human rights in much of the world
11. International understanding	Leaders such as J. Wm. Fulbright and institutions such as NSF, USIA, Carnegie and other foundations; U.S. openness to cross-cultural fermentation	Wide ignorance of and apathy to the world in the United States; many cultural exports giving unbalanced picture of U.S. life	Isolationism, materialism, hedonism
12. Reputation for dependability as ally (NATO, Israel,	Good leaders with strong values and commitments;	Deceptions by many U.S. leaders sullied U.S.	Cold War pressures; political competition;

(continues)

Table 3.3 *(continued)*

Successes	Sources	Failures	Sources
Japan, ROK, ROC); as negotiating partner with rivals	lobbies for Israel and Taiwan; open society that makes room for many opinions	reputation, e.g., in Iran-Contra affair	Nixon-Kissinger penchant for secret diplomacy; sophistry and opportunism
Some underlying factors	Policies that synthesize realism, Wilsonian ideals, and realities of interdependence; wise leaders with high conversion power; openness; modesty	Some underlying factors	Unilateralism; ignorance and misperception; wishful thinking or worst-case fear; hubris and self-righteousness; isolationism or messianism; unnecessary secrecy

Yet there were also similarities. Both the ERP and the Cuban crisis emerged from a bipolar structure of power with intense U.S.-Soviet competition. American diplomacy in each case sought and got support from U.S. allies. Both in 1947 and in 1962 U.S. policy was well planned by experts with diverse skills.

The ERP was a coordination game—a problem of coordinating convergent interests. The missile crisis looked more like a game of "chicken"—a collision course that promised catastrophe if neither side veered. Still, both Washington and Moscow converted their confrontation into a coordination game. Each avoided backing the other into a corner. Having made a deal, they found ways to implement it. Thus, when Castro refused to permit UN verification that the missiles were gone, Moscow and Washington cooperated on shipboard inspection from the air.

The near catastrophe of October 1962 confirms the view that zero-sum politics and deception are inferior to joint strategies of mutual gain and open diplomacy.[43] Still, policymaking toward tough guys requires more caution than policymaking with established partners, as suggested in the box.

American successes abroad—in rebuilding Europe and in coping with Soviet expansionism—required leadership but not dictation;

Box 3.4 Guidelines for Dealing with Tough Guys[44]

1. *Pursue mutual gain and openness.* Even with strong rivals, explore conditional cooperation buttressed with safeguards against defection. Better to compromise and create joint values than to retreat or to march toward war.

2. *Blend firmness and flexibility, potential punishment and reward.* Be sure your strength is evident and credible but do not bluster needlessly. Consider what the changing balance of power means for potential foes as well as for the United States Be aware how hard it is to communicate. Another Khrushchev or Saddam Hussein may read conciliatory gestures as weakness and ignore stern warnings.

3. *Strive to see ourselves as others see us.* Had the Kennedy team in 1962 seen itself through Khrushchev's eyes—as materially strong but irresolute—Washington might have anticipated—perhaps prevented—Khrushchev's gamble.

4. *Expect surprise.* Beat down preconceptions and wishful thinking. Investigate how "worst-case" and "least likely" scenarios might unfold. Ask whether "rationality" and "value" for the other side may differ from your definition.

5. *Expect duplicity—certainly from foes who endorse any means to their ends—but try to prevent it.* Do not trust assurances, especially when they involve ambiguous terms such as "offensive" weapons.

6. *Do not stereotype others. Allow that they may change.*

7. *Things often go wrong. Do not assume that crises can be readily managed.* Luck as well as skill avoided a catastrophe in 1962. Do not count on good fortune.

8. *Distance major foreign policy issues from partisan politics.* Election-year rivalry between Republicans and Democrats set the stage for the 1962 crisis.

9. *Learn. Do not make the same mistakes twice. But do not learn the wrong lessons.* Review assumptions and standard operating procedures to cope with change. Decide beforehand what evidence would count for or against your expectations. Weigh competing hypotheses. Integrate new data methodically with your existing beliefs. If an event comes as a surprise, reevaluate your expectations. Discuss misjudgments internally and perhaps with the other side.

10. *Do not merely adapt to circumstances but seek deep learning and new solutions.* If substantive changes are required, do not be satisfied with a mere change of tactics.

confidence but not hubris; knowledge tempered by and coupled with experience. Leaders need many qualities but in a certain balance: willingness to use force but only when needed; tolerance for ambiguity but ability to act under uncertainty; ability to get advice without producing "groupthink" or paralyzing splits among their team. They need both memory and openness. They dare not flow like driftwood nor move like a bullet on an unchangeable path. If leaders and society do everything right, they may also need luck.

Notes

1. The biosphere may also be regarded as a level of action and analysis, because it shapes and is shaped by international politics and economics. But its impact is too long-term to account for the ups and downs of U.S. policy in the twentieth century.

2. This table builds upon the approach used in Joseph S. Nye, Jr., *Bound to Lead: The Changing Nature of American Power* (New York: Basic Books, 1990). The rankings combine the author's judgment about real and perceived power in each era, starting with statistical surveys in *The Statesman's Year-Book* (London, annual) and, for recent decades, in annual reports of the World Bank, the International Institute for Strategic Studies, the U.S. Central Intelligence Agency, and other cross-national studies. Boston University students Justin Schardin and Shawn O'Neil helped compile comparisons, e.g., of coal and steel production. For economic history, see Paul Bairoch's works such as "International Industrialization Levels from 1750 to 1980," *Journal of European Economic History* 11 (1982); see also Paul Kennedy, *The Rise and Fall of the Great Powers: Economic Change and Military Conflict from 1500 to 2000* (New York: Random House, 1987) and his extensive bibliography.

3. Fareed Zakharia, *From Wealth to Power: The Unusual Origins of America's World Role* (Princeton, N.J.: Princeton University Press, 1998), pp. 183–184.

4. See Stephen D. Cohen et al., *Fundamentals of U.S. Foreign Trade Policy: Economics, Politics, Laws, and Issues* (Boulder, Co.: Westview, 1996), esp. chapter 8.

5. Alan Gilbert, *Must Global Politics Constrain Democracy? Great-Power Realism, Democratic Peace, and Democratic Internationalism* (Princeton, N.J.: Princeton University Press, 1999).

6. For an update, see essays in the special issue "Democracy in the World: Tocqueville Reconsidered," *Journal of Democracy,* 11, 1 (January 2000).

7. Manfred Jones, "Isolationism," *Encyclopedia of American Foreign Policy* (3 vols.; New York: Scribner's, 1978), 2, 496–506.

8. Walter A. McDougall, *Promised Land, Crusader State: The American Encounter with the World Since 1776* (Boston: Houghton Mifflin Co., 1997).

9. McDougall, *Promised Land*, p. 4.

10. Adam Clymer, "House Vote on China Trade: The Politics Was Local," *The New York Times*, May 27, 2000, p. A3.

11. About one-third of the special assistants who served from 1953 to 2000—five of seventeen—came from the academic world. One cartoonist suggested that presidents come and go but that "Kissinbundys" never change.

12. Henry Kissinger, *The White House Years* (Boston: Little, Brown, 1979), p. 26. For other comments on the organization of the State Department and the personalities at work in the Nixon years, see ibid., chapter 2.

13. Daniel Patrick Moynihan, *Secrecy: The American Experience* (New Haven, Ct.: Yale University Press, 1998), pp. 69–71 and elsewhere in this volume.

14. From Max Weber, *Economy and Society* (1920), quoted in Moynihan, *Secrecy*, p. 143.

15. For one interpretation, see Arthur M. Schlesinger, Jr., *The Cycles of American History* (Boston: Houghton Mifflin, 1986).

16. William Howard Taft, for example, made a fine chief justice but a clumsy president—at least in the circumstances he faced. Alexander L. George, *Presidential Decisionmaking in Foreign Policy: The Effective Use of Information and Advice* (Boulder, Co.: Westview, 1980), p. 7.

17. Evaluations based on formal ratings by retired U.S. ambassador Hermann Fr. Eilts, professors Roger Kanet and David Mayers, Dr. Jun Zhan, and the author. For rankings of other world leaders, see Walter C. Clemens, Jr., *Dynamics of International Relations: Conflict and Mutual Gain in An Era of Global Interdependence* (Lanham, Md.: Rowman & Littlefield, 1998), p. 211.

18. For a portrait, see David McCullough, *Truman* (New York: Simon & Schuster, 1992).

19. James Reston in *The New York Times*, quoted in David Fromkin, *In the Time of the Americans: FDR, Truman, Eisenhower, Marshall, MacArthur—The Generation That Changed America's Role in the World* (New York: Alfred A. Knopf, 1995), p. 6.

20. Robert Beisner, "History and Henry Kissinger," *Diplomatic History*, 14 (Fall 1990), p. 526 quoted in Lafeber, *American Age*, p. 673.

21. Wilson's doctoral dissertation was published as *Congressional Government* (1885).

22. Senate majority leader Henry Cabot Lodge was also well educated. He said of the League Covenant, "This might pass at Princeton [Wilson's alma mater], but never at Harvard [Lodge's]."

23. Juliette L. George and Alexander George, *Woodrow Wilson and Colonel House: A Personality Study* (New York: Dover, 1964); Edwin A. Weinstein, *Woodrow Wilson: A Medical and Psychological Biography* (Princeton, N.J.: Princeton University Press, 1981); for the Georges' comments on Weinstein, see *Political Science Quarterly,* 96, 4 (Winter 1981–1982), pp. 642–665. Several Wilson biographies published in the late 1980s downplay the Georges' thesis.

24. David Fromkin, *In the Time of the Americans*; W. Averell Harriman was also one of this generation. See Walter C. Clemens, Jr., "Of generations, experience, and peace," *Christian Science Monitor,* August 7, 1986, p. 18.

25. David H. Halberstam, *The Best and Brightest* (New York: Random House, 1969) and his *The Making of a Quagmire: America and Vietnam in the Kennedy Era* (New York; A. A. Knopf, 1988); Paul Johnson, *The Intellectuals* (London: Weidenfeld and Nicolson, 1988).

26. See Deborah Shapley, *Promise and Power: The Life and Times of Robert McNamara* (Boston: Little, Brown, 1993).

27. Conversation in 1965 with Jerome B. Wiesner, science adviser to President Kennedy and, briefly, to President Johnson.

28. See the conflicted conversations with Robert McNamara, James Rowley, Dean Rusk, George Ball, McGeorge Bundy, and J. William Fulbright on March 2, 1964, in Michael R. Beschloss, ed., *Taking Charge: The Johnson White House Tapes, 1963–1964* (New York; Simon & Schuster, 1997), pp. 257–265.

29. Lyndon B. Johnson, *The Vantage Point—Perspectives on the Presidency, 1963–69* (New York: Holt, Rinehart and Winston, 1971); Doris Kearns, *Lyndon Johnson and the American Dream* (New York: Harper and Row, 1976).

30. Henry A. Kissinger, *A World Restored: Metternich, Castlereagh and the Problems of Peace, 1812–1822* (Boston: Houghton Mifflin, 1957).

31. For his version, see Kissinger, *The White House Years* and other writings.

32. See Jimmy Carter, *The Blood of Abraham* (Boston: Houghton Mifflin, 1985).

33. Richard E. Neustadt and Ernest R. May, *Thinking in Time: The Uses of History for Decision-makers* (New York: The Free Press, 1986), pp. 113, 132.

34. For their narratives, see Zbigniew Brzezinski, *Power and Principle: Memoirs of the National Security Adviser, 1877–1981* (New York: Farrar Straus & Giroux, 1983); Cyrus Vance, *Hard Choices: Critical*

Years in America's Foreign Policy (New York: Simon & Schuster, 1983); for an outsider's analysis, Jean A. Garrison, *Games Advisors Play: Foreign Policy in the Nixon and Carter Administrations* (College Station: Texas A&M University Press, 1999).

35. Lou Cannon, *President Reagan: The Role of a Lifetime* (New York: Simon & Schuster, 1991). See also George P. Shultz, *Turmoil and Triumph: My Years as Secretary of State* (New York: Scribner's, 1993).

36. By contrast, Tsar Nicholas II and top Soviet leaders Leonid Brezhnev and Konstantin Chernenko were not driven by any political goals. They spent much of their days waiting for lunch and napping afterwards, with an occasional stroll or—for Brezhnev—a boar hunt, usually from a safe tree house. See diary excerpts in Dmitri Volkogonov, *Lenin: A New Biography* (New York: The Free Press, 1994), pp. 456–466.

37. Frances FitzGerald, *Way Out There in the Blue: Reagan, Star Wars, and the End of the Cold War* (New York: Simon & Schuster, 2000), p. 429.

38. See Walter C. Clemens, Jr., "Intellectual Foundations of Reagan's Soviet Policies," in Bernard Rubin, ed., *When Information Counts* (Lexington, Ma.: Lexington Books, 1985), pp. 155–172, 227–231.

39. For details, see FitzGerald, *Way Out There.*

40. For the memoir of his top general, see Colin L. Powell, *My American Journey* (New York: Random House, 1995); his longest serving secretary of state, James A. Baker, III, *The Politics of Diplomacy: Revolution, War & Peace, 1989–1992* (New York: G. P. Putnam's, 1995).

41. The contributors to the C-SPAN Survey of Presidential Leadership ranked Clinton's moral authority lowest among U.S. presidents, just behind Nixon's. But neither Clinton nor Nixon spawned the large-scale corruption that took place under U.S. presidents Grant and Warren Harding, and even Clinton did not sleep with a Mafia moll.

42. "Philosophy and timing have to come together," Condoleezza Rice told an interviewer as she briefed George W. Bush for the year 2000 elections.

43. For his part, Khrushchev counted on deception to achieve a one-sided triumph, and dismissed a Cuban suggestion to deploy the missiles openly. In a simulated replay of the Cuban missile crisis by Boston University students in February 2000 the Cuban team announced to the world in September 1962 that it had invited the USSR to deploy medium-range missiles in Cuba. Apart from the Monroe Doctrine, never part of international law, the U.S. team could not think of a justification to take firm action to remove the missiles.

44. For a more detailed exposition arising from study of the Cuban confrontation, see Clemens, *Dynamics of International Relations,* pp. 85–86.

PART TWO

The Twenty-First Century

4.

Power, Fitness, and Influence at the Cusp

Who Has What

While the Reagan Administration set its face against the "evil empire," historian Paul Kennedy warned that the United States was declining relative to other powers and would continue to do so. Like sixteenth century Spain, nineteenth century England, and the twentieth century Soviet Union, the United States suffered from global "overreach." Whenever imperial appetites and commitments exceed abilities, decline is just a matter of time. The task of U.S. leaders over the next decades, Kennedy argued in 1986, was "to 'manage' affairs so that the *relative* decline of the United States' position takes place slowly and smoothly, and is not accelerated by policies which bring merely short-term advantage but long-term disadvantage."[1] Many other "declinists" agreed with Kennedy: They pointed to America's vast military commitments, its domestic social stresses, and its exploding levels of public debt.

A decade or so after Paul Kennedy wrote *The Rise and Fall of the Great Powers,* it appeared that he was correct in one respect: The United States did not preserve its position as the

---

Box 4.1 The Breakup of
Empires in the Twentieth Century

As the twentieth century began, most great powers were seeking to expand their realms, and most Africans and Asians lived under European rule. By the end of the century most peoples had their own governments, and most Western governments focused on enhancing the economic and social welfare of their people.

Many but not all empires died in the twentieth century. Five empires perished between 1912 and 1918: China, Tsarist Russia, Austria-Hungary, Germany, Ottoman Turkey. Three empires died in World War II—those of Italy, Germany, and Japan. After World War II Europe's other great powers lost most of their overseas possessions: The Netherlands, Belgium, France, Britain, and Portugal. Britain lost Hong Kong in 1997 but retained Gibraltar, the Falklands, Diego Garcia, and other islands. Portugal transferred Macao to China in 1999—the last bit of a 500-year old empire. France and other European powers continued to exercise imperial control over distant places such as Tahiti and the Canary Islands.

Multiethnic Indonesia lost East Timor in 1999, inspiring other parts of Jakarta's empire to demand autonomy. Tamils demanded independence or at least autonomy from Sri Lanka. One of the largest empires ever, the Soviet, evaporated in 1989–1991, leaving in its wake the Russian Federation—also an empire. Serbia's empire, known as Yugoslavia, suffered a similar fate in the 1990s. Each empire suffered from a mix of internal decay and overreach. All neglected internal fitness in the quest for external greatness. These empires failed to produce value for a majority of the peoples they ruled or at home in the metropole.

The Russian Federation and People's Republic of China were also empires. Each denied independence to subject peoples struggling for national self-determination.

---

world's leading power. Instead, U.S. dominance increased. As we see from table 4.1, America's absolute strengths in 2000 were similar to those in 1990, but they improved in relation to those of other actors. How long U.S. preeminence would last was unknown. But as the century began, the U.S. economy functioned as the world dynamo while Japan, Europe, and China drifted. The Gulf War and NATO interventions in the Balkans brought to light the gaps between European and U.S. military assets. Meanwhile, Russia weakened in nearly every way.

Table 4.1 Parameters of Power, 1990–2000

	Actor	Basic Resources	Economic Power	Political Cohesion	Military Power	Brain Power	Universal Culture	International Institutions	Fitness at Home	External Fitness
1990	USA	H	H	M	H	H	H	H	M	H
After the Afghan War	USSR	H	L	L	H	M	M	M	L	M
	European Community	H	H	M	M	H	H	H	M	M
	Japan	L	H	H	M	H	L	M	H	M
	China	M	M	M	M	M	L	L	L	M
2000	USA	H	H	M	H	H	H	H	M	H
After the Gulf War, the dissolution of the USSR, and the wars in Bosnia and Kosovo	Russian Federation	H	L	L	M	M	M	M	L	M
	European Union	H	H	M	M	H	H	H	M	M
	Japan	L	H	H	M	H	M	M	H	M
	China	M	M	M	M	M	M	L	L	M
1939	USA	H	M	M	M	H	H	M	M	M
Eve of World War II	USSR	H	M	L	M	H	M	M	M	M
	Germany	M	H	H	H	H	M	M	H	H
	Britain	M	M	M	M	M	H	H	M	M
	Japan	M	M	H	M	H	L	L	M	M
	China	M	L	L	L	M	L	L	L	L
1962	USA	H	H	H	H	H	H	H	H	H
Cuban Crisis	USSR	H	M	M	H	M	M	M	M	H

(continues)

Table 4.1 (continued)

Period	Actor	Basic Resources	Economic Power	Political Cohesion	Military Power	Brain Power	Universal Culture	International Institutions	Fitness at Home	External Fitness
	European Community	M	M	M	M	M	H	H	M	M
	Japan	L	M	H	L	M	L	L	M	L
	China	M	L	M	M	L	L	L	L	L
1976	USA	H	H	M	H	H	H	H	M	H
	USSR	H	M	M	H	M	M	L	M	H
After the Vietnam War	European Community	M	H	M	M	H	H	H	H	M
	Japan	L	M	H	L	M	L	M	M	L
	China	M	L	M	M	L	L	L	L	L
1990	USA	H	H	M	H	H	H	H	M	H
	USSR	H	L	L	H	M	M	M	L	M
After the Afghan War	European Community	H	H	M	M	H	H	H	M	M
	Japan	L	H	H	M	H	L	M	H	M
	China	M	M	M	M	M	L	L	L	M

Note: H = high; M = medium; L = low strength

As the twenty-first century began, much of humanity lived in one of two domains—a zone of democratic peace, prosperity, and relative tranquility or a zone of chronic trouble and hardship.[2] The first zone included the United States, Canada, Western and much of Eastern Europe, Japan, Australia, New Zealand, and—at least for the time being—Singapore, Hong Kong, Taiwan, South Korea, and Israel. The second zone included most of Asia, Africa, and the Middle East. Parts of Latin America were closer to the first zone than to the second, but political and economic instabilities south of the U.S. border were severe and unresolved. Russia, Ukraine, Turkey, and China had a foot in each zone.

Many thousands of nonstate actors crowded the world stage. They strengthened prospects for "global governance," a scenario discussed in the next chapter. Still, states remained the most weighty actors. States formed a hierarchic structure resembling a pyramid, as suggested in figure 4.1. Each unit in the pyramid could be ranked in terms of its relative economic, military, and political-cultural power. The pyramid combined a single superpower with successive levels of great, medium, regional, and rising powers.[3] The United States was preeminent in all three kinds of power at the turn of the millennium. The great powers in the second rung were strong in two kinds of power but preeminent in none. Many regional powers such as India, Brazil, and Iran could become major or even great powers if they tapped their vast human and

Figure 4.1 The Pyramid of Power as the Twenty-first Century Began

Superpower
The United States

Great Powers
Japan, China, Germany, Russia

Major Powers
United Kingdom, France, India, Italy

Regional Powers
Argentina, Brazil, Egypt, Indonesia, Iran, Iraq, Israel, Kazakstan,
Nigeria, Pakistan, South Africa, South Korea, Taiwan, Ukraine

Potential Great or Superpower
European Union

India After 50 Years of Independence

For computer tycoons in Bangalore, socialist values gave way to the those of Silicon Valley in the 1990s.

material resources more effectively. The strengths and weaknesses of other potential powers such as Kazakstan and Brazil depended on a host of factors difficult to predict—from the price of oil to climate change.

The world's richest states at the outset of the twenty-first century were not empires but those that competed effectively in a global economy.[4]

According to the World Economic Forum in Davos, the U.S. economy in the late 1990s moved from fourth- to second-most competitive in the world—just behind the special case of Singapore.[5] Hong Kong remained near the top (third) as did Switzerland (sixth). The other two NAFTA members also moved up: Canada from eighth to fifth; and Mexico, from 33rd to 31st. Five other economies rose several ranks in the late 1990s: Taiwan (to number 4 rank); the United Kingdom (8); Netherlands (9); Ireland (10); Finland (11). Many other countries were losing competitiveness in the late 1990s. They included Japan (down to number 14); Norway (15); Malaysia (16); South Korea (22); Thailand (30); China (32); Indonesia (37);

Argentina (42); Brazil (51); and Russia (59). In the late twentieth-century Brazil, Argentina, South Korea, Malaysia, and Indonesia were referred to as Newly Industrializing Countries. After the financial and political meltdowns of the late 1990s, however, their prospects looked uncertain.

Another survey showed Denmark and Finland as the world's least corrupt countries; the United States as 18th-least corrupt—just after Ireland and Austria and just above Chile and Israel. Among leading exporting countries, U.S. exporters tied with German as ninth-least likely to pay bribes to senior government officials.[6]

The Asian financial crisis of 1998–1999 drove Thailand, Malaysia, Indonesia, and South Korea to the IMF for bailouts. Malaysian Prime Minister Datuk Seri Mahathir blamed the troubles on currency speculators—some of them Jewish—in the United States.

The United States

Let us examine U.S. assets more closely. No other country or coalition rivaled America's combined hard and soft power at the cusp of the millennium. But America's overall fitness was weakened from within.

Basic Resources.   America's physical setting, resources, and distance from potential foes were unmatched. But critics worried that Americans had become complacent about the need to conserve energy and harness renewable energy. The United States accounted for 25 percent of the world's energy use—consuming 30 percent more energy than it produced. A myopic President Clinton in March 2000 said he might tap the U.S. strategic oil reserve if other options failed to reduce prices—still far below those of the late 1970s. Americans complained about paying more than $1.50 per gallon for gasoline, but Europeans had long paid several times that amount.

Until about 1970 the United States had been the world's leading oil producer, but it then fell to second or third place. In A.D. 2000 the United States produced nearly three-fourths of its total energy and met half its own petroleum requirements. The United States produced nearly twice as much energy as China and one-third more than Russia. But U.S. energy imports were rising as the century ended—up more than 4 percent just in 1998, with most of the increase due to oil products. OPEC countries provided half of U.S. petroleum imports.[7]

The United States in 2000 imported more than 75 percent of 28 nonfuel minerals it used. China was a major source for nine minerals, from arsenic to yttrium. Russia was the leading source of palladium and the fourth major source of platinum (after South Africa, the UK, and Germany); the second major source of potash (after Canada); and the second major source of tungsten (which Americans bought also from China, Germany, and Bolivia).[8]

But mutual dependence was a fact of life for most countries. America depended on imports much less than Japan or Europe, both of which imported most of their oil. Japan imported not only such basic resources as iron ore, coal, and oil but also fuel for its nuclear reactors. Americans were phasing out nuclear power in the early twenty-first century while a less self-reliant Japan—despite its "nuclear allergy"—planned to build some twenty new reactors. China looked far and wide for energy, hoping to pipe oil all the way from the Caspian Sea. Energy consumption in the developing countries of Asia was expected to exceed that of North America by 2020. Russia possessed abundant minerals but was short of dollars, technology, grain, and other foods. Its production of oil and gas slumped in the 1990s. The oligarchs who took over these industries stashed their profits in foreign banks instead of investing to update a decrepit infrastructure. Absent such investment, Russian oil firms had difficulty tapping the oil reserves beneath permafrost, in offshore deposits, and in wells flooded and abandoned in Soviet times.

Economic Strength.   At the onset of the twenty-first, as for most of the twentieth century, the United States produced more than one-fifth of the world's goods and services. After World War II the United States produced nearly half the world's GDP. As Europe and Japan recovered from World War II, America's share of GDP declined. Still, as the twenty-first century began, some 4 percent of the world's population—less than one-twentieth of humanity—produced and consumed nearly one-fourth of its wealth! America's economy was nearly twice the size of Japan's and four times Germany's. The combined European Union had a larger population and produced more than the United States, but of single countries, only China displayed a capacity to overtake the United States in total GDP in the foreseeable future.

Measured in what they could buy ("real" GDP), average per capita incomes in the United States exceeded those in all other countries except for a few oil exporters. In A.D. 2000 the United States had the lowest inflation and lowest unemployment of any large industrialized state. Productivity hit new records, thanks in part to computerization of the work place.

The U.S. federal budget in the late 1990s equaled one-twentieth of world GDP. In Fiscal Year 1999 net budget outlays exceeded $1.7 trillion. The key items relevant to internal and external fitness included:

- Social Security Administration $420 billion
- Health and Human Services Department $360 billion
- Interest on public debt paid by Treasury Dept. $354 billion
- Defense Department $261 billion
- Veterans Affairs Department $43 billion
- Department of Education[9] $33 billion
- Intelligence (estimated) $29 billion
- Energy Department $16 billion
- National Aeronautics and Space Administration $14 billion
- International military and economic assistance $10 billion
- Environmental Protection Agency $7 billion
- State Department $5 billion
- National Science Foundation $3 billion

As Richard N. Gardner showed in *Foreign Affairs* (July/August 2000), only one percent of the federal budget (more than $1.8 trillion in FY 2000) went to the nonmilitary aspects of foreign policy. Funding for the State Department and foreign economic assistance had declined since the 1980s—leaving U.S. embassies understaffed and poorly equipped for global-age diplomacy and were vulnerable to terrorist attacks. The reductions reflected Congressional disdain for world affairs but were also part of a broad effort to cut deficit spending. Interest payments on the federal debt in the late 1990s exceeded 20 percent of the total—up from 10 percent in the 1970s. The debt burden pressured the government to cut back on discretionary spending so as not to add to interest payments.

The federal government had often run budget deficits. It did so to pay for the War of Independence; the War of 1812; the recession of 1837; the Civil War; the depression of the 1890s; the New Deal; World Wars I and II; the Vietnam War; and the arms buildup of the early 1980s.

Government became a major player in economic and social life in the 1930s. As a share of GDP, the federal budget increased from less than 5 percent in the 1920s to more than 10 percent during the New Deal; soared to over 40 percent during World War II; declined and then reached 20 percent during the Korean War; declined a little in mid-1950s; kept to a range between 19 and 25 percent after 1959; peaked again at 25 percent under President Reagan, and stayed at 21 percent in the mid-1990s.

Between 1945 and the late 1990s the yearly U.S. federal budget usually showed a deficit. The budget deficit grew as government outlays exceeded tax collections. Accumulating over the years, the annual deficits generated the national debt. Thanks to President Reagan's arms buildup and tax cuts, the debt doubled between 1980 and 1986—from less than $1 trillion to more than $2 trillion. By 1998 it had nearly trebled again—to more than $5.5 trillion—a burden exceeding $20,000 for every U.S. citizen—and more than half the value of current GDP.

In the early 1980s the United States became the world's largest debtor. As investors lost confidence in the dollar, it weakened. A dollar traded for barely 100 Japanese yen in the mid-1990s compared to more than 200 in the early 1980s. As a fraction of GDP, however, the U.S. deficit in the mid-1990s was only 2 percent—the same as in Japan, and much less than in the United Kingdom (7 percent of GDP) or Italy (10 percent).

When America's economic growth picked up after 1996, the budget deficit shrank and then disappeared. In Fiscal Year 1998 the federal budget enjoyed a surplus—the first time since 1969. And in FY 1999 the surplus doubled to $123 billion or 1.4 percent of GDP. In 1999–2000 the dollar again exceeded 100 yen. Europe's new currency, the euro, started life higher than the dollar but soon fell to below parity with the dollar.

Besides a budget deficit, the United States in the 1980s and 1990s ran a large trade deficit—the imbalance between the value of imports and exports. The trade deficit approached $300 billion in A.D. 2000—thanks to huge imbalances with China and Japan.

Americans imported more office equipment than they sold; Boeing sold fewer planes; American consumers splurged while those in Asia and Europe held back.

The trade deficit in 2000 amounted to some 4 percent of GDP—more than the narrowly defined Pentagon budget. The U.S. economy depended far less on world trade than the Japanese or German. This was a mixed blessing, since trade can bring wealth but also dependency. Imports helped keep down inflation; ease demand for labor in a tight job market; and slow GDP growth. But some economists worried that financing the trade imbalance could become unsustainable. The dollar could weaken; interest rates rise; and expansion stop. In late 1999–early 2000 leading Japanese mutual funds were pulling their investments from U.S. markets and investing more in Japan.[10]

The U.S. budget and trade deficits fed the image of a declining hegemon spending beyond its means, but this was misleading. America's total public debt in 1998 was 57 percent of its GDP (and declining)—less than the debt/GDP ratio elsewhere. In Italy the public debt was 120 percent of GDP; in Belgium, 116; Greece, 106; Japan, 100; Canada, 90; France, 67; Germany, 63; Denmark, 59; the same as the UK, 57, but more than Switzerland, 48, or Taiwan, zero.[11]

The United States had the means to fund public goods if it chose to do so. Many budget cutters failed to distinguish between spending for today and investing for the future. Borrowing to spend today can burden future generations; borrowing to *invest* in infrastructure, health, and education can benefit future generations. Was there some residue of Puritanism that blinded Americans to this distinction?

Clinton wanted to use most of the surplus in FY 2000 to reduce the federal debt, but he also wanted to invest some of it in health and education; Republicans favored radical tax cuts. A balance was needed between debt reduction that could reduce burdens on later generations, and investments that could benefit them.

Political Cohesion.   Despite the country's rising GDP, the 1990s were not boon years for political cohesion in the United States. Many Americans turned their backs on politics—national as well as foreign. Liberals despised Newt Gingrich and Jesse Helms Republicans; the Christian Coalition condemned liberals. People of many stripes disliked Clinton's words and deeds, the budget impasses that paralyzed Washington from time to time, and campaign financing.

Foreign policy suffered from ideological polarization. Conservatives who opposed Clinton on many grounds utilized the abortion issue to block his policies at the United Nations.

More Americans "bowled alone."[12] Not many voted. Few of the brightest ran for public office. Only the richest or those backed by special interests could afford television time. The U.S. Army TV slogan "Be All That You Can Be" was dropped because it did not generate sufficient enlistments.

The rising tide of globalization added to the cacophony of opinions regarding U.S. foreign policy. Since external threats were diminished, particular interests rather than the "national interest" could claim primacy. Since global forces affected life across the United States, foreign policy could no longer be dominated by an "establishment" based between Washington, New York, and Cambridge. Some observers were happy to say good-bye to the "wise men" who had dominated U.S. foreign policy since World War II.[13] Centers of international studies became stronger across the country,

Service pay often had to cover a spouse and children. Would enlistments increase if volunteers knew that their families might qualify for food stamps?

many with an eye to regional concerns—for example, Latin America in Miami; the Pacific rim in San Diego.

The growing ethnic and cultural complexity of the U.S. population also shaped foreign policy. Cuban refugees played a large role not just in Florida but in hemispheric politics. Other Hispanics in California, New Mexico, and Texas raised their voices on immigration and NAFTA as well as on language issues. Some Chinese refugees demanded that Washington be more vigilant about human rights in China.

It was both an asset and a liability that "national identity" in the United States hinged far more on shared ideals than common ethnicity. The presence of more people from non-European cultures added variety to the American mosaic. In principle, they helped the descendants of white Europeans to understand better the Qu'ran and Ramayana. But some observers worried that, awash in multiculturalism, Americans were losing their cultural roots.[14] More new arrivals had ties to Bogota or Bangalore than to Berlin, Bruges, or Boston (England). Most had less occasion to be steeped in the values of the Renaissance, Reformation, and Enlightenment than European immigrants. Even the primacy of English was questioned. Hispanics and others wanted the U.S. government to use and to subsidize their language—sparking a countermovement to make English the one "official" tongue.[15]

Fragmentation resulted also from new philosophical-literary fads. Deconstructionists tore apart once-sacred texts. Feminists and others bemoaned traditions made by "dead white males." Bill Clinton in 1993–1994 seemed to regard gay rights as the most pressing problem in the Armed Forces. Bits and bytes of news on computer screens added to cultural erosion. Why read books by dead people— white or otherwise—or quality newspapers when the latest stock prices, news headlines, and hit recordings could be accessed with a mouse click?

While the chattering classes chattered, racial tensions remained strong—abetted by increasing waves of Latino and Asian immigrants. Thousands of self-styled "patriots" armed to protect white supremacy. Many wanted to attack a government that, they asserted, had sold out to the United Nations. Exploiting e-mail and the web, hate groups became larger, better informed, and more deadly. One or more "patriots" blew up a government building in Oklahoma City, killing hundreds.

The end of the Cold War left Americans uncertain where and when to risk U.S. lives abroad. Without a clear and obvious danger from Russia or some other foreign foe, many Americans seemed to know and care less about international relations than in previous decades.

But the nature of public and elite opinion was in flux. In the late 1990s a much larger share of the American public saw a wide range of possible threats to U.S. interests as "critical" than did a cross-section of U.S. leaders. These threats ranged from international terrorism to global warming to economic competition from Japan. Leaders, however, perceived a much stronger U.S. interest in many foreign countries—from France to South Korea—than did the general public.[16]

Presidential leadership remained the essential element in molding public opinion regarding such cases as Somalia and Bosnia.[17] When President Clinton said that Kosovo counted, he got broad support; when he remained nearly silent on East Timor and on Chechnya, few strong voices cried out for more U.S. intervention. Still, a claim that public opinion is "clay, made to be shaped by pres-

Not all Americans worried about resources and the environment.

idential leadership backed by the Congress" exaggerated and even distorted the reality.[18]

Military.   In the early twenty-first century the United States and Russia were the only states with thousands of nuclear warheads; the British, Chinese, French, and Israeli arsenals numbered in the hundreds. American forces were downsized in the 1990s, but the U.S. deterrent stood on three strong legs—more than 315 long-range bombers; 701 intercontinental ballistic missiles (ICBMs); and 464 submarine-launched ballistic missiles (SLBMs) with multiple warheads. These systems were well maintained.[19] The trends in U.S. strategic force structure and numbers of strategic warheads are shown in table 4.2 and figure 4.2.

Figure 4.3 shows a large rise in capital outlays for the Air Force strategic forces in the mid-1980s. In the mid- and late 1990s, however, aggregate capital and operating costs for U.S. strategic forces leveled off at less than $10 billion per year.

Even after downsizing, Russia retained a somewhat larger number of ICBMs and SLBMs than the United States, but fewer long-range

Table 4.2 U.S. Strategic Forces, 1994–2002

	FY 1994	FY 1995	FY 1996	FY 1997	FY 1998	FY 1999	FY 2000	FY 2001	FY 2002
Land-Based ICBMs									
Minuteman II (1 warhead each) plus Minuteman III (up to 3 warheads each)	625	535	530	530	500	500	500	500	500
Peacekeeper (10 warheads each)	50	50	50	50	50	50	50	50	50
Heavy Bombers									
B-52	64	74	56	56	56	56	56	56	56
B-1	84	60	60	60	70	74	80	82	82
B-2	3	6	9	10	12	13	16	16	16
Submarine-Launched Ballistic Missiles									
Poseidon (C-3) and Trident (C-4) missiles on pre–Ohio-class submarines	48	0	0	0	0	0	0	0	0
Trident (C-4 and D-5) missiles on Ohio-class submarines	336	360	384	408	432	432	432	432	432

Source: U.S. Department of Defense in 2000.

Figure 4.2 Strategic Forces: Air Force and Navy Bombers and Missile Warheads, 1980–2000

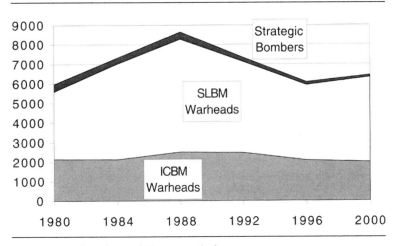

Source: Institute for Defense and Disarmament Studies

Figure 4.3 Strategic Force Funding by Service, 1980–2000 FY 1990 Through 2007 (constant $B, FY 2000 price)

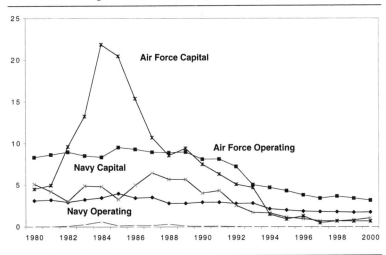

Source: Institute for Defense and Disarmament Studies

bombers—just 74. Its most reliable deterrent was ICBMs. Russia deployed ten or twenty new *Topol*-M2 ICBMs in the late 1990s, but much of its nuclear arsenal was deteriorating from age and poor care. Unpaid electric bills sometimes led to power outages at missile bases.

The START 2 agreement, conditionally ratified by the Duma in 2000, obliged Moscow and Washington by the year 2007 to reduce their arsenals of strategic nuclear warheads to 3,000 (for Russia) and 3,500 (for the United States). As shown in table 4.3, neither country could deploy more than 1,750 warheads on SLBMs.

However, there was no treaty constraint on substrategic ("tactical") nuclear weapons, of which Russia still had more than 10,000. Russia's new strategic doctrine (both the 1997 and 2000 versions) allowed for first-use of nuclear weapons to make up for Russia's weaknesses in conventional forces. The United States had withdrawn most of its tactical nuclears from Europe and from all naval ships. It preferred to fight with nonnuclear, precision-guided munitions. One could imagine contingencies when Washington might find it expedient to use tactical nuclear weapons, but the expected public outcry and other consequences made this unlikely.[20]

In 1999 China had 15 to 20 ICBMs; more than 60 intermediate-range missiles; and one submarine with twelve missiles; the UK had 48 SLBMs; France, 64 SLBMs and 60 Mirage aircraft

Table 4.3 Reductions in U.S. Strategic Nuclear Arsenal Force Levels

	FY 1990	FY 2000	START I (December 5, 2001)	START II (December 31, 2007)
ICBMs	1,000	550	550	500
Attributed Warheads on ICBMs	2,450	2,000	Not over 2,000	500
SLBMs	568	432	Not over 432	336
Attributed Warheads on SLBMs	4,864	3,456	Not over 3,456	Not over 1,750
Ballistic Missile Submarines	31	18	Not over 18	14
Attributed Warheads on Ballistic Missiles	7,314	5,456	Not over 4,900	Not over 2,250
Heavy Bombers	324	113	95	95

Source: U.S. Department of Defense in 2000.

with air-to-surface missiles. Israel had a small but powerful nuclear deterrent. India and Pakistan also had some nuclear weapons and delivery systems.

No other country besides the United States had large conventional forces, able to fight anywhere on short notice. To deploy a sizeable force in the Persian Gulf in 1979 would have required three months; in 1991, three weeks; in 1995, three days—thanks in part to prepositioned equipment and some twenty ships stationed in or near the Persian Gulf. No other country had even one U.S.-style aircraft carrier group, but the United States had eleven plus one in reserve.

By comparison, in A.D. 2000 the European members of NATO had difficulty conducting operations outside their borders—even in the nearby Balkans. Russia's air- and sea-lift capability declined in the 1990s. China still lacked amphibious forces even to attack Taiwan. In 2000 China purchased a missile-firing frigate from Russia that could damage if not sink a U.S. aircraft carrier. China also considered buying one rusting Russian aircraft carrier to flaunt in the South China Sea.

The next three figures show the total number of Russian, Chinese, and U.S. warships, battle tanks, and combat aircraft from 1972 to 2010, based on current evidence. But total numbers hide qualitative

Figure 4.4 Naval Ships, 1972–2010 (Russia, PRC, USA)

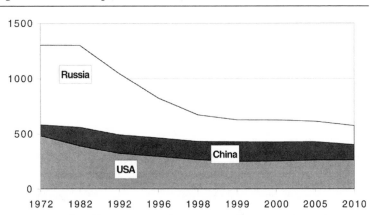

Source: Institute for Defense and Disarmament Studies in 2000.

Figure 4.5 Main Battle Tanks, 1972–2010 (Russia, PRC, USA)

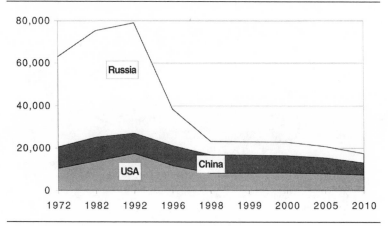

Source: Institute for Defense and Disarmament Studies in 2000.

differences. Thus, figure 4.7 reveals that most Chinese aircraft are quite old—Soviet MiG or Sukhoi models dating from earlier decades. Russian equipment is poorly maintained and few Russian ships are at sea. Another difference is that U.S. pilots and other forces train much more intensively than those of most other countries.

The American military benefited from continuing advances in C⁴ISR four C's—command, control, communications, and computer processing and ISR—intelligence collection, surveillance, and reconnaissance. These technologies sought to gather, sort, process, and display information in real time about complex events occurring in all kinds of weather over wide areas. Such technologies were becoming widely available through commercial sources. But the United States led in coordinating them in a system of systems—the kind that facilitated the use of precision force during the Gulf War and kept U.S. casualties low.

The bills for C4ISR were not trivial—nearly $16 billion in operating costs per year in the 1990s (figure 4.9) and more than $7 billion for research and development, testing and evaluation (figure 4.11). Besides these outlays, the country spent an estimated $29 billion on intelligence gathering and analysis by the National Security Agency and Central Intelligence Agency.

Figure 4.6 Combat Aircraft, 1972–2010 (Russia, PRC, USA)

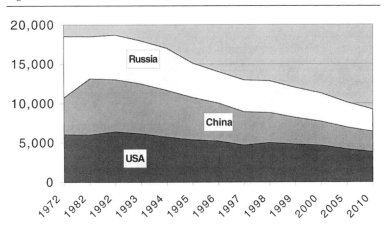

Source: Institute for Defense and Disarmament Studies in 2000.

Figure 4.7 China Numbers vs. Technology: The Case of Combat Aircraft

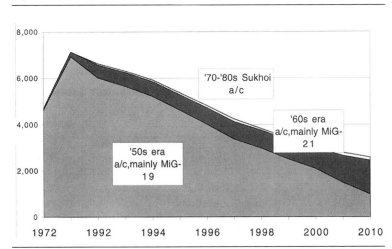

Source: Institute for Defense and Disarmament Studies in 2000.

Figure 4.8 A System of Systems for Battlefield Operations

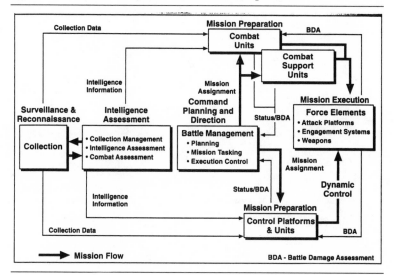

Source: U.S. Department of Defense in 2000.

Figure 4.9 C⁴ISR Operating Costs (Aggregated), 1980–2000 (constant $B)

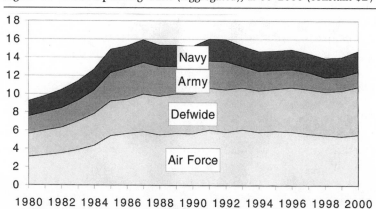

Source: Institute for Defense and Disarmament Studies in 2000.

Figure 4.10 Intelligence and Communications RDT&E, 1980–2001 ($B)

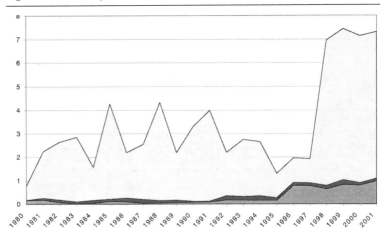

Source: Institute for Defense and Disarmament Studies in 2000.

The blend of quantity and quality in U.S. forces was unrivaled, but the country's vulnerability was increasing. The United States could attack and deter others but had weak or no defenses against the missiles, airplanes, bombs, poison gas sprays, bacteriological agents, or the truck and suitcase bombs of major powers, rogue states, and nonstate terrorists.

In A.D. 2000 Pentagon expenditures exceeded the combined military outlays of the other eight leading industrial powers. Still, President Clinton proposed to increase spending for defense by $112 billion for the period 2000–05, reversing years of decline. Of this amount, $37 billion would go for pay increases and other outlays meant to recruit and retain personnel. As table 4.4 shows, the Navy and Air Force received more of the pie than the Army.

Procurement of more modern weapons was set to reach nearly $62 billion in 2001. The biggest outlays were for air capability modernization, centered on the Joint Strike Fighter. The 509th Bomber Wing acquired its twentieth B-2 bomber in 2000—at $1.3 billion per aircraft. The army was upgrading its Abrams tank and *Bradley* fighting vehicle. The navy was procuring new destroyers, docking

Table 4.4 U.S. Department of Defense Budget Authority by Component (in millions of constant FY2001 dollars)

	FY1985	FY1990	FY1996	FY1997	FY1998	FY1999	FY2000	FY2001
Army	116,028	104,469	73,195	71,500	69,435	72,229	71,471	70,569
Navy	149,975	130,061	89,348	87,196	86,476	88,374	89,861	91,688
Air Force	148,653	120,608	81,716	80,169	81,616	86,036	83,754	85,298
Defense Agencies/ OSD/JCS	20,342	23,788	24,280	24,072	24,733	25,445	24,914	25,297
Defense-wide	1,391	3,607	15,936	19,479	14,923	20,478	17,843	18,234
Total, Constant $	436,390	382,533	284,475	282,416	277,184	292,562	287,843	291,087
% Real Growth								
Army	13.2	-2.2	-0.5	-2.3	-2.9	4.0	-1.1	-1.3
Navy	16.0	-0.6	1.7	-2.4	-0.8	2.2	1.7	2.0
Air Force	11.5	-4.5	-3.4	-1.9	1.8	5.4	-2.7	1.8
Defense Agencies/ OSD/JCS	17.6	-1.1	3.3	-0.9	2.7	2.9	-2.1	1.5
Defense-wide	-95.1	28.9	-29.1	22.2	-23.4	37.2	-12.9	2.2
Total	6.3	-2.1	-2.6	-0.7	-1.9	5.5	-1.6	1.1

Source: U.S. Department of Defense in 2000.

ships, and nuclear-powered attack submarines. The ninth and last *Nimitz* class aircraft carrier was to be delivered in 2003. A new type of aircraft carrier was not expected to enter service before 2015.

Actual military outlays in A.D. 2000 totaled some $480 billion—more than any other budget category—and amounted to more than 5 percent of GDP. Besides Defense Department outlays of $261 billion, other military expenditures included: veterans, $43 billion; intelligence, $29 billion; half of Energy Department outlays, $8 billion; half of NASA, $7 billion; half of international assistance, $5 billion; and half the interest on the national debt (resulting from previous wars and arms buildups)—$127 billion. Beyond these actual outlays by the federal government, there were other costs: disruption in the work place when reservists and National Guard units were called to active duty for months at a time; stress on families from poor accommodations on and near military bases; psychological and physical trauma for family members of those killed or wounded in military service. These costs easily raised the share of "defense" to more than 6 percent of GDP.

The Pentagon's guiding rationale in the 1990s was that the United States needed the ability—without allies if need be—to prevail in two medium-sized regional wars at the same time (for example, against Iraq and North Korea), while conducting a major peacekeeping or humanitarian operation. In 1997 the Pentagon's *Quadrennial Defense Review* said the U.S. military should be able to respond to current crises; it should also shape the strategic environment and prepare for the future, especially the emergence of a new peer rival. Former Defense Secretary William J. Perry and his colleague Ashton B. Carter urged the Pentagon to give more emphasis to "shaping" by what they termed "preventive defense."[21]

But many of the weapons still being purchased in the late 1990s, such as B-2 bombers, looked like they were meant for the "last war"—a potential strike against Russia. Many tanks and helicopters being produced were too large, heavy, and valuable to be used against third-rate foes in the Balkans.

Were the U.S. Armed Forces ready for two regional wars and a major peacekeeping or humanitarian mission? Table 4.5 and figure 4.11 show the decline in U.S. military personnel in the 1980s–1990s.

In A.D. 2000 the U.S. Army active duty force numbered 479,000 men and women, but two of its ten divisions classified themselves as

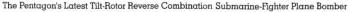

The Pentagon's Latest Tilt-Rotor Reverse Combination Submarine-Fighter Plane Bomber

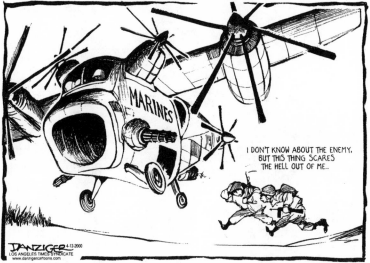

The Pentagon sought cutting-edge machinery

unready for war because so many of their troops were committed to Bosnia and Kosovo. Given its many tasks, the Army drew heavily on the 564,000 members of its National Guard and Reserve. Of 150,000 troops that served in Bosnia from 1995 to 2000, some 33,000—22 percent—belonged to the Guard or the Reserve. Nearly one in four of the forces that served in Kosovo (10,016 of 46,160) came from reserve units. In Haiti the ratio was nearly one in three (8,100 of 23,400). Forces engaged in fighting or monitoring Iraq since the Gulf War numbered 193,884—of which more than 19,000 came from reserve units. In A.D. 2000 the Army pledged to restrict overseas deployments of such units to six months.[22]

All this gave grist to debate by strategic and policy analysts: whether U.S. defense spending was too high or too low; whether the allocation of resources among different defense missions was prudent; whether the United States should invest more in the non-military dimensions of security, such as the environment.[23] A related question: Was it wise to allow women to serve in combat units?

Table 4.5 U.S. Department of Defense Military and Civilian Personnel (in thousands)

	FY 1989	FY 1992	FY 1994	FY 1996	FY 1998	FY 2000	FY 2001
Active Component							
Army	769.7	611.3	541.3	491.1	483.9	480.0	480.0
Navy	592.7	541.9	468.7	416.7	382.3	371.8	371.3
Marine Corps	197.0	184.6	174.2	174.9	173.1	172.1	172.0
Air Force	570.9	470.3	426.3	389.0	367.5	360.9	354.4
Total	2130.2	1808.1	1610.5	1471.7	1406.8	1384.8	1377.7
Reserve Component Military (Selected Reserve)							
Army National Guard	457.0	426.5	369.9	370.0	370.0	350.0	350.0
Army	319.2	302.9	259.9	226.2	205.0	205.0	205.0
Naval	151.5	142.3	107.6	98.0	93.2	90.3	89.6
Marine Corps	43.6	42.3	40.7	42.1	40.8	39.6	39.5
Army National Guard	116.1	119.1	113.6	110.5	108.1	106.6	160.7
Air Force	83.2	81.9	79.6	73.7	72.0	73.7	73.9
Total	1170.6	1114.9	9971.3	920.4	881.5	865.2	864.7
Civilian							
Army	401.5	364.5	289.5	258.6	232.5	219.9	216.4
Navy/Marine Corps	350.2	319.5	276.5	239.9	207.6	199.5	192.2
Air Force	258.6	215.0	196.6	182.6	172.8	162.6	161.6
DoD Agencies	97.1	139.4	154.0	137.6	118.0	118.4	114.3
Total	1107.4	1038.4	916.5	818.7	730.9	700.2	684.5

Source: U.S. Department of Defense in 2000.

Figure 4.11 U.S. Land Forces: Army and Marine Division Equivalents, 1980–2000

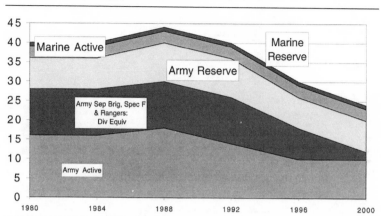

Source: Institute for Defense and Disarmament Studies in 2000.

Brain Power. America's intellectual resources were strong but uneven. U.S. scientists and economists won more than half of Nobel prizes in chemistry, physics, medicine, and economics (and more than their share in literature and peace). As the twentieth century ended, however, an increasing share of researchers in the United States were foreign born. A dwindling number of American-born scholars pursued advanced study in science or mathematics.

Public outlays for science were critical to wealth and health as well as to military strength. America's preeminence in world science was due in part to a federally funded science-and-technology establishment. In science, as in other fields, Japan, Europe, and other regions were catching up.

In the 1990s U.S. government spending on research and development was declining, but privately financed R&D was increasing. But while industrial researchers spent more dollars than those funded by government and private foundations, patents for inventions in all fields credited publicly funded science far more than they did industrial. The Internet, for example, was a spin-off of Defense Department research.[24]

Figure 4.12 shows the downward trend in U.S. government-sponsored research by the Defense Department, NASA, National Institutes

Figure 4.12 Investment in Research and Development for FY 1981
            Through FY 2002 in Constant 1992 Dollars ($Billions)

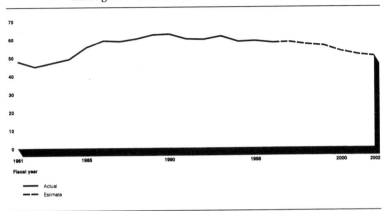

Source: Budget Trends: Federal Investment Outlays, Fiscal Years, 1981–2002 (Washington, D.C.: U.S. General Accounting Office, May 1997).

of Health, the Department of Energy, and other agencies. Outlays for R&D in constant dollars increased from $48 billion in 1981 to $63 billion in 1990 and then decreased to an estimated $50 billion in 2002.

While American public school students held their own in science and reading, they lagged behind those of other industrialized countries in mathematics. More than one-third of Americans aged 25 to 65 graduated from college, but many others were functionally illiterate. The country's foremost educator—television—glorified consumerism, violence, sexism, and promiscuity.

U.S. government outlays for education and training (by the Departments of Labor, Veterans Affairs, and Education) declined sharply in the early 1980s and then remained flat at about $30 billion through 1990. They were expected to exceed $40 billion by 2002. The trend is sketched in figure 4.13.

Despite the shortfalls of U.S. schools, the country's greatest comparative advantage in A.D. 2000 was its leadership in the information revolution. Thanks to Cold War investments and to America's open society, the United States stood at the cutting edge of communications and information processing technologies. This leadership was a force multiplier of both hard and soft power. It un-

Figure 4.13 Investment in Education and Training for FY 1981 Through FY 2002 in Constant 1992 Dollars ($Billions)

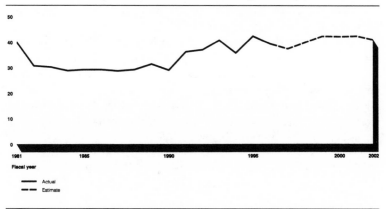

Source: Budget Trends: Federal Investment Outlays, Fiscal Years, 1981–2002 (Washington, D.C.: U.S. General Accounting Office, May 1997).

derlay military prowess and enhanced the soft power attraction of democracy and free markets.[25]

If the United States shared some information, this could add to soft power leadership. Information gathered by U.S. reconnaissance was shared not just with allies (as in the 1982 Falklands conflict between the UK and Argentina) but with the United Nations Special Commission and the International Atomic Energy Agency, helping and pushing both agencies to intensify and broaden their respective investigations in North Korea and Iraq.

America's lead in technology and its domination in pop culture intertwined. Music and image merged with the medium. For most of the century, English was the world's lingua franca for commerce and science. At the end of the century, English ruled the Internet.

Fitness at Home.   America's domestic fitness did not equal its material assets. At century's end public goods got less funding than in earlier decades. School buildings, bridges, and public transportation cried out for new investment. Scientific research and funding for the arts were cut back. Welfare programs were in flux.

U.S. government spending on physical assets (federally funded highways, airport facilities, research facilities for the Department of Energy and NASA) was relatively stable from 1980 to 1995 and then declined, as shown in figure 4.14.

The president's Council of Economic Advisers brought him good news for most of the 1990s. If the president also had a Council of Social Advisers, it would have reported at the end of the century that the country's social health was improving in some ways, for example, fewer homicides and fewer babies born to unwed mothers; also, declining rates of infant and maternal mortality. But social health was deteriorating in many ways:

- The income gap between America's rich and poor expanded in the 1980s and 1990s, exceeding that in any Western country, Japan, or Taiwan.
- More American babies died in their first year and more American children were deprived than those in most other industrialized countries. A larger share of American children lived below the poverty line than in most industrial democracies, and their disposable income was far less than comparable children elsewhere.[26]

Figure 4.14 Investment in Physical Assets for FY 1981 Through FY 2002 in Constant 1992 Dollars ($Billions)

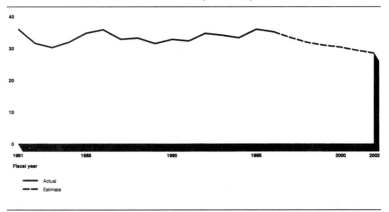

Source: Budget Trends: Federal Investment Outlays, Fiscal Years, 1981–2002 (Washington, D.C.: U.S. General Accounting Office, May 1997).

- Suicide rates among young people were 36 percent higher in 1998 than in 1970 and nearly triple the rate in 1950.
- Income disparities were at their third worst level in fifty years. More than 41 million Americans lacked health insurance.
- Violent crime remained almost double the level in 1970, despite a decline in the 1990s.
- Average wages for workers fell sharply since the early 1970s. The number of children living poverty was up by one-third since 1970.[27]
- America's prison population increased to nearly 2 million by 1999 (25 percent of the *world's* prisoners!)—a 42 percent increase over 1990—and included a huge fraction of young black males.

Could even a well-endowed country remain a superpower if racial and class cleavages multiplied? When guns ruled some streets and schools? When more than a third of its people were obese? When ever more citizens distrusted their own government?

Fitness in the World.   Despite its many problems, the United States dominated world affairs as the twenty-first century began. Except for the British Empire, no other country had ever towered so over the entire globe. It drew on the affinity of others for U.S. culture and on the compatibility of U.S. and international institutions. The Roman, Ottoman, and Mongolian empires were large but bounded. Most other hegemons exercised a direct rule based on commands and coercion. None inspired statues to the goddess of liberty in far-away places—as in China in 1989. Not even the British Empire could rely so heavily on consensus and cooption across the planet.

None of the great powers approached the lone superpower's overall assets, but each had regional and global strengths. All faced the fundamental challenge of complexity theory: How to achieve a flexible and creative fitness between the poles of rigid order and anarchy.

Japan

Recovering from World War II, Japan became a model "trading state," exporting far more than it imported. In the final decades of the twentieth century Japan's GDP was second only to America's. Japan's economy, education, and social cohesion were strong. Japanese nationals lived longer than most other peoples, even though Japan's consumers received less protection than their Western counterparts.[28] Shielded by the U.S. nuclear umbrella, Japan conquered markets rather than foreign territories.[29] Japan invested about one percent of GDP on its "Self-Defense Forces" and another one percent in support of U.S. forces stationed in Japan. Just this sliver of Japan's wealth yielded the world's third- or fourth-largest military budget.

After decades of growth, Japan's economy stalled in the 1990s, and the ruling party lost its grip. In the late 1990s, however, Japan underwent many changes. Some observers said that Japan resembled the United States a decade before, when businesses made painful changes and workers' real incomes fell. Confident that the reduction by Japanese firms of their excess capacity, labor, and debts would rekindle economic growth, the Japanese stock market rose in 1999. Despite government cheer-leading and public works outlays, however, Japanese consumers proved reluctant to resume their erstwhile free-spending ways.

Despite its economic clout, Japan's external influence was curtailed by its inward-looking culture; dependency on the United States; a post–1945 allergy to militarism; and neighbors' fears of revived Japanese imperialism. Critics said that Japanese dynamism suffered from a monoculture and from hedonism. Japanese firms sent bright young people to MIT to become innovators, but their creativity wilted when they returned home. The country's pampered youth refused to work like and for their elders.

Germany

In A.D. 2000 Germany was strong in most respects except military power. Its population and GDP were Europe's largest but less than one-third of America's. Domestic cohesion was strained by the burdens of integrating East and West Germany; discontent over "guest workers" and political refugees; high unemployment, which reached over 20 percent in the provinces of former East Germany. A corruption scandal pulled the props from under the Christian Democratic Union in 1999–2000, but led to a double revolution: A woman from the former East Germany became CDU leader.

The European Union

As the twenty-first century began, the European Union (EU) had great economic power and internal fitness but modest influence abroad. The EU countries had a larger population and GDP than the United States. The EU pioneered the "common marketization" of international relations—downgrading security/sovereignty issues while cooperating in a single trading bloc. Despite much talk and some action, however, the EU still had no common military or foreign policy. EU members denounced Austria's government for including Jörg Haider's right-wing Freedom Party in A.D. 2000, but then debated their right to meddle in Austria's domestic affairs.

Austria's Mr. Haider Explains the Freedom Party's Position

The EU resembled a troika—the strongest horse, Germany, continued to run straight ahead; the French horse pulled to the left (toward big government); the British to the right (toward less government). Both London and Paris possessed nuclear forces, but neither was willing to share them. The European "union" split on how far to expand its membership. If more countries were admitted, the consensus rule would have to be relaxed to get decisions made. If poorer countries from Eastern Europe were admitted, there would be strong pressures to increase agricultural and other subsidies. Few Europeans except business elites and a few politicians were keen on closer integration and a single currency. In 1999 there was much gnashing of teeth when the euro rapidly slid lower than the dollar.

A united Europe could be strong in most realms (though never able to match the U.S. physical setting). Would Europe remain a loose assembly of "fatherlands" or become an integrated federation? As of A.D. 2000 Europe's potential remained far from fulfilled.

Russia

Though the USSR looked fit in the 1970s, it stood on clay feet and collapsed in 1991. The Russian Federation emerged as a separate state, along with fourteen or more other independent states on its borders. But the core of the former Soviet Union, the Russian Federation, was still the world's largest country, with vast resources and a huge nuclear arsenal.

Non-Communist Russia experienced a relatively peaceful movement toward multiparty democracy in the 1990s. M. S. Gorbachev's campaigns for economic reform and glasnost' (openness) had helped prepare the country for change. But Russia's transition to multiparty politics in the 1990s fell far below any ideal mark. When not bedridden, Boris Yeltsin ruled with a strong arm. He prorogued parliament in 1993, issued a new constitution, and arranged new elections. When the Duma still did not follow Yeltsin's wishes, he ignored or bypassed it.

Russia moved toward crony capitalism rather than free enterprise. Accelerating a trend begun in the 1970s, Kremlin favorites won personal control of what had been state monopolies. Some Russians became rich in the 1990s, but most became poorer. Oil, gold, and arms were sold abroad, but industrial and agricultural production decreased. Corruption and criminality mounted. Not just bankers but reformist journalists and politicians were assassinated.

The country's internal fitness plunged. Civil society was weak. Post-Communist Russia possessed few institutions or habits to buffer ordinary citizens from the whims of government and the hurricanes of raw market forces. Russians drank more spirits (including home brew, often toxic) than before. Infant mortality continued to rise while male life expectancy fell in the 1990s from about 63 to 57 or 58.

Though Russian officials felt compelled to beg for loan extensions and sometimes for food aid in the 1990s, the Kremlin still demanded political treatment equal to that of other great powers. Russians seemed unsure of their political identity. Could they be real Russians without an empire—without control of the borderlands they now called the "near abroad"?[30] Russian bullying alienated many members of the Commonwealth of Independent States, driving several, including Kazakstan and Ukraine, into an anti-Russian alignment.

President Yeltsin appointed and fired many prime ministers in the 1990s. The last three appointees included two heads of the secret police and one minister of the interior. Ignoring the lessons of Afghanistan and international norms, the Kremlin waged a brutal and ineffective war against Chechnya in 1994–1996 and then resumed it in 1999. The near genocidal campaign against Chechens waged by Acting President V. V. Putin made him very popular among Russian voters and helped him win the presidency in the 2000 elections.

Meanwhile, the Davos World Economic Forum in 2000 ranked Russia the world's least competitive major economy—just below

Which way would Putin travel?

Ukraine, Zimbabwe, Bulgaria, Bolivia, Colombia, Ecuador, and India. Many business people rated it one of the most corrupt. President Putin, however, promised a "dictatorship of the law."

China

In the 1990s China was medium-strong in hard power but weak in soft. Its economy grew rapidly in the 1980s and 1990s, but its growth might slow or stall for many reasons. Even if China's economic growth continued at a rapid clip and overtook Japan in GDP, most Chinese would be poor compared to most Americans, Japanese, and Europeans. China's per capita income in the late 1990s did not exceed $600.

In A.D. 2000 China had the world's largest army. Its troop strength was nearly double that of Russia, India, or the United States. China also boasted a modest nuclear arsenal, including regional and intercontinental ballistic missiles and some missile-firing submarines.

China's influence fluctuated. In the late 1990s China regained Hong Kong and Macao. President Jiang Zemin received red carpet treatment in Washington. But China looked like a paper tiger when it "test"-fired missiles into the Taiwan Straits in 1996 and made threatening noises in 2000 in a vain attempts to influence Taiwan elections. When the most independence-minded candidate won Taiwan's presidency in 2000, he offered to relax ROC barriers to direct investment in China, and Beijing backed away from its threats.

China's Problems.   Still, China had multiple vulnerabilities: too many people cultivating too little land; environmental degradation; rampant corruption; discontent among Tibetans and other subject peoples; and no visible alternative to one-party dictatorship.

The very means by which China hoped to meet these problems in the twenty-first century opened up new challenges. Let us review some of them:[31]

1. The Information Age: China had to cope with revolutions not just in information technology but in agriculture and industry. How could the Chinese Communist Party (CCP) retain political dominance *and* allow the free flow of information needed for innovation? Photo-

copying helped undermine the Soviet dictatorship; how much more potent is the modem!

Most Chinese had little access to any information except what came from state-controlled media. In A.D. 2000, however, there were more than one million Internet accounts, each shared by several users. For many Chinese with access to outside resources, the gap between party line and reality widened, eroding the legitimacy of CCP rule.[32]

2. Modernization: How could a one-party dictatorship foster the application of rationality and science in social development? Subjective whim, ambition, and greed generated many major PRC decisions—for example, on the Three Gorges Dam.[33]

   A former Chinese technocrat wrote in 1998 that the country's present system could not endure because China was moving toward a crossroads where, without complete transformation, it could not continue its push toward modernization.[34] Crony capitalism engendered inefficiency as well as corruption. Loans and tax breaks given for political and personal considerations presaged economic difficulty.[35]

3. Morality-Legality. Chinese society in A.D. 2000 was no longer held together by a common ideology. Communism as well as Confucianism had been replaced by Deng Xiaoping's slogan "glorious to become rich." Even filial piety and family solidarity often gave way to rugged individualism.

   Economic hardship contributed to crime. Crime rates in the 1980s and 1990s were two or three times the magnitude of previous crime waves.[36] Gone were the old restraints of a neighborhood policing system and a regimented work-unit system. Crime waves encouraged "campaign-style policing" and human rights abuses.

   More than half a large sample of European companies investing in China complained in 1997 that corruption, unfair taxation, and other manifestations of exploitative attitudes impeded good business practice in China.[37] Transparency International in 1999 ranked

China as the 58th least honest country in the world,
tied with Belarus and Senegal. Bribery of senior officials in China was more common than in any other
major exporting country.[38]

4.   Civil Society: In A.D. 2000 virtually all social institutions were still controlled by the Communist regime.
Many nongovernmental organizations (NGOs) existed
in the economic and social arenas, but the institutional
space for politically oriented NGOs was extremely limited. The CCP did not welcome intermediate institutions that could buffer individuals from the tyrannies of
governments and raw market forces. As private owners
and managers become more important in China, workers needed trade unions or other institutions to shield
them from the tyranny of the market. Chinese workers
confronted alliances between local entrepreneurs and
local officials who collaborated not only against the
central state but also against local workers.[39]

5.   Quality of Life: How could China combine economic
growth with environmental protection and social justice? Deal humanely with its aging population? Mobilize for constructive pursuits the huge numbers of
persons arrived from the countryside in the cities and
the large numbers of high school and college graduates—at a time when state-owned industries were lay-
ing off workers?

China's leaders showed great flexibility in dealing
with such challenges, but the top-down, command system impeded an optimal response. The system inhibited
open discussion of gains and losses from alternative
courses of action. It did not tap the energies of women,
minorities, entrepreneurs, and creative thinkers.

Communist ideology encouraged a narrow realpolitik blind to the potential advantages of mutual gain.
This zero-sum outlook (what Russians called *kto
kovo*—"who will do in whom?") made it harder to cultivate mutual advantage with Taiwan, the United
States, and other rivals.

China in the early twenty-first century was less well
prepared for democracy than were the USSR and Rus-

sia, where relatively free elections were held for the Congress of People's Deputies in 1990. A multiparty system was functioning in the USSR two years before the Soviet Union ended. Yeltsin's presidency of Russia (still a republic of the USSR) dated from 1990, making him a bridge from Soviet to post-Soviet times. Many Soviet citizens were familiar with Western democracy and set out to emulate it. Very few Chinese had comparable knowledge in A.D. 2000.

China's Options.   China's future course was probably the biggest external question mark for U.S. policymakers in the early twenty-first century. Let us examine six options.

1. Communist Capitalism. The Chinese leadership in A.D. 2000 seemed to hope that it could maintain its political monopoly while promoting a more liberal economy. While China undertook sweeping economic reforms in the 1980s and 1990s, the CCP regime avoided any Gorbachev-style campaign for glasnost' or democratization. China's mass media remained under tight central control. China gave token representation to a few non-Communist parties, but permitted no real challenge to CCP hegemony. Instead, Beijing relativized or ridiculed Western concepts of human rights, emphasizing China's commitment to eliminating poverty. In the late 1990s Beijing signed the two UN human rights conventions but did not immediately ratify them. Chinese human rights activists lacked a legal anchor like that which the "Helsinki Process" gave to Soviet dissidents after 1975.[40]

2. Authoritarian Capitalism Singapore-Style. If the present system of Communist capitalism could not hold, many top CCP leaders hoped that China could follow Singapore's model of authoritarian capitalism.[41] But this model was not feasible for China. Singapore was tiny; China, huge. Singapore was urban; most of China, rural. Singapore had four major ethnic groups; China was far more diverse, with many regions and ethnic minorities at different levels of development.

Singapore resembled Hong Kong more than China as a whole. Singapore benefited from its location, but geography was cruel to China. The English language united Singaporeans more than Mandarin united Han Chinese (with their regional dialects) and non-Hans of China.

3. The Soviet Imperial Model. The Soviet system took power in Russia in 1917 and collapsed in 1991, having lasted 74 years. The world's largest state disintegrated—not with a bang but a few whimpers. Change could overtake China more quickly than the USSR, for history's horse gallops ever faster.

But China in the early twenty-first century was spared many of the problems that undermined the Soviet empire. Unlike the USSR, the PRC had never tried to outdo the United States militarily or in other ways.[42] China developed its capacity for modern technology and a modern military establishment, but without placing a dead weight on the entire economy and society.

Unlike the USSR, Communist China did not attempt to control regions much beyond realms controlled by Chinese governments for centuries. China did not expend life and treasure in a fruitless war as in Afghanistan. It did not subsidize clients (whether Czechoslovakia or Ethiopia) to keep them loyal and afloat.

Compared to Soviet leaders, Communist Chinese made a very modest commitment to leading the Third World. In the 1960s the Chinese were pleased to win accolades from Phnom Penh and Havana and from pro-Beijing splinter groups in Communist parties around the world. They welcomed kowtows from African and other foreign visitors. But Beijing never staked its political success as Moscow did on winning the devotion of foreign leaders. The Chinese were acutely aware of their material constraints and the limited influence possible by aiding others. Also, they equaled or surpassed Russians in racism and ethnocentrism. Beijing downgraded its efforts to win Third World favor and concentrated on China's internal development. But China courted overseas Chinese, attracting investors even from Taiwan.

Far more confident than Russians, the Chinese have seen their state as the Middle Kingdom, blessed with all heaven's favors and little need to rule others. Only in the late twentieth century did China see much need to trade with others. Were Beijing to lose Inner Mongolia, as Moscow lost Central Asia, most Chinese would still know who they are politically and culturally.

The upshot was that China did not suffer from imperial overreach like the former USSR. Beijing could allocate its resources more rationally than the Soviet system between domestic needs and external ambitions.

4. The Russian Model: Anarchic Capitalism. China faced a real danger that, like post-Soviet Russia, it could slide from rigidity into anarchy. China, like Russia and most former Soviet republics, lacked institutions of civil society and moral consensus to halt the drift toward chaos.[43] Should the "center" crack, there was little to take its place. Like the former USSR, Communist China had almost no institutions to mediate between the power elite and its subjects.

Weak institutions of civil society make it easier for dictatorships to keep all powers. But this weakness also renders a social system brittle; minimizes information flow and dialogue between rulers and ruled; and reduces the chances of constructive feedback. Some Chinese intellectuals and dissidents won the right to exit (for example, on the next plane to a Minneapolis hospital); but few if any enjoyed the right openly to dispute the Party line and suggest other paths.

5. Internal Dissolution. For thousands of years China's unity was challenged by regional centers. The pressures for dissolution may increase in the twenty-first century, because a dynamic society cannot rely on centralized plans and top-town direction of economic life. If society as a whole cannot "self-organize," it may break up.

Even more than the Russian Federation, China in the early twenty-first century suffered from uneven economic development. Both Russia and China had large spaces inhabited by minorities dwelling near precious mineral resources but lacking control over them and having no direct access to foreign markets. Non-Hans made up only 9 percent of the Chinese population in A.D. 2000, but many lived in the Tarim River Basin rich in oil and minerals and close to ethnic cousins in the new states of Kyrgyzstan and Kazakstan.[44] China often repressed Kazaks, Uighurs, Tibetans, and other minorities. Communization combined with the arrogant hegemony of a master ethnic group threatened physical and cultural genocide in China, as it did in the USSR/Russia and the Balkans.

But what if Kazakstan became prosperous due to its oil wealth? What if Turkic culture turned vibrant in Central Asia? The ability of Kazakstan to influence and even to intervene in Chinese Turkestan would increase. If China comes to depend on Caspian oil, the PRC will be the more vulnerable to pressures from Central Asia.

Russia in the early 1990s granted Tatarstan limited "sovereignty," an approach that could be adapted by China toward Tibetans and Uighurs. But Beijing wishes to maintain a unitary state without allowing more autonomy to its minorities. Beijing probably believes it can keep the lid on regional separatism without resorting to the full-scale wars that Moscow waged against Chechnya.

More than 90 percent of China's population is Han. But Hans speak different dialects, exhibit some cultural differences, and have very different income levels. Some Chinese—including non-Han Muslims—flourished in coastal economic zones that look outward; others languished inland where they were limited by poor resources and infrastructure and circumscribed by many restrictions. Some regions of China grew richer, pleased with the direction of life; others were poor and resentful. In southern China peasants maintained or strengthened their dialects, lineage groups, and religious cults despite official efforts to promote class consciousness and nationalism.

The more affluent rather than the poorer provinces may demand autonomy or secession. In the USSR and in Yugoslavia it was the richest units—Estonia, Latvia, Lithuania, Slovenia, Croatia—that pressed for separation. They felt exploited and retarded by the "center," and wanted greater freedom to make their way westward. But none of China's ethnic minorities is positioned so favorably as Estonians or Slovenes. In the late 1990s there were few signs that China's affluent coastal regions might seek greater autonomy or independence. But neither was there much sign in the 1970s that the Baltic peoples would soon demand—and get!—sovereignty. If Beijing increases taxes or restrictions on the rich coastal regions, if its language policy is felt to be oppressive, or if Beijing's rulers fight among themselves, centrifugal forces will probably multiply.

A regional breakup of China could pit Han against Han and non-Han against Han. Averting this tendency will not be easy. If Beijing grants the regions more freedom, they may want still more—a revolution of rising expectations. But if the center represses the regions, the periphery may become more restive. Exploitation backfires.

6. Democratic Capitalism Taiwan-Style. The sands of time were probably running out for any regime—whether in Singapore or Beijing—trying to combine authoritarian rule with economic and social modernization. Taiwan offered a model of gradual transition to meet the demands of modernization.[45] The Taiwan experience showed how an authoritarian regime can permit a gradual devolution of power—economic and political.

Unlike Russia's precipitous shift from one-party rule to anarchic capitalism, change in Taiwan was gradual. One-party rule gave way to multiparty democracy, but not overnight. Whereas the Communist Party was suddenly stripped of its privileges in the USSR and Russia, the long-time ruling party, the Guomindang, remained the dominant force in Taiwan in the 1990s. In A.D.

2000, however, its main rival, the Democratic Progressive Party, won the presidency.[46]

Taiwan's government played a large role in the economy in the second half of the twentieth century, but gradually permitted private enterprise to take control of large as well as small industries. Education and general prosperity strengthened democratic impulses. Most cabinet officers had doctorates from U.S. universities.

Taiwan was seven times more populous than Singapore in A.D. 2000, but tiny compared to mainland China. Equally or more important, divisions within Taiwan by income, region, and culture were trivial by comparison with China's. Taiwan could recognize and subsidize the cultures of ethnic minorities with no risk that they would secede.

In the 1990s many mainland Chinese—even educated youth—seemed to yearn less for democracy and more for national glory and personal wealth. Meanwhile, many Taiwanese thought less about unification and more about independence. Such sentiments would be affected by developments in Hong Kong, where, after returning to Chinese rule, many freedoms waned.

Despite these caveats, the imperatives of modernization and global interdependence could push China toward political as well as economic reform. Cross-straits exchanges would improve mutual knowledge in Taiwan and the mainland. If mainland China gravitated toward the Taiwan model, tensions between the two entities would probably recede and federation become more feasible.[47]

Chinese might learn from others and adapt foreign ways to their own needs. But whatever course the country took, China would remain stamped by the special features of its history, culture, and geography.

Competitiveness and Wild Cards

This survey of the pyramid of power touches only on a few highlights. In A.D. 2000 many countries faced choices as complex and difficult as those facing the United States, Japan, the EU, Russia, and China. Also, the world's deck was loaded with wild cards that could disrupt visible trends. Some actors would make the most of their potential while others wasted their assets. The personal qualities of individuals—their vision or blindness, heroism or cupidity, energy or sloth—would boost some countries, firms, and movements and harm others. Bad luck—an earthquake, a drought, a flood—would knock some actors to their knees—as happened to Nicaragua in 1999 and to Mozambique in 2000.

Let us consider in chapter 5 the dynamic factors that could usher in a more orderly or chaotic world by 2025.

Notes

1. Paul Kennedy, *The Rise and Fall of the Great Powers: Economic Change and Military Conflict from 1500 to 2000* (New York: Random House, 1987), p. 534.
2. *New World Coming: American Security in the 21st Century: Supporting Research and Analysis* (Washington, D.C.: The United States Commission on National Security/21st Century, 1999), p. 138.
3. See also Brian Nichiporuk, "Pivotal Power: America in the 1990s," Cambridge, Ma.: MIT Defense and Arms Control Studies Working Paper, May 1991; Joseph S. Nye, Jr., *Bound to Lead: The Changing Nature of American Power* (New York: Basic Books, 1990); for a different approach, see Lars-Erik Cederman, "Emergent Polarity: Analyzing State-Formation and Power Politics," *International Studies Quarterly*, 38, 4 (December 1994), pp. 501–533.
4. On the changing nature of power, see Thomas L. Friedman, *The Lexus and the Olive Tree: Understanding Globalization* (New York: Farrar Straus & Giroux, 1999); Richard N. Rosecrance, *The Rise of the Virtual State: Wealth and Power in the Coming Century* (New York: Basic Books, 1999). Many critics contend that the state is still the most important actor and that governments must step in to protect even the Internet from abuse.
5. The ranking takes into account assets and liabilities with respect to openness, government, finance, infrastructure, technology, labor, and institutions—for example, trust in politicians' honesty and the extent of government favoritism. See 2000 World Economic Forum, *Global Competitiveness Report* (Davos, Switzerland): www.weforum.org/rep
6. The *1999 Transparency International Corruption Perceptions Index:* www.transparency.de/documents/cpi-

7. *The World Almanac and Book of Facts 2000* (Mahwah, N.J.: Primedia, 1999), pp. 163–164.

8. *The World Almanac,* p. 132.

9. Most educational outlays came from town and state budgets and from private sources.

10. They reduced U.S. shares from 45 to 38 percent of their portfolios, increasing shares in Japanese companies to 26 percent in February 2000 from a low of 15 percent in 1998. "Managers shift funds out of US," *Financial Times,* March 1, 2000, p. 6.

11. See entries for each country in International Institute for Strategic Studies, *The Military Balance, 1999–2000* (London: Oxford University Press, 1999). These magnitudes existed earlier in the decade, as seen in E. Gerald Corrigan, "Building Blocks to Strengthen the International Financial System," *Trialogue: 48* (New York: Trilateral Commission, 1995), pp. 31–43 at 34–35.

12. Robert D. Putnam, *Bowling Alone: The Collapse and Revival of American Community* (New York: Simon & Schuster, 2000); see also Mark E. Warren, ed., *Democracy and Trust* (Cambridge, UK: Cambridge University Press, 1999).

13. Michael Clough, "Grass-Roots Policymaking: Say Good-Bye to the 'Wise Men'," *Foreign Affairs,* 73, 1 (January-February 1994), pp. 2–7.

14. James Kurth and other authors made this point in the quarterly *The National Interest.* See also Arthur M. Schlesinger, Jr. *The Disuniting of America: From Pluralism to Fragmentation* (New York: W. W. Norton, 1992).

15. Seekers of unemployment benefits in Massachusetts got instructions in more than a dozen languages.

16. Survey sponsored by the Chicago Council on Foreign Relations summarized by John E. Rielly, "Americans and the World: A Survey at Century's End," *Foreign Policy,* (Spring 1999), pp. 97–114. See also *American Public Opinion and U.S. Foreign Policy 1999* (Chicago: Chicago Council on Foreign Relations, 1999) and the Chicago Council web site www.ccfr.org

17. See essays by Catherine M. Kelleher and others in Daniel Yankelovich and I. M. Destler, eds., *Beyond the Beltway: Engaging the Public in U.S. Foreign Policy* (New York: W. W. Norton, 1994).

18. Walter A. McDougall, "America and the World at the Dawn of a New Century," *Foreign Policy Research Institute WIRE,* 7, 12 (December 1999).

19. The following analysis depends upon U.S. Department of Defense Annual Reports and the International Institute for Strategic Studies, *The Military Balance, 1999–2000* (London: Oxford University Press, 1999) and previous editions.

20. Stansfield Turner, *Caging the Genies: A Workable Solution for Nuclear, Chemical, and Biological Weapons* (Boulder, Co.: Westview, 1999), pp. 57–59.

21. Ashton B. Carter and William J. Perry, *Preventive Defense: A New Security Strategy for America* (Washington, D.C.: The Brookings Institution, 1999).

22. Steven Lee Myers, "Army to Shorten Tours of Reserves Serving Overseas," *The New York Times,* March 5, 2000, pp. 1, 20.

23. See, for example, Carl Conetta and Charles Knight, "Post–Cold War US Military Expenditures in the Context of World Spending Trends"; Conetta, "Commentary on the QDR [Quadrennial Defense Review]: Backwards Into the Future"; Conetta, "Future Tense—An Assessment of the Report of the National Defense Panel," all done for the Project on Defense Alternatives, Commonwealth Institute, Cambridge, Massachusetts in 1997.

24. But high technology for the civilian economy was driven by research funded by the government and by foundations—not by industry-sponsored research. One study showed that 73 percent of the scientific papers cited by U.S. industrial patents were based on U.S. and foreign research financed by government or nonprofit agencies—and only 27 percent by private agencies. William J. Broad, "Study Finds Public Science Is Pillar of Industry," *The New York Times,* May 13, 1997, pp. C1, C10.

25. Joseph S. Nye, Jr. and William A. Owens, "America's Information Edge," *Foreign Affairs,* 75, 2 (March/April 1996), pp. 20–36; also Eliot A. Cohen, "A Revolution in Warfare," in the same issue, pp. 37–54.

26. Lee Rainwater and Timothy M. Smeeding, "Doing Poorly: The Real Income of American Children in a Comparative Perspective," Luxembourg Income Study Working Paper No. 127 (Walferdange, Luxembourg: Centre d'Études de Population, de Pauvreté et de Politique Socio-Économiques, August 1995).

27. Marc Miringoff and Marque-Luisa Miringoff, *The Social Health of the Nation: How America is Really Doing* (New York: Oxford University Press, 1999), p. 5 and supporting data in the rest of the book.

28. Japan Tobacco Inc., owned and operated by the Ministry of Finance, was the largest corporate taxpayer in Japan in 1993. Lung cancer killed 3 out of 100,000 in 1955; 31 of 100,000 in 1991.

29. The sharing of burdens was uneven. The United States spent a much greater share of its GNP on defense than Japan or Germany. Still, America also gained: Japan and Germany aligned with Washington on nearly every security issue of the Cold War.

    Absent ties with Washington, Japan and Germany would surely have felt compelled to build a nuclear deterrent. Had this happened, neighboring states—recalling World War II—would probably have been far cooler toward their ex-foes.

30. Before and after the Soviet era the Russian state has been referred to with a term larger than Russian, a term meant to include non-Russians. The pre-Soviet tsarist empire was known as the *Rossiiskaia Imperiia;* the post-Soviet state is called the *Rossiiskaia Federatsiia.* Had these states been meant for Russians alone, they would have been called *russkaia*—as in *russkaia literatura.* The distinction resembles that between British Empire and English literature. The "China" in PRC, however, is also inclusive. It does not translate as "Han" but as "Middle Kingdom" or "Middle Glory."

31. For elaboration of the following analysis of China, along with bibliographic references, see Walter C. Clemens, Jr., "China: alternative futures," *Communist and Post-Communist Studies,* 32 (1999), pp. 1–21.

32. In 1998 there were more than 250,000 addresses in China receiving—even if they did not request them—electronic newsletters on Chinese affairs sent from the United States. PRC officials attempted to block this flow by electronic firewalls—filters and electronic disturbances—but waged a losing battle.

33. Suffering from gigantomania, top PRC officials committed their prestige and vast resources. They compared the Three Gorges project with the Great Wall and claimed that their ability to carry out such undertakings proved the intrinsic abilities of socialism. Prevented from publishing critical analyses within China after 1989, some Chinese scientists published their views abroad. Of 2,600 delegates to the 1992 Congress, 177 voted against the dam and 664 abstained.

34. This is the conclusion of a proposal of the Democratic Faction signed by Fang Jue and submitted to China's National People's Congress in March 1998. The essay was entitled "China Needs a New Transformation."

35. "We say that the board of directors makes the main decisions, but it's really the Hebei Party Committee," said the president of North China, a pharmaceutical company chosen by the central authorities to become a world-class giant.

    A Chinese economist, He Quinglian, wrote a devastating critique of "reforms" initiated by Deng Xiaoping in the late 1970s. Her book, *China's Pitfall,* was published in Hong Kong in 1997 and in Beijing in 1998. It argues that the country's economic growth since the late 1970s had slowed if not stalled in the countryside. Given the huge role still played by state industries, only 10 percent of urban economic activity was due to private enterprise. The entire process benefited a limited number of people who, thanks to their positions, plundered public goods—the savings of the masses and the environment.

36. A police analysis meant for internal use reported that a wave of serious crime developed in the late 1980s—the fourth after 1949, 1958, and 1966. The number of serious crimes (thefts, robberies, frauds) increased from an average of 60,000 per year in the early 1980s to more than 160,000 in 1988. The police report said that the major perpetrators of crime in the 1980s were peasants who had come into cities; the second source, idlers. The report said that these trends probably continued in the 1990s. See "The Basic Character of Crime in Contemporary China," *The China Quarterly* 149 (1997), pp. 160–177.

37. "Gemischtes Bild von China-Engagements," *Neue Zürcher Zeitung*, February 12, 1998.

38. *1999 Corruption Perceptions Index* and *Bribe Payers Index* at www.transparency.de/documents

39. Nearly one in three potential workers in China was unemployed or underemployed in 1998. China's state-owned enterprises laid off millions of employees in the late 1990s. The enterprises are supposed to provide benefits to the those laid off, but when the enterprises are themselves collapsing, benefits are meager or nonexistent. Some discharged workers find jobs in the private sector, but if the economy stalls, private sector jobs will also shrink.

40. In 1975 the Brezhnev regime signed the Helsinki Final Act with its human rights provisions as well as its "baskets" for security and economics. Moscow hoped to stabilize Eastern Europe and promote West-to-East technology transfer. It did not anticipate the consequences of the Helsinki commitment authorizing Soviet citizens as well as foreign monitors to scrutinize the observance of human rights in the USSR and Soviet client states.

41. As some Chinese saw it, the Singaporean system maintained order but spawned wealth. One party dominated politics, with token representation for other parties. A paternalistic interpretation of Confucianism maintained consensus. Children obeyed fathers; fathers obeyed bosses and governors; everyone obeyed the ruling elite. Rising prosperity offered proof that the elite retained the mandate of heaven.

42. Though it is difficult to imagine in A.D. 2000, Khrushchev claimed in the late 1950s that the USSR would soon surpass the U.S. in production of various goods. When it later appeared that the USSR could not keep up with any First World economy, the Kremlin sought at least military parity. It invested far more of its resources in arms than the United States, undermining still more the Soviet ability to compete economically.

China too experienced a slogan euphoria in the late 1950s when Mao Zedong predicted that the Great Leap Forward would permit China to surpass various capitalist countries in the production of steel and other goods. Indeed, Mao called on his countrymen to advance more quickly than the USSR, telescoping development so as to enter directly into the glories of communism. But the Great Leap brought chaos and famine, and Mao's next campaign called for Cultural Revolution—not material uplift.

43. Some Western writers redefine "civil society" to make it fit China; others look for changes in China to fit the concept; still others drop the concept entirely. Some suggest that civil society may be an obsolete term, because the nation-state is obsolete: The fulcrums of action are situated in localities and in transnational forces.

44. In March 2000 China announced plans for a 4,200-kilometer pipeline to transport natural gas from Lunnan gas field in Xinjiang to Shanghai. The pipeline, expected to cost more than $20 billion, was to be completed by 2007 or soon thereafter.

45. Four transformations of politics made democracy possible in Taiwan: a responsible opposition, a political culture compatible with democracy, competing political parties participating in free elections, and respect for a constitution.

46. The Guomindang held onto the presidency and kept a majority of seats in parliament through the 1980s and 1990s. But it permitted opposition parties to contest local and national elections. When the Guomindang majority became too liberal for conservatives, the latter formed the New Party. The Democratic Progressive Party (DPP) defeated the Guomindang or reduced its dominance in many local elections. In November 1997 the DPP received 44 percent of the ballots cast; the Guomindang, 42 percent. The DPP claimed then to govern 47 percent of Taiwan's area, 71 percent of its population, and 83 percent of its revenues. Vote-buying and other forms of political corruption remained, particularly at the local level, but the overall trend was toward election integrity and transparency.

47. While Washington would breathe a sigh of relief if Taipei and Beijing reconciled, some Japanese policymakers concluded in the late 1990s that Taiwan's unification with the mainland could harm Tokyo's interests. Tokyo in November 1998 refused to affirm for visiting PRC President Jiang the "three no" principle toward Taiwan already accepted by U.S. President Bill Clinton.

5.

Alternative Futures,
A.D. *2000 to 2025*

The onset of another millennium spurs reflection on the future as well as the present and the past. What alternative futures should Americans nurture? Which should they try to avoid? To answer these questions, we shall stretch our minds across the first quarter of the twenty-first century and trace six scenarios.

Change is certain, but let us start with the basic facts of international life in A.D. 2000—the division of humanity into those living in a zone of democratic peace and those living in a zone of chronic trouble and hardship; the pyramid of power sketched in chapter 4; the realities of global interdependence; and the cross-border forces of globalization.

Global interdependence means that *states* are mutually vulnerable—in military, economic, public-health, and in other terms. Even physically distant actors can hurt or help one another.

Globalization refers to the process by which transnational forces cross and ignore borders—in some ways weakening and diminishing states. Some of these forces are intangible—knowledge, values, skills, and tastes. Others are so tangible as drugs and viruses. All are spread by transportation and communication technologies— airplanes, ships, the Internet, satellite broadcasting, electronic mail, and electronic banking.

Global interdependence coexists with globalization. In some ways states are more important than ever; in other respects, their importance recedes. Transnational forces integrate humanity but also divide it. Neither the forces of Jihad nor of McWorld bode well for democracy.[1] Some nongovernmental organizations (NGOs) support the tribe and tribalism; many others have wider allegiances.

Modems can be used by the Ku Klux Klan as well as by Human Rights Watch.

Each scenario that follows assumes that technology continues to reduce distance and time, that many means of locomotion and of destruction become cheaper and more widely acceptable, and that mutual vulnerabilities increase. Science and technology continue to advance and become more widely used around the world, though their benefits are not equally distributed. Weapons of mass destruction proliferate. Some state and nonstate actors commit horrific violence to impose their will or make a point. The United States and other countries will have to cope with the global trends outlined in box 5.1.

The zones of democratic peace and chronic trouble will not be frozen. The quality of life in each zone will evolve. Each zone will gain or lose members. Some peoples straddling each zone in A.D. 2000 will advance or fall into one zone or the other. In theory the two zones might exist in isolation, but this is unlikely. The relative tranquility of the first zone will probably experience the pain, heartbreak, refugees, and diseases of the second. Will members of the first zone try to help those who live in a zone of chronic trouble? Can those who inhabit the first zone help these in the second—or must each people save itself?

All actors—governments, firms, NGOs, movements, individuals—have a basic choice. As suggested in the initial framework to this book, they may claim and try to seize values at others' expense or strive to create values with others for mutual gain. They can see life as a zero-sum contest or a cooperative endeavor.

All our scenarios except the fourth and sixth assume that governments dominate the world scene; the fourth scenario posits that the processes of globalization elicit world governance by combinations of national, international, and transnational agents; the sixth scenario posits anarchy.

Each scenario blends elements of conflict and mutual gain. The scenarios define clusters of likelihood derived from what we know about how the world works.[2] None is a prediction. But scenarios can serve as heuristics. They can help us anticipate how the world may evolve. Given these possible scenarios, we can then strive for policies that make preferred outcomes more likely and disagreeable outcomes less likely.

To maximize credibility, let us portray each scenario as a fact—not what "could," "would," or "should" be. We begin by extrapolating from the pyramid of power in A.D. 2000.

Box 5.1 Global Trends, 2000–2025, as Seen by the U.S. Commission on National Security/21st Century

1. Even though it remains militarily superior to all adversaries, the United States will become increasingly vulnerable to attack or destabilization.

2. Rapid advances in information and biotechnologies can be used against U.S. interests.

3. New technologies will divide the world as well as draw it together.

4. The security of all advanced states will be affected by the evolving global economic infrastructure.

5. The United States and most other countries will continue to depend heavily on fossil fuels.

6. All borders will become more porous; some will bend and some will break.

7. The sovereignty of states will come under pressure but endure.

8. Some states will fragment or even "fail," destabilizing their neighbors.

9. Demands for self-determination will increase, backed by violence, pressing the major powers to devise effective institutional responses.

10. Outer space will become a critical and competitive military environment.

11. The essence of war will not change. Some groups will use violence against societies with a lower tolerance for casualties.

12. U.S. intelligence will face challenging adversaries and be subject to strategic surprises.

13. The United States will often be called upon to intervene militarily in a time of uncertain alliances and with fewer forward-deployed forces.

14. America and its partners will need many instruments of diplomatic, economic, and military power, backed by technological innovation, adjusting capabilities to emerging threats.

Source: New World Coming: American Security in the 21st Century. Supporting Research and Analysis (Washington, D.C.: The United States Commission on National Security/21st Century, 1999), pp. 141–145.

I. Unipolar Stability

The unipolar "moment" lasts for decades—perhaps much longer. American power is rooted in tangible and intangible assets that show no sign of weakening—a splendid geographical setting occupied by a diverse and well-educated population with freedom to create.[3] Americans can respond to unipolarity in three ways: by retreating to a Fortress America; by bullying their foes and even their friends; or by leading mainly by persuasion and example. They opt for this third approach.

The United States is a new kind of hegemon on the world stage. A rarity in history, the dominant power seeks neither territory nor empire. The sole superpower seldom acts alone. It seeks and obtains cooperation from other actors to maintain peace, thwart violations of human rights, and sustain prosperity.

The combination of unipolarity with multilateralism gives rise to the most peaceful, stable, and prosperous era in human history. This form of unipolarity proves to be more conducive to peace among the great powers than other distributions of power—the multilateral balancing of the nineteenth century, the rival alliances of 1914, or Cold War bipolarity. It is a world in which actors deal with global interdependence and with globalization so as to generate mutual gain. It begins to follow the principle: "From each according to her or his ability, to each according to her or his need." Relations between most actors on the world stage begin to embody more the Canadian-Mexican-U.S. model than the tensions that existed in A.D. 2000 between India and Pakistan or Iraq and Israel.[4]

No country or region has the wish or the means to challenge the global hegemon. A deal takes shape: Washington does not abuse its power and other countries do not gang up against it. This deal is facilitated by the fact that the United States is closer to the United Kingdom, Germany, Japan, China, Russia, Brazil, India, Ukraine, and Kazakstan than any of them to each other.

The United States and Russia go beyond START 3 and cut arsenals to 1,000 strategic nuclear weapons for each country. The other nuclear powers accept even lower ceilings.

The major powers have no deep reason, as in 1914, to rush to battle as if linked and locked in the same chain; nor have they a strong incentive, as in 1938–1939, to hold back and pass the buck.[5]

The era of a universal democratic peace, however, has not arrived. The zones of tranquil prosperity and chronic trouble have much the same membership as in A.D. 2000. Russia, China, and many countries of Latin America still have a foot in each zone. Turkey, Ukraine, and India have pulled closer to the zone of democratic peace, but still suffer from severe internal fractures and weaknesses.

Japan's standing in the pyramid of power declines as China's strengthens. Japan faces severe constraints: Its archipelago remains crowded; the population becomes grayer, with fewer workers to support retirees; Japan's foreign markets shrink as Korea and other neighbors fill the same demands at lower prices. Alliance with the United States is still the linchpin of Japan's security.[6]

Europe remains a confederation rather than a unitary state. Real union is infeasible due to language, cultural, and economic differences. The European states do designate forces for collective actions in which the United States and Canada do not take part, but NATO is still intact—much as in A.D. 2000. Most Europeans are more likely to converge against one of their own, Germany, than against the United States. To make sure this never happens, Germany abjures advanced weapons and remains dependent upon the nuclear forces of its NATO partners. Some French and German leaders call for formation of an inner-core—a "Euro-Europe" within an expanding European Union, but this does not happen. The EU expands and becomes more rule-bound without becoming more efficient. Many people in Great Britain feel closer to English-speakers far away than to the polyglot European Continent.

Russia is more democratic than in A.D. 2000 and has begun to realize its economic potential. Its free press, along with offshore radio and television, help to keep politics clean. Liberal reform parties have gained the upper hand over ultranationalists and wolf-in-sheep's-clothing Communists. But a millennium of dependency upon an iron fist leaves a heritage difficult to erase.

Unipolarity does not prevent conflict between China and its great power neighbors India, Russia, and Japan. But all these countries focus on their internal development and do not permit their disagreements to threaten the peace or interfere with trade. Mainland and island China are still separate political entities, but Taiwan investors and industrialists are active in mainland China.

Great power stability does not prevent conflict in the zone of chronic trouble and hardship. Backed by the United States and other great powers, the United Nations intervenes diplomatically and sometimes militarily to quash threats to peace and to human rights.

New economic giants arise—Argentina, Brazil, Indonesia, Iran, Kazakstan, Nigeria, Ukraine. Fear and resentment toward regional powers such as Nigeria mount but do not erupt in major violence.

The World Trade Organization becomes more powerful and smites the barriers to free trade. The world is sufficiently rich and well informed to find paths to sustainable development. The World Bank formulates dependable guidelines by which countries can enlarge their GDP and improve their Human Development Index ratings.[7] Rich countries help many less developed countries (LDCs) to surmount transitional problems. Infant mortality and AIDS deaths continue to decline worldwide.

World population levels off at about 8 billion people. Economic prospects for most of the world are positive.

II. Bipolar Cooperation

China and the United States have equivalent GDPs by 2025, but average Chinese incomes are much lower than average American. The two economies are more complementary than competitive. The two countries have no territorial claims on each other. Cooperative projects convince people in both countries that mutual gain is possible in culture and science as well as in commerce.[8]

The U.S. economy does not suffer as China becomes richer. The two countries trade goods and services in ways that generate value for each party. The U.S. as well as the PRC government wanted China to join the World Trade Organization in A.D. 2000, with the difference that Washington pressed Beijing to drop barriers to foreign investment. Openness and transparency turn out to benefit China's competitiveness.

The erstwhile Middle Kingdom keeps to its late-twentieth-century borders and focuses on internal problems. It wrestles with severe economic and environmental challenges such as shortages of fuel and water. But the United States and other countries give or sell much of what China needs to make up its food and other deficits. China is not active at the United Nations but rarely objects to peacemaking, peacekeeping, or peace-enforcement activities sponsored by the United States and other powers.

The Taiwan issue no longer troubles PRC-U.S. relations, because China confederates with Taiwan—one people living in two systems. As happened in Taiwan in the 1980s, one-party rule begins to give way to pluralism in mainland China. Technocrats supplant ideologists. China is not a democracy but neither is it a dictatorship.

III. Multipolar Cooperation

There are multiple centers of power. The centers are diverse but, on the whole, complementary. The strengths of one help compensate for the weaknesses of another.

The zone of democratic peace has expanded while that of chronic trouble has shrunk. Countries such as Turkey and Ukraine that once straddled the two zones are firmly in the region of democratic peace. Russia and China have a much firmer grounding in this zone than in previous decades.

Democracy and peace reinforce each other—sustained by the synergistic trends anticipated by Immanuel Kant.[9] Cyberspace joins scientists, cultural figures, business people, relatives, and e-mail pals across the world. More and more peoples belong to a grid of complex interdependence and trade.

By 2025 Russia and the United States have cut their nuclear arsenals to 500 strategic warheads; China agrees to a ceiling of 300; other nuclear powers agree to limits no higher than 175.

The military requirements set out in Articles 43–47 of the UN Charter have been fulfilled. At last the UN Security Council has a Military Staff Committee; and most UN members have earmarked forces for use by the Security Council. Collective security is becoming a reality. The tough action taken by the United Nations against Saddam Hussein in the 1990s and early twenty-first century encourages confidence in collective security and discourages rogue attacks on the evolving world order. Israel and most of its neighbors are learning how to coexist and trade. The Palestinian Republic is becoming the Singapore of the Middle East.

More Asian, African, Middle Eastern, and Latin American countries have entered a path of rapid and sustainable development. New strains of hybrid wheat, rice, maize, and other crops permit nearly every region to become self-sufficient in basic foods—without heavy irrigation or chemicals. Few countries still depend on any single commodity such as jute or cocoa. Investment in health and education rises dramatically as developing and industrialized countries shift resources from defense to development needs. Biodiversity in the Amazon and other tropical regions is protected and becomes profitable.

IV. Global Governance without World Government

A transnational civil society is evolving. Like civil society within countries, it shields individual humans and groups from the raw powers of government and market. The transnational civil society develops in tandem with complex interdependence across many countries and regions. Common values—political choice, trust in free markets, respect for human rights—are shared by more than three-fourths of humanity. Territoriality weakens as a principle of organization.

There is no world government by a supranational authority. Independent states remain. But they share power with a medley of business and labor groups as well as NGOs. Together they form expanding networks of institutions designed to meet a wide range of human needs.[10]

States retain sovereignty, but every state is permeable—from Albania to the United States. Many transnational corporations control more wealth than most countries. Already in A.D. 2000, of the world's hundred largest economies, 51 were companies and 49 were countries.

National governments confer among themselves and with responsible specialists from national, international, and transnational agencies. This is functionalism writ large—decision making informed and managed by experts (an "epistemic community"), mediated and supervised by representatives of elected governments. The twenty-first century builds upon the efforts of governments and industrial leaders in the late twentieth century to forge a consensus on shared concerns.[11]

To cope with epidemics, for example, government experts form a committee drawn from national medical boards, the World Health Organization, the International Committee of the Red Cross, and the recently formed International Academy of Health Sciences. To deal with economic issues—currency fluctuations, debt, volatile commodity prices—government experts form a committee drawn from the World Bank, the IMF, leading commercial banks, and the recently formed International Academy of Economic and Social Scientists.

In Africa the Diamond Trade Buys Arms for Cruel and Endless Wars

International governance by a wide range of global actors is needed to curb wars fueled by the sale of diamonds, gold, or cocaine.

To deal with threats to peace and security, governments depend heavily on the UN Security Council and the UN Secretary-General. Some governments retain nuclear arsenals, but the Security Council has its own rapid reaction force, backed by designated units from most UN members. The UN Secretary-General has a panel of mediators whom she/he can propose to disputants. A committee of elders drawn from Nobel Peace Prize laureates advises the Security Council and the Secretary-General. The International Peace Academy has graduated many diplomats skilled at conflict resolution.

By 2010 the University of the Middle East, founded by Arabs and Israelis who met while attending U.S. graduate schools in the 1990s, has received help from some governments and foundations. Its pilot college in Morocco proved a great success, inspiring comparable institutions in Tunisia, Jordan, and Egypt. By 2025 it has trained a generation of men and women more concerned with peaceful development than with sectarian passions. By 2025 they have launched several projects that knit Israel and its neighbors in networks of mutual gain.

World governance is more than the "common marketization" of international relations. It is global public policy responding to the dangers and opportunities inherent in globalization.

V. Challenge to the Hegemon

Nothing lasts. When the United States appears weak or overbearing, the rising power of China strives to overthrow the hegemon.

Most Chinese remain poor, but the country's enormous GDP permits Beijing to build formidable armed forces. China's scientists and engineers move the country to the leading edge of technology. China's oil requirements deepen its motives to dominate Central Asia and the South China Sea.

China has moved away from dictatorship toward a more nationalistic democracy. Deep political transitions are dangerous for peace—whether from or toward dictatorship.[12] There are liberal strains in China, but they resemble Europe's nineteenth-century liberal nationalism rather than the universalist nationalism envisioned by theorists of a democratic peace.[13]

While China has not sought to change the world and implant a large empire Soviet-style, Beijing has sought to extend China's sovereignty. The National People's Congress in 1992 incorporated the entire South China Sea and the Diao Yu Do islands, reserving the right to use force. This orientation threatens violent confrontation with others—for example, over oil resources.

Problems multiply when China insists that Japan stop building antimissile defenses. But a more serious threat to stability arises when China demands that Taiwan join in a Beijing-dominated federation. Washington again sends aircraft carriers to the Taiwan Straits. The danger to peace is far greater than when an Austrian archduke died in Sarajevo.

Here the road forks: One direction sees China back down before the U.S. show of force. Like Russia's rulers in 1911 and 1962, however, Beijing swears "never again"—never again to retreat before a rival power. Since the 1990s PRC strategists have studied how to defeat "a powerful opponent with a weak force in a high tech war."[14] China steps up investment in the sinews of war and prepares for a confrontation one or two decades hence.

The other fork also leads to trouble: Washington pulls back while Beijing incorporates Taiwan into China. The PRC proceeds to bully other neighbors—Vietnam, Korea, Japan, Russia, India. Washington wants to contain China, but blows hot and cold—as it did toward Khrushchev in 1958–1962. Emboldened, China marches toward a collision with the enfeebled hegemon, believing it will triumph in the next game of chicken.

VI. Fragmented Chaos

Extrapolations from the relative calm and prosperity of the late twentieth century miss the mark. Humans stand at the brink: Mutual

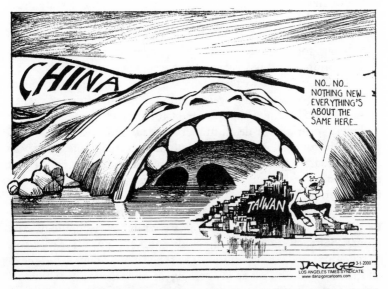

The United States tried to maintain good relations with Beijing and with Taipei as the Taiwanese alternated between complacency and deep anxiety over their relationship with the PRC.

vulnerability means that a serious change in any part of the system can ripple and multiply throughout the whole. Unipolar stability rapidly succumbs to fragmented chaos—division and mayhem.

The United States looks either like a bully or a giant with feet of clay. When Americans use their muscle aggressively, they antagonize followers as well as rivals. If the United States weakens or fails to lead, its followers jump off the bandwagon. Americans get the worst of both worlds as they oscillate between hubristic arrogance of power and do-nothing complacency.

The extent of anti-American animus was evident at the onset of the twenty-first century. A former French president and German chancellor asserted that nationalists in Washington would be pleased if the EU overreached by taking in one or two waves of additional members. This could generate crises and dilute the Union into a mere free-trade area. This "would satisfy those in Washington who aspire to maintain some control over Europe in order to facilitate America's global aims—and, sometimes, illusions."[15]

The U.S. home front deteriorates as racial and class cleavages multiply; as many Afro-Americans, Hispanics, and others reject the long dominant Anglo-European culture; as guns rule some streets and many schools; and as Congress and the public refuse to invest in science, public health, or even in basic infrastructure. Couch potato–fast food obesity and drug dependency undermine intellectual, emotional, and physical well-being.

The U.S. military weakens from the conflicting requirements of doing social work, putting down rogue states, and deterring peer rivals. The poor are not happy to fight for the rich. With patriotism and civic spirit all but dead, money does not suffice to entice high quality enlistments. Physical standards are lowered in the military to accommodate women who wish to serve in combat units. "Don't say and don't ask" policies aggravate morale problems and undermine fighting efficiency.

The economic imperatives of capitalism conflict with realpolitik. Capitalism thrives on free flows of labor, technology, and money. But each state wants greater wealth and power; each wants to sell, grow, and possess more. Unless the United States stands head and shoulder above all rivals combined, movement toward global integration will be reversed.[16]

Contrary to the disciples of Adam Smith, international trade does not prove to be win-win. In many cases, as neomercantilists

Every day in 1996 two U.S. children (age 14 and younger) were shot to death. In the entire year nearly 34,000 Americans died by firearms (compared to 44,000 in auto accidents).

warned, some actors gain more than others and use their new wealth to press their advantages. Regardless where technological breakthroughs occur, others master the know-how and use it to generate competitive advantage or threaten others.

As Lenin predicted, capitalists export their advanced technologies worldwide and then struggle against one another for market share. Contrary to Kant, representative democracy does not assure the absence of war.

The logic of collective action takes its toll. Many actors try to free-load and pass the buck. While more and more individuals "bowl alone"—some of them lost in cyberspace—a global time of troubles engulfs humanity. Democracy is weakened by the insidious role of free markets and by the power of mass-media technology.[17] Some countries withdraw from the WTO and erect protectionist barriers to keep out imports.

The peace and prosperity enjoyed by some humans is not shared by most others. The zone of chronic trouble expands. Tensions

Western Drug Firms Agree to Sell Aids Drugs in Africa at Cost
(About $2.00 a day)

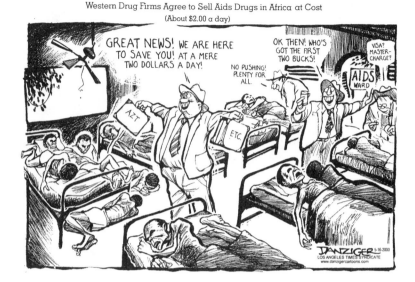

between haves and have-nots sharpen. Unemployed youth in many LDCs are furious in the knowledge that others live far better than they. Religious and ethnic zealots incite violence. In failing states the road to economic development is derailed by civil strife. As in Tajikistan and Sri Lanka in the 1990s, many groups continue to fight despite local exhaustion and foreign mediation.

Several rogue states resemble Iraq in the 1990s. Their leaders throw down the gauntlet against the United States and other "have" nations.

Both environmental and economic barriers impede growth. It is easier to preach and propose "sustainable development" than to practice it. Global epidemics spread and undermine both human and financial health. H.I.V. infections impose a heavy economic burden in many countries where workers die young or require expensive drugs to survive.

The biosphere fails to support human life in some places where it flourished in the 1990s. The affluent Pacific rim sits on a ring of fire—volcanoes and fault lines—that devour life and property. Storms and droughts increase due to climate change abetted by pollution and deforestation. The Republic of the Maldives and several other island states are submerged.

Economic growth on the Pacific rim stalls as fresh inputs of labor, capital, and energy become more costly. Authoritarian rule stills the once vibrant energies of Singapore and Hong Kong. Japan and South Korea resurrect nontariff barriers to keep out imports.

Russia reverts to its old ways. Its economy lags behind Europe, but Moscow seeks to reimpose imperial controls on borderlands such as Estonia, Ukraine, and Kazakstan. At the same time, however, regions facing the Pacific Ocean try to break from Moscow's control.

When the awakening giant China trembles, there are global repercussions. Millions are unemployed as the country's economy slows. Malthus strikes: China cannot feed itself because too much scarce farmland has been sacrificed to industrialization. Serious environmental problems undermine public health. China's border peoples become more restive. China cracks down on Uighurs, Kazaks, and Tibetans, but they mount a Chechen-style resistance, with aid from abroad. China lurches toward Russian-style anarchy and then disintegrates into regions—south against north, east against west.

Weapons of mass destruction become more accessible. A single nuclear explosion near a city—set off by mechanical accident, human error, or design—makes Chernobyl and Oklahoma City look like child's play. Besides local deaths, large areas suffer from radiation and disruption. Reports that Iraq is ready to launch anthrax-filled warheads create panic in Iran and Israel. The United States experiences large-scale devastation and death on a far wider scale than the World Trade Center bombing some decades before.

A Mixed Model

Elements of each scenario materialize at different times and places. A stable unipolar world exists for a decade or so but then gives way to other trends. The United States and China may cooperate for a time, only to see China challenge the hegemon as it becomes stronger. Alternatively, China and the United States may cooperate but face a strong challenge from a third party—perhaps Russia, India, or Japan.

Economic and environmental uncertainties loom. Man-made strife and natural disasters can sweep away years or decades of economic progress. In some places new seeds and farming techniques may bring abundance; other regions—wasted by desertification, floods, or earthquakes—remain in zones of chronic hardship.

The biggest questions concern the zones of democratic peace and chronic trouble. Which one will become stronger and bigger, and which weaker and smaller? And what will be the ties between them?

Which Scenario Is Best? Which Is Most Feasible?

It is easy to say which scenarios are the worst—Scenarios V and VI. Either a collision between hegemon and challenger or fragmented chaos could destroy many lives and waste valuable assets. The more violence, the greater the suffering and the more difficult the tasks of reconstruction. Wise planners will act to block the roads that lead in these directions.

Any scenario that promotes peace and prosperity is acceptable. But scenario IV—world governance—has two advantages. First, it postulates development of a truly transnational society. Without such a society, the state system may eventually break down. World governance both requires and contributes to a well-integrated global society.[18]

Second, global governance is more likely to cultivate a rich emergent structure able to cope with complex challenges than any scenario that leaves basic tasks mainly to governments. Fitness requires an ability to cope with complexity. Cooperation between governments and nongovernmental bodies is more likely to embody the flexibility and reach needed to deal with emerging needs.

What can we do to strengthen prospects for a more peaceful and prosperous world? Lessons from the past and guidelines for the future are examined in the final chapter.

Notes

1. Benjamin R. Barber, *Jihad vs. McWorld: How Globalism and Tribalism Are Reshaping the World* (New York: Ballantine, 1996).
2. This method is articulated in *New World Coming: American Security in the 21st Century: Supporting Research and Analysis* (Washington, D.C.: The United States Commission on National

Security/21st Century, 1999), p. 133. The commission sketches four scenarios: Democratic Peace, which may evolve into Globalization Triumphant; Protectionism and Nationalism, which could provoke Division and Mayhem. These four scenarios find their way into this book's six alternative futures. Many other alternatives can be imagined. But future realities may outstrip our imagination because they depart so far from known trends.

3. See Zbigniew Brzezinski, *The Grand Chessboard: American Primacy and Its Geostrategic Imperatives* (New York: BasicBooks, 1997).

4. A sad exception to the overall relationship, Canadian-U.S. fishing disputes embodied heavy doses of local as opposed to national politics.

5. Thomas J. Christensen and Jack Snyder, "Chain gangs and passed bucks: predicting alliance patterns in multipolarity," *International Organization,* 44, 2 (Spring 1990), pp. 137–68; also Randall L. Schweller, "Tripolarity and the Second World War," *International Studies Quarterly,* 37, 1 (March 1993), pp. 73–104.

6. Brzezinski, *Grand Chessboard,* p. 152.

7. The Human Development Index (HDI) aggregates three measures: life expectancy; educational attainment; and real income per capita. The Gender-related Development Index (GDI) adjusts the HDI for gender. See United Nations Development Programme, *Human Development Report* (New York: Oxford University Press, annual).

8. Westinghouse and General Electric by 2025 have built state-of-the-art nuclear power plants in China. Boeing and Chinese companies together are building entire 100-passenger planes there. Collaboration between the Guandong Modern Dance Company and the American Dance Festival in Durham, North Carolina has set a model for cultural cooperation. The U.S.-sponsored School for Advanced International Studies at Nanjing has produced generations of Chinese and Americans familiar with each other's thinking on world affairs.

9. As noted in the framework, Kant's *On Perpetual Peace* (1795–1796) pointed to the combined impact of representative government, a federation of nations, international law, the spirit of trade, and the growth of a common, enlightened culture. Text in Immanuel Kant, *Perpetual Peace and Other Essays* (Indianapolis, Ind.: Hackett, 1983), pp. 107–143.

10. See Inge Kaul et al., eds., *Global Public Goods: International Cooperation in the 21st Century* (New York: Oxford University Press, 1999); Wolfgang H. Reinicke, *Global Public Policy: Governing without Government?* (Washington, D.C.: Brookings Institution, 1998); *Our Global Neighborhood: The Report on the Commission on Global Governance* (New York: Oxford University Press, 1995); Mihaly Simai, *The Future of Global Governance: Managing Risk*

and Change in the International System (Washington, D.C.: U.S. Institute of Peace Press, 1994).

11. Thus, the Trans-Atlantic Business Dialogue between industrial leaders and officials from the European Union and the United States agreed on how to reduce a major nontariff barrier to cross-Atlantic trade: duplicate sets of regulations. Governments and CEOs found a simple remedy—mutual recognition agreements: If a product passes inspection on one side of the Atlantic, it is ordinarily approved on the other. In 1997 the United States and EU ratified mutual recognition agreements in five domains including pharmaceuticals, medical devices, and electromagnetic equipment.

Corporate leaders and governments also discussed uniform standards for taxation, investment, and prosecution of business corruption. Drug companies wanted laws to ban dissemination of their trade secrets on the Internet; other groups lobbied against any form of censorship.

Did all this amount to collusion between bureaucrats and technocrats? Consumer advocates and environmentalists demanded transparency and full reporting. Perhaps they too would gain seats in the trans-Atlantic dialogue.

12. Jack L. Snyder, *From Voting to Violence: Democratization and Nationalist Conflict* (New York: W. W. Norton, 2000).

13. Bear F. Braumoeller, "Deadly Doves: Liberal Nationalism and the Democratic Peace in the Soviet Successor States," *International Studies Quarterly*, 3, 41 (September 1997), pp. 375–402.

14. See Michael Pillsbury, ed., *Chinese Views of Future Warfare* (Washington, D.C.: National Defense University Press, 1997).

15. Valéry Giscard d'Estaing and Helmut Schmidt, "Time to Slow Down and Consolidate Around "Euro-Europe'," *International Herald Tribune,* April 11, 2000.

16. Benjamin C. Schwarz, "Is Capitalism Doomed?" *The New York Times,* May 23, 1994, p. A15.

17. Jacques Attali, "The Crash of Western Civilization: The Limits of the Market and Democracy," *Foreign Policy,* 107 (Summer 1997), pp. 54–64; also Claude Moisy, "Myths of the Global Information Village," ibid., pp. 78–87.

18. See the alternative paths to world order in Hedley Bull, *The Anarchical Society: A Study of Order in World Politics* (New York: Columbia University Press, 1977), chaps. 10–14.

6.

Lessons from the Past, Guidelines for the Future

Let us assume that Americans wish to avoid chaos and conflict on the world stage and instead to foster scenarios conducive to peace, prosperity, and freedom. What can they learn from the past? Let us apply the theoretical perspectives advanced in the first pages of this book to America's record of achievement and failure. This blend of theory and experience may suggest ways to promote positive over destructive tendencies.

Lessons from the Past

The ultimate condition for American successes at home and abroad was fitness—a capacity to cope with complex challenges and opportunities. Fitness depended on intangible and tangible assets—the capacity of Americans to convert their hard and soft power to shape their lives and others'. Since its founding the United States enjoyed great human and material human strengths. Still, success in world affairs often required consummate skill and sustained, titanic effort, braced by commitment and credibility. Victories in peacetime usually depended on the creative use of economic and intangible assets. Victory in major wars required the United States to mobilize its military, technological, and industrial potential and to forge sturdy coalitions with allies.

United States achievements in peacetime usually flowed from a strategy of conditional cooperation and openness. A fusion of political realism, idealism, and recognition of interdependence shaped the most successful U.S. foreign policy ever—the Marshall Plan. The

European Recovery Program became a model of mutuality in planning, inputs, and perceived gain. Like the Marshall Plan, other successes such as the Fulbright exchanges and 1994 Mexican peso bailout were investments quickly recouped by good returns.

A quest for mutual advantage helped even in tough negotiations with the Kremlin regarding arms control and a pullback from Cuba. Americans learned not to back adversaries such as the USSR into a corner. They grasped that international relations is not a one-shot affair. The game goes on. Whatever happens today sets the stage for more encounters tomorrow. Major actors like Russia and China do not go away. Distrust and misunderstandings will persist but can be reduced by improved communication and collaboration.

America's foreign policy blunders usually arose from an arrogant unilateralism that took little notice of others' interests, intentions, or capabilities; often, one that ignored others' nationalist aspirations or visions of justice. This syndrome helped explain both America's sometime passivity and its bouts of hyperactivism—its refusal in the 1920s–1930s to take part in collective security and its later Cold War interventions and fruitless campaign in Indochina. Secrecy and deception often made matters worse. The blunders of the Cold War era were usually hatched and often implemented with little public debate. The White House even deceived Congress and the public on the Indochina War and the Iran-Contra affair.

The ups and downs of America's material power did not explain outcomes, for the United States was always a great power in the twentieth century. Even if its military forces were weak, as before each world war, they could be quickly mobilized. The crucial variable was the policies themselves: Successful policies were usually oriented to mutual gain and were openly debated at all stages. Unilateralism and secrecy spawned failures.

Limited political capital was a greater problem for U.S. foreign policy than limited financial capital. America's greatest achievements in the world took shape in the late 1940s when farsighted Democrats and Republicans forged an enlightened, bipartisan foreign policy. Many failures arose when Congress kept its heads in the sands or resolutely opposed the president, no matter what—as in the Senate's rejection of the comprehensive nuclear test ban. Thus, partisan politics sometimes strengthened unilateralism and weakened U.S. credibility abroad.

The historical record warns against unilateral withdrawal to an imagined Fortress America, but it also counsels against one-sided efforts to manage the world. Balancing self-reliance and conditional cooperation, of course, is not easy.

Guidelines for the Future

At the dawn of the twenty-first century Americans felt secure and did not worry much about the world around them. But their sense of well-being could quickly erode.

Taking things for granted is a common curse. We are tempted to say that the most probable future is "more of the same." But the least likely future is that nothing important will change. Unthinkables can become thinkable: Democracy's advances can be reversed; semi-democracies fight other democracies; China falls apart; Russia reverts to meaner ways; food surpluses become shortages; stock bubbles burst; and apparent wealth evaporates.

A good premise: Americans are less secure than they think. Dangers already visible may grow faster than expected. Dangers not yet visible may materialize and strike without notice. Dangers may come not just from rogue states and great power rivals, but from within the body politic or from the global environment.

How can governments and publics learn and become sensitive to dangers before they become acute? Is learning possible? How can decision-makers become more responsive to the need to abandon a familiar path or logic and choose a new one before the roof crashes? Openness is a sine qua non.

The decision-making process within governments and international organizations should be made transparent to reduce errors and achieve maximum consensus. Standard operating routines should include hearing out advocates of conflicting views—each making the best case possible. When policies go wrong, assumptions and practices should be reviewed. Simulation exercises can be used to suggest policy alternatives. Problems should be analyzed to see how they are nested—what aspects should be linked or kept apart.[1]

An ounce of prevention is worth tons of cure. The United States and its partners should establish routines that identify and address problems before they become crises.

Minimize Conditions That Conduce to Dangerous Instability

The big picture is that United States must reduce conditions conducive to dangerous instability—a world of intense great power rivalry or of fragmented chaos. At the same time it should make good use of unipolar stability while fostering bipolar or multipolar cooperation with other states and, beyond that, new forms of global governance.

Avoid a World of Hostile Rivalries and Confrontations.   Both China and Russia teeter between authoritarian rule and pluralism. Both are partners and challengers to the United States, as well as to each other. The long-term remedies are clear but difficult: Promote democracy and try to build a relationship of complex interdependence with potential peer rivals such as China and Russia and other potential adversaries such as Iran. Cultivate joint ventures to create values for each side. Recognize, however, that some situations may appear to be zero-sum to other actors. If so, they will see no room for mutual benefit. Thus, either China or Taiwan could view U.S. policies in East Asia as contrary to its vital interests. If China regards incorporation of Taiwan in the near future as a high priority, Beijing may not be influenced by trade treaties or bank loans.

Since push could come to shove, Americans must keep their powder dry—maintain strong military forces. Bolster NATO and U.S. security treaties with Japan and South Korea. Arm Taiwan to maintain its defenses.

But Americans should not provoke China, Russia, or other potential foes unnecessarily or worry NATO allies, for example, by pursuing the chimera of a national missile defense (NMD). The various plans for NMD offer no magic wand against an ICBM attack and would do nothing to defend against weapons smuggled into the country or delivered by cruise missiles or airplanes. But they could trigger a PRC and Russian arms buildup, spurring a chain reaction in New Delhi and Islamabad.

Learn to let well enough alone. Europe in the early 1990s was pretty stable, except for the Balkans. But the Clinton administration opted to open a pandora's box. It pushed to enlarge NATO up to Russia's border at Kaliningrad. This infuriated Russians and left many countries, from Estonia to Ukraine, in a no-man's land be-

Clinton Offers US Anti-missile Technology to Mr. Putin

tween NATO and Russia. What to do about them is a huge problem. At the onset of the century there were six options:

1. Leave the borderlands in limbo, fearful of neoimperialist tendencies in Moscow.

2. Buttress their security without formally bringing them into NATO. Continue the Partnership for Peace and other training programs to prepare the Baltic republics and other would-be NATO members for coordinated actions with the Western alliance. Count on expanding ties with the European Union to give them an additional security umbrella.

3. Use the Partnership for Peace to foster habits of cooperation in peacekeeping and search-and-rescue missions among NATO, Russia, and the countries in between. Promote sound economic as well as security cooperation with Russia.

4. Establish a belt of neutral states from the Baltic to the Black Sea—the 1955 Austrian model writ large. Some states might choose to be heavily armed, like Sweden; others not, like Austria.

5. Bring into NATO former Soviet republics such as Estonia and Ukraine and former Soviet allies such as Romania, thus drawing a deeper line against Russia.

6. Include in NATO not just former Soviet republics and allies but Russia itself—jettisoning the alliance's original raison'être.

Each option has drawbacks. So long as no clear and present danger takes shape in Moscow or elsewhere, perhaps it is wiser to avoid radical measures and hope that incremental change will transcend present anxieties and past hurts.

Avoid a World of Fragmented Chaos.   First, utilize diplomacy, economic incentives and sanctions, and force to contain rogue governments and control terrorists. But give hope to have-nots that the international system can meet their needs without violent change. Demonstrate that globalization will not leave them in permanent

North Korea

Negotiating with the Democratic People's Republic of Korea was not easy. The Pyongyang government hung tough in negotiations with the United States, Japan, and South Korea in the mid- and late 1990s, even though famine ravaged North Korea.

economic thrall. A model for containment-engagement is the U.S.-Japanese-South Korean policy toward North Korea which, in the 1990s, combined toughness with creative efforts to assist and engage Pyongyang—conditional on its renunciation of nuclear weapons.

Second, reduce the poverty, ignorance, and disease that help to breed chaos. Reduce trade barriers to exports by poor countries and promote direct foreign investment. Help LDCs wipe out illiteracy among both sexes. Tap the information revolution to bring LDCs into the twenty-first century. Foster education for public health. Make available preventive measures such as mosquito netting, saline solutions against dehydration, and polio vaccines. Provide drugs at or below cost to control H.I.V.

Third, reverse the environmental degradation that also spawns chaos. At home and abroad, Americans need to curtail emissions of carbons and other pollutants; protect forests, croplands, and biological diversity; assure adequate supplies of clean water, clean air, and clean foods. If global warming is partly human induced, and if Americans contribute more to the greenhouse effect than any other people, they probably bear some responsibility for the increasingly

Mozambique made a good start on developing in the late 1990s but was then hit by unprecedented floods. One of the most useful forms of foreign assistance by industrialized countries would be to curtail global warming.

frequent floods and droughts devastating LDCs from Nicaragua to Mozambique.

Fourth, strengthen (and fund!) the United Nations. Make Germany, Japan, and India permanent members of the Security Council. Relax the veto power so that the Security Council can deal with human rights problems as in Kosovo. Bolster UN mechanisms for conciliation, arbitration, and mediation of disputes—if possible, before they erupt in fighting. Mediation by U.S. officials and private citizens can be helpful, but an institutionalized capability for the United Nations should be the first resort.

No one country could mediate all the world's conflicts.

Fifth, strengthen UN and regional capabilities for peacekeeping and peace enforcement. If Americans will not allow their regular forces to serve under a UN commander, the United States could still foster, underwrite, and offer logistical support to a rapid reaction force under the UN Secretary-General. This would be a lot cheaper than mobilizing another Desert Storm or even a "stabilization" force for Bosnia, Albania, or Kosovo.

Finally, prevent further spread of weapons of mass destruction. Use carrots and sticks to lower the demand and supply of loose nukes, fissionable materials, and weapons know-how. Cultivate civil defense as seems prudent. If North Korea or some Middle Eastern country acquires nuclear-armed missiles, deploy antimissile systems above them or on their periphery to destroy them in boost phase.

Maximize Conditions That Conduce to Peace and Prosperity

Make Good Use of Unilateral Stability. Maintain and strengthen U.S. fitness—both tangible and intangible power. But use American assets in cooperation with others to foster mutual gain. Demonstrate to other actors that their interests can be well served by the present order. Do not employ force to compel or coerce others to change their behaviors unless grave interests are at stake. Do not needlessly goad others to organize against U.S. power. Avoid hubris, wishful thinking, and irrational exuberance in world affairs.[2]

Pax America was not Pax Romana. Virgil in *The Aeneid* advised his fellow Romans: "Make your task to rule nations by your government—these shall be your skills: to impose ordered ways upon a state of peace, to spare those who have submitted, and to subdue the arrogant." Let others shape bronzes and make marble come to life; let others plead their cases in court; let others analyze the heavenly bodies.

Americans, by contrast, would not so much rule as lead. They asked no one to submit. They tried to persuade and coopt rather than subdue—except in extreme cases such as Saddam Hussein. They also wished to excel in the arts, at law, and in sciences—and did.

But hegemony breeds resentment. Americans will be damned if they use their power and damned if they do not. In some situations the United States may have to choose between doing nothing and acting in ways that others resent. If Washington leads efforts to make a better world, some critics will fault it for bullying. If Americans withdraw to the sidelines, some will chastise them for ignoring the rest of humanity. When the Clinton Administration kept Dr. Boutros Boutros-Ghali from serving a second term as UN Secretary-General, however, this did not prove devotion to the United Nations but petulance.

U.S. or U.S.-led actions for just causes may threaten third parties. If Americans help Kosovars today, tomorrow they may try to intervene in Tibet, Chechnya, or Kashmir. Indian critics took umbrage at NATO's new strategic doctrine adopted in 1999 justifying out-of-area intervention even when it violates traditional norms of national sovereignty and lacks authorization by the United Nations. A doctrine that Washington and its partners lauded for advancing the cause of human rights struck others as a fig leaf for neoimperialism.

Worries that Washington and its NATO partners intend to police the world could provoke much closer cooperation between Russia and China and possibly even India. To be sure, sharp differences on other issues would remain between Beijing and Moscow, Beijing and New Delhi. But even if a triple entente proved impossible, the three might still take joint stands against the United States and its partners on particular issues. If so, we are talking about the world's two most populous countries and its largest territory facing off against smaller but richer Western countries.

When President Clinton traveled to India and Pakistan in 2000, he urged each side to negotiate on Kashmir and to avoid a nuclear arms race. He wanted to be "constructive," but Indians objected to words that implied their course of action was dangerous if not wrong; and they objected to advice on nuclear weapons from a country more noted for expanding than reducing its nuclear arsenal.

When to intervene? And how? Here are six rules of the road: First, never view any form of intervention—military or other—in a short-term time frame. Interventions that achieve their immediate goals may leave open wounds that fester for decades or even—as with Cuba—more than a century! Thus, Americans helped Cubans defeat Spain in 1898 and, for their trouble, got a base in Guantanamo and a right to intervene if Cubans proved unable to govern themselves. Over time, U.S. actions—private as well as official—inspired an anti-Yankee revolution that triggered generations of fruitless conflict between Castro and Washington and permitted Khrushchev to breach the Monroe Doctrine.

Second, do not fight unless vital U.S. interests are at stake. Neither human rights violations, as in Kosovo, nor mass hunger, as in Somalia, directly jeopardized vital U.S. interests.

Third, do not use U.S. military force to promote "social work."[3] Rather, support human rights and humanitarian relief through the United Nations and other multilateral channels.

Social work can easily put Americans on a slippery slope. To deliver humanitarian aid can require military action—even, occupation. When the world sent food to Somalia in the 1990s, armed force was needed to assure that it reached all the needy—a force much stronger than Washington had imagined.[4] U.S. leaders thought they could do good on the cheap. Instead, Americans got hurt and soon pulled out, leaving Somalis and NGOs to their own devices.

Do not bypass the United Nations. Interventions without UN backing may seem necessary to evade a veto in the Security Council, but NATO's 1999 war to help Kosovars seriously worsened U.S. relations with Beijing and Moscow and left Kosovo (Kosova in Albanian) in limbo.

Third, if you intervene militarily, try to form a multilateral coalition with UN authorization. Use sufficient force to prevail quickly and decisively. Engage as many partners as possible; dissuade the uncommitted from backing the other side. This approach helped oust Iraq from Kuwait.

If you intervene militarily, do not promise an early withdrawal. Do not count on being able to follow an "exit strategy." Despite a near-term victory over Iraq in 1991, the Saddam Hussein regime remained a menace. And do not count on a low-cost win. Other countries picked up most of the $60 billion tab for Desert Storm, but Americans had to pay for their veterans' medical and other costs, and for the continued U.S. presence and military actions against Iraq. Victory in war followed by years of UN arms controls and economic sanctions left many problems unresolved and generated many new ones.

Fourth, do not pursue contradictory principles. In the Balkans the Bush and Clinton administrations favored territorial integrity *and* respect for human rights. But whose territory—and whose rights? After years of watching and preaching, America finally intervened to uphold the integrity of Bosnia-Herzegovina and keep its Muslims from being massacred by Serbs or Croats. But then the United States tried to compel Bosnian Croats and Bosnian Serbs to live within the boundaries of a new Bosnian state—even though many of them would have preferred to join Croatia or Serbia. Soon Washington was attempting a similar feat in Kosovo—hoping that two peoples with historic enmities and different cultures could learn to live in peace.

The accords that stopped most of the killing in Bosnia and in Kosovo were near-term successes for the United States and its partners. But how would they look in ten or in fifty years?

Fifth, preventive diplomacy is a better bet than peace enforcement. In the 1990s the United States provided one-fifth of just over 1,000 troops from 27 countries in a UN Preventive Deployment Force (UNPREDEP) based in Macedonia to monitor and report any developments along the Serbian border that could threaten the territory or stability of Macedonia. Macedonia remained comparatively calm in the 1990s, even when many Kosovars fled across the border in 1999. Consider the economics: Prevention by UNPREDEP cost about $50 million a year—compared to $4.5 billion a year for post-operative NATO Stabilization Force (SFOR) in Bosnia and Herzegovinia.

Sixth, do not ignore possibilities for automated monitoring of peacekeeping. Thus, in the mid-1970s a single post manned by U.S. civilians (the "Sinai Field Mission") supervised electronic sensors that monitored a long stretch of the demilitarized Sinai peninsula. Americans also conducted aerial reconnaissance and shared photos of suspected violations with both Egypt and Israel.[5]

Similarly, unmanned seismic stations can help verify a ban on underground nuclear tests. Scanning machines monitored the portals to Soviet and U.S. missile factories under the 1987 INF Treaty and were used to monitor Iraqi facilities after 1992.

Welcome a World of Bilateral and Multilateral Cooperation.

Do not expect unipolarity to last forever. Therefore seek a soft landing—a graceful transition to another distribution of power. Seek multifaceted cooperation that can lead to relationships of complex interdependence in which resort to force is virtually excluded. The path to complex interdependence follows the same synergistic route endorsed by Immanuel Kant as the way to peace and international civil society—representative government, federalism, law, trade, and hospitality to other cultures. An emergent property that blends complex interdependence and Kantian ideals probably offers the sturdiest known foundation for peace.

Bilateral and multilateral cooperation can be nourished in countless ways. Thesis and antithesis characterized the early twenty-first century. Calls for going-it-alone competed with movement toward complex interdependence. But experience showed that insularity was infeasible and unilateralism counterproductive. If Americans accepted these propositions, their best strategy was to promote mutual gain with other actors so as to deal effectively with shared vulnerabilities and global forces.

The European Union has a population and a GDP larger than the United States. If China continues the economic growth trends of the 1980s–1990s, its GDP could also exceed the American. The vast human and material resources of Russia await self-organization. The same is true for India and Brazil. Many small states are also powerhouses—Taiwan (just over 22 million people, with the world's largest cash reserves per capita) and Singapore (just over 3 million people, but a world leader in many domains).

Transatlantic ties were strong at the onset of a new century. Europe and the United States, as a German official put it, were like a quasi-domestic society. "The distinction between foreign and domestic policy has blurred as our societies have interwoven."[6] Instead of worrying about the Berlin Wall or Euromissiles, Europeans and Americans debated genetically modified food, child custody laws in Germany, capital punishment in the United States, and the best ways to deal with one-crop economies (bananas) in the Caribbean and Central America.

Each side of the Atlantic needed a strong euro. If the euro fell too far against the dollar, European goods would become cheaper for Americans, generating stiffer competition for U.S. manufacturers at home and abroad. The U.S. government was supposed to hold its tongue, but American business interests applauded any moves by the European Central Bank to prop up a declining euro.

America's NATO partners worried that an American NMD would scuttle the foundations of international security and leave Europeans "sitting ducks" without comparable defenses. In turn, some Europeans said they wanted to build a European Security and Defense Identity so strong that it could act without the United States. French intellectuals denounced American arrogance—*hyper-puissance*—but they would object even more were Washington to pull its remaining troops from Germany.

Complex interdependence also emerged between the United States and Japan in the second half of the twentieth century, despite cultural differences. This was a relationship to be nourished in the twenty-first century, tapping the strengths of each society, and avoiding any conditions that could lead to a remilitarization of Japan.

At the outset of the twenty-first century the outlines of complex interdependence were also present in U.S. relations with China and with Russia. To give flesh to these bones, however, would take hard work and skill. It would not be "order for free."

Consider the Hong Kong-PRC-USA-WTO-Taiwan connections: Hong Kong's exports rose by 21 percent in the first quarter of 2000, even though the Hong Kong dollar was pegged to the American at a fixed rate—making Hong Kong goods relatively costly to others. Hong Kong's GDP grew in the first quarter of 2000 by 14 percent— its most torrid advance since 1987. American investors played a large role in Hong Kong and a growing role in China. An analyst in Hong Kong predicted: "The longer the U.S. keeps booming, the faster Asia will grow." Hong Kong expected its GDP to gain an extra 5 percent over ten years after China joined the World Trade Organization. On the other hand, a more open China could erode Hong Kong's traditional role as entrepôt between China and the world, especially if Taiwanese investors put more money into cash-hungry China, And if Taipei and Beijing moved toward conciliation, Americans would face less risk of being sucked into an Asian conflict.

Strong or weak, Russia still stretched from the Baltic and Black Seas to the Pacific Ocean. Better to have Russia as a partner than as a foe. Much of the news from Russia was bad—for Russians and others—but some Russian and Western leaders recognized the need for cooperation. Consider the arrangements by which the USEC, a private company managing U.S. Department of Energy plants, contracted to buy from the Russian Ministry of Atomic Energy, over twenty years, 500 tons of enriched uranium recovered from dismantled ex-Soviet weapons. When the agreed price fell below spot market prices in 1999 and caused losses for USEC stock holders, the American company and TENEX, the Russian agent, negotiated in A.D. 2000 to lower the price but increase the amount purchased. American producers of uranium objected that Russian exports would kill their business. All this pushed the parties into ever more complex interdependence, with a growing stake in each other's well-being.

Despite Western encouragement, however, two key ingredients of Kantian synergy were weak or missing in China and Russia—representative government and law. Each country lacked institutions of civil society. Neither had a tradition placing law above party and interest. Neither showed much interest in strengthening the United Nations.

The one element in the Kantian approach that appealed to many Chinese and Russian elites was the spirit of commerce. Both China and Russia saw international trade as a way to riches, higher living standards, and cutting edge technology. Optimists hoped that the demands of the WTO for openness and transparency would push China and then Russia, if it joined, toward a rule of law.

There was still a rub. As Kant recognized, "from the crooked timber of humanity no straight thing can ever be made." So long as humans can do evil, the need for force to deter or compel others will persist. Who should possess this coercive force and decide on its use remains an unresolved problem. Washington said that it sought the rule of law, but did not want foreigners to judge U.S. actions; it also refused to put U.S. troops under foreign command. Americans could not even agree on modest domestic gun controls to keep their children from shooting each other and their teachers. "*Quis custodiet ipsos custodes?* Who will guard the guardians?" Juvenal asked. This question may be finessed but (along with many others raised in this chapter) will probably not be resolved in the twenty-first century.

Foster a World of Global Governance.   World government was not feasible in the early twenty-first century and probably not desirable, given the diversity of values and levels of income and power across the planet. Was some other form of self-organization possible to meet the challenges of global interdependence and globalization? Could the many players on the world stage—governments, international organizations, NGOs, multinational corporations—coordinate their actions for mutual gain?

Some trends were encouraging. Networks of global governance began to form in the nineteenth century to regulate navigation on the great rivers of Europe and Africa; to curtail the slave trade; to regulate and tap the power of the telegraph; to nurse the wounded and mitigate the horrors of war. The number and importance of nonstate actors grew rapidly in the nineteenth and twentieth centuries. The trend continued into the twenty-first century, abetted by Internet communications that permitted each actor to broadcast its message and talk to other actors far and wide. Humanity's capacity for self-organized fitness was growing by leaps and bounds.

Americans could be proud of their number who had already done much for global governance. Ralph J. Bunche won the Nobel Peace Prize as a UN mediator. American officials such as Theodore Roosevelt, Charles Dawes, and Henry Kissinger won the prize, but so did many others outside government. Jane Addams, Nicholas Murray Butler, Linus C. Pauling, Martin Luther King, Jr. and Elie Wiesel won the prize for their leadership of social movements or their influence on minds and conscience. Norman E. Borlaug won the prize for his contributions, financed by the Rockefeller Foundation, to the Green Revolution. Most of these individuals pricked the conscience of Americans and others on the planet, pushing and pulling them toward a more humane existence. Most winners of the Nobel Peace Prize, of course, were not Americans. But many were officially welcomed in Washington—from Anwar Sadat and Menachem Begin to Nelson Mandela, Lech Walesa, Desmond Tutu, and the Dalai Lama (not officially a guest of the president, to minimize hurt feelings in Beijing).

Many Americans also contributed to some of the movements and organizations that won the Nobel Peace Prize—the International Red Cross (1917, 1944, 1963); the Quakers (1947); the UN High Commissioner for Refugees (1954, 1981); UN Children's Fund (1965); International Labor Organization (1969); Amnesty International (1977); International Physicians for Prevention of Nuclear War (1985); Pugwash Conferences on Science and World Affairs (1995); and the International Campaign to Ban Landmines (1997).

Societal fitness, complexity theory suggests, thrives on self-organization rather than top-down rule. As the century began, the global picture offered a virtuous circle congenial to American values and interests: representative government—>rule of law—>spirit of commerce—>cultural openness—>complex interdependence—>self-organized fitness. Private American citizens, NGOs, and businesses as well as the U.S. government could do even more to cooperate with their counterparts across the globe to promote this kind of global governance.

But if others become more fit, would this jeopardize American interests? Realpolitik says yes. The spirit of value-creating says no. Human needs and desires are vast. The pie can be expanded without limit. If others provide a service or good more efficiently than Americans, let Americans find and then fill other niches. For Americans to do this, of course, they must enhance their fitness in many domains—a task that requires vast improvements in education and training programs to update or learn new job skills.

What Paradigm Works Best?

Realists and neorealists assert that world politics is still a jungle—an endless struggle for power. States are the key actors as they joust to maximize their national interests. International law, multilateral regimes, and other forms of cross-border cooperation are ephemeral. Even economic interdependence fails to prevent mayhem—witness not only World War I but America's Civil War. "Accords" endure only so long as states' interests overlap. Nonstate actors shape the periphery—not the vital center—of world politics. Functional cooperation makes life more convenient, but will never supplant the contest of all against all.

Some idealists and neoidealists, however, counter that sovereignty is a deeply eroded myth and that every state is permeable—even hermit dictatorships such as Myanmar. More and more persons act on convictions of human solidarity—as if they were the keepers not only of their brothers and sisters but of distant cousins and absolute strangers.[7]

A theory of international relations rooted in an understanding of global interdependence provides a broader framework than realism or idealism for analyzing the past and planning the future. "Self-help" on a narrow scale is not optimal. Nearly every state depends upon others near and far. Mutual dependency drives states and other global actors into networks of cooperation—regimes and organizations. Functional cooperation overshadows politics, as in the European Union.

The concept of interdependence underlines both the dangers and the opportunities inherent in mutual vulnerability—the need to think about means and ends, practicality and morality. It does not presume that humans are good or bad, but hopes that they learn to act on principles of enlightened self-interest.

Policy Implications: Mutual Gain Theory

Mutual gain theory integrates key assumptions from the theories of interdependence, complexity, and liberal peace. It starts with the assumption that most actors on the world stage interdepend with others—in their region if not globally. How actors respond to their mutual vulnerability, however, is up to them.

Unlike fish and other inhabitants of coral reefs, humans can consciously plan and decide whether to go it alone or cooperate with neighbors. They may seek to create values with others for mutual gain or claim and seize values for private gain. "Value-claiming" signifies an effort to treat other actors as though life were a zero-sum game in which one side's gains must equal what the other loses. "Value-creating" assumes that the "pie can be expanded," permitting each side to gain ever more.

America's record confirms the basic expectation of mutual gain theory: Policies oriented to conditional cooperation are more likely to enhance an actor's interests than zero-sum competition. Americans, like other global actors, are more likely to enhance their objectives if they can frame and implement value-creating strategies aimed at mutual gain than if they pursue value-claiming policies for one-sided gain.

Making cooperation conditional on reciprocity encourages policies oriented to mutual gain but erects barriers against abuse by exploiters. Other approaches to foreign policy—hard-line value-claiming and unconditional cooperation—are likely to backfire. The win-lose negotiator risks losing the benefits of long-term cooperation. The win-win idealist risks destruction by Machiavellian lions and foxes.

A fit society is likely to be one self-organized for the mutual gain of its members and across borders for cooperative value-creation with other societies. If actors on the world stage interdepend and co-evolve, the best predictor of success or failure is whether an actor pursues and achieves conditional cooperation.

Notes

1. See Ernst B. Haas, *When Knowledge Is Power: Three Models of Change in International Organizations* (Berkeley: University of California Press, 1990), pp. 72, 208–212.
2. Professor Kenneth Waltz in his 1987 reply to the survey on American foreign policy attributed U.S. achievements to modesty and failures to hubris. More than two thousand years before, Thucydides recorded how overweening pride undid the Athenians.

3. Michael Mandelbaum, "Foreign Policy as Social Work," *Foreign Affairs.* 75, 1 (January/February 1996), pp. 16–32.
4. America's role in Somalia began in the 1970s when Washington backed Somalia's dictatorship as a counterpoise to leftist Ethiopia. But when "our S.O.B." (who used to be Moscow's man) was thrown out, clan chaos and hunger engulfed the land.
5. Former U.S. Ambassador to Egypt Hermann Fr. Eilts recalled in spring 2000 that Israel wanted seven, five, or at least three posts manned by Americans, but finally settled for one, which proved quite adequate. Most of the personnel were U.S. Foreign Service Officers. Texas Instruments provided housekeeping. Some of the negotiating history may be found in Henry Kissinger, *Years of Renewal* (New York: Simon & Schuster, 1999), pp. 448–449.
6. Karsten Voight quoted by Roger Cohen, "Tiffs Over Bananas And Child Custody," *The New York Times,* May 28, 2000, Section 4, pp. 1, 4.
7. The Chernobyl Children Project USA, Inc. was founded in Boston in 1994 to help children affected by radioactive leaks at Chernobyl to receive relief, compassion, and medical care. More than 100 children from Belarus and Russia stayed with volunteer families in summer 2000. Another group brought polio victims from Vietnam to the Shriner's Hospital for Children. But these projects paled next to the magnanimity of the parents of Ali Jawarish, a Palestinian child inadvertently killed by Israeli soldiers in 1997. The parents donated the boy's organs to the Israeli national organ tank. Soon the child's heart, liver, a lung, and one kidney were transplanted into two Israeli boys. Ali's father, Mohammed Jawarish, said he wanted his son's death to give life to others.

INDEX

Japan, 14, 157; economy of, 19n19, 34–35, 35–36, 48, 97- 99, 121, 154, 161, 163, 164, 167, 181, 186, 190, 200n10, 200n28, 216; as great power, 158, 209; and Russia, 75; and United States, 32, 35–36, 47, 55, 97, 102, 108, 109, 145, 161, 204n42, 208, 219, 226, 235; and World War II, 30, 63, 67, 68, 112, 136, 154

Jiang Zemin, 85, 190
Joffe, Josef, 2, 34–35
Johnson, Lyndon B.: administration of, 106, 124, 132–134, 138; and Vietnam, 65, 131, 135, 137
Jordan, 213
Juvenal, 237

Kaliningrad, 226
Kanet, Roger 150n17
Kant, Immanuel, 12, 13, 14, 21n29, 144, 211, 221n9, 234, 237. *See also* liberal peace theory
Kauffman, Stuart, 17n15
Kazakstan, 40, 79, 80, 87, 157, 158, 189, 196, 208, 210, 218
Kellogg-Briand Pact, 69, 96
Kennan, George F. 2
Kennedy, John F., 138, 141; administration of, 36–37, 37–38, 89, 130–133 *passim,* 137, 144, 148; and Cuba, 111n4; personality

of, 136, 139, 140; and Vietnam, 65, 137
Kennedy, Paul, 153
Khatami, Mohammad, 87. *See also* Iran
Khrushchev, Nikita S., 122; and Cuba, 68, 152n43; and Egypt, 83; and Kennedy, J. F., 140, 148; and Nixon, R. M., 140; and world revolution, 82
King, Martin Luther Jr., 42, 238
Kissinger, Henry: and China, 85; and GRIT 39–40, 42; and Nixon R.M., 53, 130–132, 135, 140, 147; and Nobel Peace Prize, 238; personality of, 126–128, 129–131; and Rockefeller, N. A., 141, 144
Korea: economy of, 159, 209, 218; North, 3, 30, 38–39, 45, 48, 92, 96, 131; South, 23, 25, 30, 55, 145, 157, 228; and Russia, 44; and United States, 23, 32, 39–40, 41, 45, 55, 85, 92, 96, 145, 167, 178, 226, 228; war, 25, 27, 30, 31, 37–38, 38–39, 68, 82, 84, 123–125, 133, 163; weapons of, 91, 181, 230.
Kosovo/Kosova: autonomy of, 46, 95; human rights in, 229, 232; and NATO, 4, 33, 71, 79, 92, 94, 167, 233; peacekeeping in,